The Webmaster's Guide to HTML

J. Ranade Workstation Series

In order to receive additional information on these or any other McGraw-Hill titles, in the United States please call 1-800-822-8158. In other countries, contact your local McGraw-Hill representative.

The Webmaster's Guide to HTML

For Advanced Web Developers

Nathan J. Muller

Illustrated by Linda L. Tyke

McGraw-Hill

New York San Francisco Washington, D.C. Auckland Bogotá
Caracas Lisbon London Madrid Mexico City Milan
Montreal New Delhi San Juan Singapore
Sydney Tokyo Toronto

McGraw-Hill

A Division of The McGraw·Hill Companies

Library of Congress Cataloging-in-Publication Data
Muller, Nathan J.
   The Webmaster's guide to HTML : for advanced Web developers / by
Nathan J. Muller.
      p.   cm.
   Includes index.
   ISBN 0-07-912273-6 (pbk.)
   1. Hypertext systems. 2. HTML (Document markup language)
   I. Title.
   QA76.76.H94M79   1995
   005.7'2—dc20   95-42869
                                                              CIP

2 3 4 5 6 7 8 9   FGR/FGR   9 0 0 9 8 7 6

ISBN 0-07-912273-6

*The sponsoring editor for this book was Jerry Papke, the executive edi-
tor was Robert E. Ostrander, and the book editor was Aaron G. Bittner.
The production supervisor was Katherine G. Brown. This book was set
in ITC Century Light. It was composed in Blue Ridge Summit, Pa.*

Printed and bound by Quebecor, Fairfield, PA

McGraw-Hill books are available at special quantity discounts to use as
premiums and sales promotions, or for use in corporate training programs.
For more information, please write to the Director of Special Sales, McGraw-
Hill, 11 West 19th Street, New York, NY 10011. Or contact your local
bookstore.

MH95
9122736

In memory of Mary and Charles Tyke

Contents

viii   Contents

Preface

The World Wide Web was conceived in the late 1980s at the European Particle Physics Laboratory in Switzerland (CERN). There, the HyperText Markup Language (HTML) was developed to provide researchers with a means to access and display documents stored on servers anywhere on the Internet. Since then, the World Wide Web (WWW) has grown to become one of the most sophisticated and popular services on the Internet.

Although no specific organization exercises sole administrative control of the Web, the World Wide Web Consortium (W3C), created by the Massachusetts Institute of Technology (MIT) and CERN, directs the development of the Web. As of February 1995, INRIA, France's national computing research institute, has replaced CERN in that effort. The goal remains the same: to promulgate a single set of standards worldwide.

An appearance of order is imposed on the Web by the languages and protocols that constitute worldwide standards, such as the HyperText Transfer Protocol (HTTP) and HyperText Markup Language (HTML). Currently there are different flavors of these standards, which causes compatibility problems in some areas, but not enough to cause chaos on the Web.

As its name implies, HTTP is used to transfer hypertext documents among servers and, ultimately, to a client (your computer). Collectively, the tens of thousands of servers distributed worldwide that support HTTP are known as the World Wide Web. HTML is used to structure information that resides on the servers in a way that can be readily displayed by clients. It makes documents portable from one computer platform to another, and is intended as a common medium for tying together information from widely different sources. Users interact with the Web through a browser, such as Netscape or Mosaic, installed on their computer.

The first version of HTML was designed to be an extremely simple way to author and render hypertext documents. Judging from the phenomenal growth of the Web since 1990, the design goals of HTML have succeeded beyond expectations. HTML 2.0 has added new features, while preserving the original intent of keeping things simple. At this writing, the HTML Working

Group of the Internet Engineering Task Force (IETF) is in the process of re-fining HTML 3.0 into a formal standard. The IETF is a volunteer group that researches and solves technical problems, and makes recommendations to the Internet Architecture Board (IAB).

HTML is expected to evolve rapidly to support multimedia. Initially lim-ited to handling a few image formats, HTML already handles video clips, an-imations, virtual reality, and eventually will be able to handle a variety of drawing formats and become a general means for embedding other applica-tions.* In the not-too-distant future, HTML may even be used to create mag-azine-style pages.

The Web itself can best be described as a dynamic, interactive, graphi-cally-oriented, distributed, platform-independent, hypertext information system.

- The WWW is dynamic because it changes daily. New server sites continu-ally are being added to the tens of thousands of sites already online. New information also is continually being added, as are new hypertext links.

- The WWW is interactive in that specific information can be requested through various search engines and returned moments later in the form of lists, often with each item weighted according to how well it matched one or more search parameters. Another example of interactivity is the exis-tence of online forms for business transactions, whereby users can select items from a catalog and fill out an order form. Credit card numbers are verified and processed through a third-party service. In the case of soft-ware purchases, the product can be downloaded from the vendor to the buyer immediately after credit card verification.

- The WWW is graphically oriented; in fact, it was designed for the exten-sive use of graphics. The use of graphics not only makes the Web visually appealing, but easy to navigate. Graphical signposts direct users to new sources of information accessed via hypertext links.

- The WWW is distributed, meaning that information resides on tens of thousands of individual Web servers around the world. If one site goes down, there is no significant impact on the Web as a whole, except to that particular site and the hypertext links that connect to documents there. Some servers are mirrored at other sites to keep information available, even if the primary server crashes.

- The WWW is platform-independent, which means that virtually any client can access the Web, whether it is based on the Windows, OS/2, Macintosh, or UNIX operating environment. This platform-independence even ap-

---

*Multimedia topics such as video, animation, and virtual reality are not covered in this book. Although there is a significant amount of interest and experimentation in these areas, they are not yet mainstream Web applications. In future editions of this book, we hope to devote whole chapters to these topics.

plies to the Web servers. Although most Web servers currently are based on UNIX, Windows NT is growing in popularity and is becoming the platform of choice among developers of new Web sites. Some application developers even offer the means for a Windows client to do double-duty as a Web server.

- The WWW makes extensive use of hypertext links. A hypertext link points the way to other information, which might be found virtually anywhere: the same document, a different document on the same server, or another document on a different server that might be located anywhere in the world. A hypertext link does not necessarily point to text documents; it can point to maps, forms, images, sound and video clips, or to e-mail programs. Hypertext links can even point to other Internet services, such as Gopher sites. A hypertext link is usually identified by an underlined word or phrase that also is rendered in a different color than the surrounding text. A graphical object, such as an icon or photographic image, also can be a hypertext link.

There are a number of good reasons for companies to publish on the World Wide Web. On a publicly accessible Web server, companies can post product announcements, advertisements, press releases, technology white papers, application notes, annual reports, quarterly financial statements—anything that can generate interest in their products and services. In the process, they can project a professional image, while meeting the routine informational needs of diverse constituents at reduced overhead expense.

Companies also can use the Web server to distribute help information, drivers, software patches and other commonly requested items. This saves staff time and mailing costs, while meeting the support needs of customers on a timely basis. Product configuration and troubleshooting advice, too, can be posted on the Web, which can reduce support costs.

Not all Web servers are open to the public. Many companies are using their LAN servers for internal document distribution over the Web. Examples include:

- The human resources department can use an internal server for making available corporate policies and procedures, as well as state and federal employment regulations, to managers at remote locations over the Web.

- The accounting department can make available forms for expense reporting, purchase orders, check requests, and other routine items. Employees call up the appropriate form, fill in the requested information, and file it electronically over the Web for processing by the accounts receivable or accounts payable group.

- A company's distributed manufacturing sites can access online documentation about various fabrication processes, component inventories, quality control procedures, and test histories—all via the World Wide Web.

- Engineering can use an internal Web server for distributing technical documentation and drawings to suppliers and customers, as well as design consultants anywhere in the world.

- The corporate library can publish an online catalog of books and periodicals, handling inquiries and requests from borrowers electronically.

- The information systems (IS) department can put its forms on an internal Web server and process information collected from users. Scripts can move the data into appropriate databases without manual key entry.

- The marketing department can post product availability and pricing information, accessible only to company salespeople and customer service operators in branch offices and, increasingly, telecommuting employees who work out of their homes.

- Network administrators can share information stored in an internal Web server to troubleshoot hardware and software problems. The Web server can make a valuable adjunct to the help desk, especially when corporate locations are spread across multiple time zones.

Specifically aimed at Webmasters, the purpose of this book is to provide a clear, concise reference for the development of sophisticated, functional and attractive Web pages using the HyperText Markup Language. As the term is used here, a Webmaster is usually any person who manages a Web site and who also may have responsibility for retrieving and responding to e-mail messages concerning the content of the site's Web pages. Whether or not the Webmaster actually manages the Web server, the term implies a high degree of expertise in HTML, forms software, and associated programs.

To make Web page development as easy and painless as possible, this book comes with HTMLdisk, which contains many of the scripts discussed in the text. A good selection of forms and tables also is included on HTML disk. Just upload the contents of HTMLdisk to an appropriately named subdirectory (i.e., \htmldisk will do nicely) in your word processor and use the cut-and-paste method to collect the items you need for your Web pages. You can then insert your own content into the structure.

HTMLdisk also contains graphical objects, including specially designed bullets, buttons, bars, frames, and screen backgrounds in GIF format—everything you need to give your Web pages a classy look from the start without having to learn a design program or scour the Internet. As you get more familiar with HTML and have more time to experiment, you can refine your Web pages accordingly.

The files on HTMLdisk are not compressed. You can view the information contained in the scripts with your favorite Web browser. From the browser's File menu, choose Open File (or something similar). You do not have to be online to view local files from within your browser. The scripts and graphics in HTMLdisk have been thoroughly tested on the Internet using the Netscape browser. You may have difficulty viewing certain files with any other browser, at least in the near term. For example, the ability to create and view tables is a feature of HTML 3.0, and most browsers available currently only support HTML 2.0.

The chapters in this book are structured to convey information in a no-nonsense manner. Wherever possible, real-world examples are used to illustrate the HTML coding under discussion. As appropriate, depending on the complexity of the function, the following information is provided for most topics:

- Functional Description: provides a brief description of the function to be formatted in HTML, such as "Creating a hypertext link to another document."

- Format: Provides the format of the HTML command that will implement the function.

- Background: Provides useful information that will help you understand the context, ramifications, or requirements of the HTML command to ensure its proper operation.

- Applications: Provides suggestions on some possible uses of the HTML command or script.

- Rules: If applicable, draws attention to specific elements of the HTML command or Perl script that will ensure its proper operation.

- Examples: Provides coding examples of how the HTM command or Perl script is actually used.

- Browser view: Provides an actual illustration of the HTML command as it appears in a Web browser.

This book cannot possibly discuss every design feature that can be coded in HTML for incorporation into your Web pages. The level of sophistication is more a function of imagination and design sense than HTML tags alone. This book will help you present information on the World Wide Web in a way that projects an image of quality and credibility. If you are using the Web to advertise your company or product, projecting a professional image is all the more important.

I must admit at the outset that I favor the liberal use of graphics, hypertext links, forms, and tables in Web pages, especially when product-oriented information is being conveyed. After all, the Web was designed to handle information in exactly these ways. Although the speed at which these items are viewed is dependent on such factors as the amount of available bandwidth on dedicated links or the speed of the modem on dial-up links, the computer's processing power, and the type of browser, I do not believe in "dummying down" Web pages by providing text-only versions and imposing a strict limit on the number of hypertext links and graphical objects.

At the same time, however, I believe links, forms, tables, and other objects should only be used when appropriate, such as to provide additional levels of detail, to illustrate a point, or to break down complex ideas and concepts to aid understanding. The obvious exception is the first Web page, usually called the home page. A visually enticing home page invites the user to browse further to see what kind of information is available. This brings up another function of objects in general—they can be used to lead the viewer from page to page or topic to topic.

I wrote this book because I was disappointed with the lack of breadth and depth I found in most HTML books. In attempting to explain HTML concepts as simply as possible, they generally failed to make the connection to real-world applications of HTML. Thus, a reader could understand the concept, but not necessarily be able to apply it to the creation of his or her own Web pages. To help correct this situation, this book provides actual uses of HTML coding, and enough of it to fully illustrate the point.

Along the way, I promise not to bore you with the history of the Internet, waste your time discussing terribly cool sites, or demonstrate my cleverness with stupid net tricks. There will be no talk of "cyberspace," the "information superhighway" (with its on- and off-ramps), the "global village," or the Internet's potential—if used for good instead of evil—to bring all humankind together in world peace. The World Wide Web is merely part of the Internet, a worldwide assemblage of networked computers of all kinds, that is intended to convey useful information in as friendly a way as possible. It's really that simple.

Out of concern for objectivity, I fully intended to make use of several different Web browsers to illustrate various points in my discussions of HTML coding. However, it quickly became apparent that if I used any other browser than Netscape, the quality of this book would be substantially compromised. Simply stated, if you are not using Netscape, you will not appreciate much of what is in this book. This is not a plug for Netscape, but merely a realistic assessment of the state of the art in browser technology. In fact, many companies would prefer not being in the browser market at all, and offer their own browsers as "obligatory offerings" to round out their product lines. They have already conceded the browser market to Netscape.

At the same time, I am fully aware of the ongoing debate concerning the use of proprietary (i.e., Netscape) versus standards-based HTML coding. Standards are always slow in coming and when they finally are issued, they are quickly outdated by continued advancements in technology. This is true in every area of the computer and communications industries. Fortunately, there are companies that insist on pushing the technology envelope, enabling progress to be made, which is of great benefit to all. Often, proprietary technologies are used as the basis for standards. The company with the largest market share will even have a lot to say about the future direction of a standard. The same is true with browser technology. Netscape has not only made the Web more useful and efficient for information delivery, it has enabled information to be published more creatively.

The information contained in this book, especially as it relates to specific vendors and products, is believed to be accurate at the time it was written and is, of course, subject to change with continued advancements in technology and shifts in market forces.

Nathan J. Muller

Basic Document Construction

The key concept in the hypertext markup language (HTML) is the use of tags, which are used to code documents for the Web. Tags encapsulate (surround) the various elements of a document, such as headings, paragraphs, lists, forms, tables, and hypertext links. These tags enable the document to be identified by Web servers and Web clients (computers that view the documents with browsers) as a hypertext document, the content of which can be rendered and navigated according to the instructions represented by the tags.

In this chapter, we will use various tags to build a single HTML document, and we will depict its renderings at various stages using Netscape Navigator, the most popular browser for viewing documents on the Web. This process will accomplish several objectives:

- You will learn how to code documents in the hypertext markup language.
- You will become familiar with the context within which the various HTML codes can be applied.
- You will become familiar with some of the attributes that can be placed within the tags to further influence the way text is rendered by the browser.

The Role of Tags

HTML is not a programming language in the normal sense. It is more like the simple notations a magazine editor uses to get an article ready for publication, which is why it is referred to as a "markup language." The markup language consists of tags to convey instructions to a browser (like Mosaic or Netscape) about how the document's various text elements should be rendered. For example, there are tags that are used to render portions of text as bold or italic. It is the use of tags that makes HTML so easy to learn. After becoming acquainted with the use of these notations or tags, information of any kind becomes easy to code for distribution on the Web.

Tags have a format of their own. They may consist of one or more characters, and are enclosed within the less-than (<) and greater-than (>) brackets. In most cases, there are start tags and end tags: the start tag turns on or opens certain features such as italics and bold, while an end tag turns them off or closes them. A feature's end tag is indicated by a slash (/). Together, the start and end tags have the following format:

```
<tag>  .  .  .  </tag>
```

There are a few things you should know about tags before you begin marking up your documents:

- Not all instructions require an end tag. For example, the paragraph tag <P> is used to indicate the start of a paragraph and, by default, the end of the previous paragraph. There are several other instructions that omit the end tag when it is clearly implied by the context.

- Tags are case-insensitive. You can use uppercase, lowercase, or mix the two throughout the same document. (In this book, tags appear in uppercase.)

- Spaces are ignored, so you can arrange tagged elements horizontally or vertically in a document, skipping spaces or skipping lines as you see fit. This can make the document easier to review and revise later on.

Document Organization

The HTML document is organized much like a memo or letter; it has a head and a body. Within the head, you can put a title and other descriptive information about the document. Within the body, you can code text as paragraphs and lists, highlight words and phrases, and create links to other places in the document or to other documents in the database. You can also create links to other documents located somewhere else on the Internet.

The first tag you will find in most documents is the HTML tag. When used, the start and end HTML tags encapsulate the entire document, with <HTML> at the top and </HTML> at the bottom. While most documents on the Web use the HTML tags, they are omissible. The reason they may be omitted is that the HTTP servers that make up the Web do not handle documents formatted in any other way, and neither do the browsers running on the various clients. So there really is no need to explicitly identify documents as being coded in HTML.

You also may come across documents that use HEAD tags. The head of a document is encapsulated with the <HEAD> and </HEAD> tags. Like the

HTML tags, the HEAD tags are omissible. However, the head of an HTML document can contain other descriptive information about the document, as in the following example:

```
<HEAD>
<TITLE>Examples of Head Elements</TITLE>
<META name="keywords" value="web, html, tag">
</HEAD>
```

In this case, the META tag is used to identify key words in the document that various indexing software on the Web can use to describe the content of your Web pages.

The first part of an HTML document that is mandatory is the title, which is encapsulated within the `<TITLE>` and `</TITLE>` tags. When rendered with a browser, the document's title does not appear in the document itself, but as a separate label within the browser's windows-based graphical user interface. Typically, the browser displays the title of the document prior to retrieving it, or while the document is being loaded, along with information on the status of the connection.

Titles are usually used in a global context. Rather than a different title for every document, the title should describe a collection of related documents. It can be the name of the entire database or service, or it can be the name of the company or individual who owns the database.

Here are some other things you should know about titles:

- The title element must appear within the head of the document.

- The title should be no more than 64 characters in length, including spaces, or it risks becoming truncated or cut off when it is rendered by some types of browsers.

- The title should be short, but descriptive. Instead of "Guide," which is meaningless out of context, a more meaningful title would be "The Web Developer's Guide to HTML."

- The title element must not contain paragraph tags, anchors, or highlighting of any kind.

- Only one title is allowed in a document.

The body of the document is indicated by the `<BODY>` and `</BODY>` tags. For most documents, the use of BODY tags is optional. However, they are essential for certain features, such as specifying the colors of backgrounds, text, and links. The use of the body tag for these purposes is discussed in chapter 5.

Although the HTML, HEAD, and BODY tags are omissible, this is not recommended because the structure allows certain properties of the document (such as the title) to be determined by the browser without having to parse (or read) the entire document. With these considerations in mind, the coding illustrations in this book include these omissible tags.

As discussed so far, a basic HTML-coded document looks like this:

```
<HTML>
<HEAD>
<TITLE>The Web Developer's Guide to HTML</TITLE>
</HEAD>
<BODY>
The World Wide Web can be an efficient and economical way to distribute
information globally. HTML-coded documents can form a vast database—all
or portions of which can be interconnected with hypertext links.
</BODY>
</HTML>
```

In this coding example, there is no <P> tag to indicate the paragraph. Because there is only one paragraph, no <P> tag is required, because it is implied by the context. If there were multiple paragraphs, the <P> tag would be used to separate them.

Here is what the document looks like so far when rendered by Netscape Navigator (Figure 1.1). Notice where the title appears: in the label at the topmost area of the screen, which is part of the browser's graphical user interface.

Right now our document looks bland and lifeless. This will change dramatically as we go on.

Paragraphs

After the first paragraph, succeeding paragraphs are indicated with the <P> tag. Although a </P> tag can be used to indicate the end of a paragraph, it is not needed, because the start of a new paragraph implies the end of the previous paragraph. Because the <P> tag also adds one line of vertical space, it can be thought of and used as a paragraph separator.

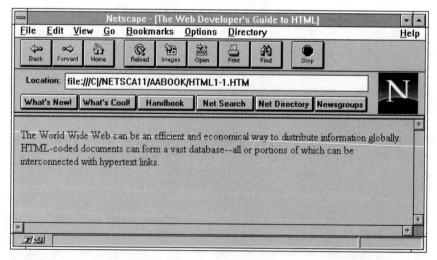

Figure 1.1

By default, paragraphs are rendered flush left. According to the draft HTML 3.0 specification, paragraphs also can be made flush right, centered, or justified on the page through the use of the ALIGN attribute, as in the following examples:

```
<P ALIGN=RIGHT>
<P ALIGN=CENTER>
<P ALIGN=JUSTIFY>
```

The use of the ALIGN attribute in the paragraph tag is not widely supported. When this attribute is recognized within the paragraph tag, often it is rendered inconsistently. For example, a browser might recognize `<P ALIGN=CENTER>`, but not `<P ALIGN=RIGHT>` or `<P ALIGN=JUSTIFY>`.

Headings

HTML defines six levels of headings, which are used in the same way as the headings in a book chapter—to organize text into appropriate topics and subtopics, making the chapter easier to read. The headings require end tags as well as start tags; the tags encapsulate the word or phrase.

The format of the heading tags are as follows:

```
<H1> . . . </H1>
<H2> . . . </H2>
<H3> . . . </H3>
<H4> . . . </H4>
<H5> . . . </H5>
<H6> . . . </H6>
```

Level 1 heading tags render the largest font size, while Level 6 heading tags render the smallest font size. Not only do the heading tags render different font sizes, they also put paragraph breaks before and after the heading.

The six heading levels, as rendered by Netscape Navigator, are compared in Figure 1.2.

As you can see, heading Levels 5 and 6 are extremely difficult to read. You might want to consider avoiding them if you possibly can. On the other hand, if you're a lawyer and your company is obligated to spell out the terms and conditions of product or service pricing in its advertising, Levels 5 and 6 might be exactly what you need.

Highlighting Text

There are a number of tags that can be used to highlight text in different ways. These tags do not cause a paragraph break; only the word or phrase encapsulated by the start and end tags is affected:

- Bold is indicated by `<B> . . . </B>`
- Italic is indicated by `<I> . . . </I>`

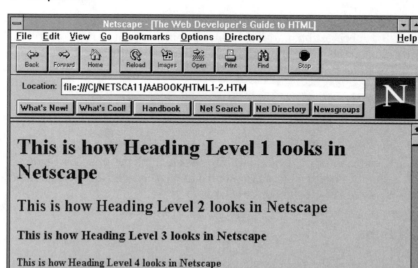

Figure 1.2

- Emphasized text is indicated by `<EM>` . . . `</EM>`
- Strongly emphasized text is indicated by `<STRONG>` . . . `</STRONG>`

These tags can be nested. For example, you could indicate bold italic text in the following way:

```
<B><I>This is bold italic text</I></B>
```

Figure 1.3 compares these text highlights as rendered by Netscape. Obviously, you should avoid overusing highlighted text; otherwise it loses its impact. Here are some general guidelines:

- To avoid projecting a psychotic image, do not highlight whole sentences, paragraphs, or documents. (If you really are psychotic, go for it!)
- Avoid highlighting acronyms, words, and phrases that already are highlighted in uppercase.
- Avoid frequent use of highlighted text in the same paragraph.
- Avoid mixing different highlight styles in the same paragraph.

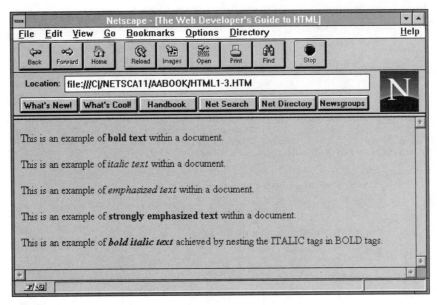

Figure 1.3

Preformatted Text

Preformatted text is indicated by the `<PRE>` . . . `</PRE>` tags. These tags cause the encapsulated text to be rendered in a fixed-width font, making them suitable for displaying things like computer screen text, sample programming code, or tabular data. The `<PRE>` tag may be used with the optional WIDTH attribute, which specifies the maximum number of characters per line and allows the browser to select a suitable font and indentation. When used, the WIDTH attribute can specify 40, 80, or 132 characters. If the WIDTH attribute is not present, a width of 80 characters is assumed. The WIDTH attribute can be used as follows:

```
<PRE WIDTH="40"> . . . </PRE>
<PRE WIDTH="80"> . . . </PRE>
<PRE WIDTH="132"> . . . </PRE>
```

There are several things to remember when using the PRE tags:

- Hypertext links and tags that are used to highlight text may be encapsulated within the PRE tags.

- Tags that are used to define paragraph formatting, such as headings and address, must not be used within the PRE tags.

- Tags that are used to define line breaks and character formatting may be used within the PRE tags.

Here is an example of how the PRE tags are used to render sample programming code:

```
<HTML>
<HEAD>
<TITLE>Programming Tips</TITLE>
</HEAD>
<BODY>
<H3>Assembling jumps and calls</H3>
This routine automatically assembles a short, near or far jump or
call, depending on byte displacement, to the destination address. You
can override such a jump or call by using a <B>near</B> or <B>far</B>
prefix, as the following example shows:
<PRE>
 -a0100:0500
0100:0500 jmp 502 ; a 2-byte short jump
0100:0502 jmp near 505 ; a 3-byte near jump
0100:0505 jmp far 50a ; a 5-byte far jump
</PRE>
You can abbreviate the <B>near</B> prefix to <B>ne</B>.
</BODY>
</HTML>
```

Figure 1.4 shows how this preformatted text is rendered by Netscape Navigator.

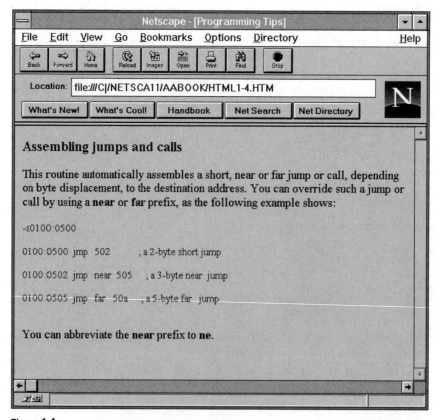

Figure 1.4

Notice how the use of the PRE tags causes the programming code to be rendered exactly the way the programmer laid it out, including the spacing within lines of code.

Despite carefully laying out text exactly where you want it within the PRE tags, there is always the possibility that it will not be rendered as you intended it—even when rendered by the same browser! This is because other factors come into play that are beyond your control. For example, the same model computer running the same version of the same browser may render the text differently if the video drivers are different and/or the screen resolution is different. If you have a large amount of information to format between the PRE tags, keep in mind that the time and effort you put into this process may not be worth the results most people get.

Using Address Tags

ADDRESS tags are used to encapsulate such information as address, signature, and document authorship, and are typically used at the top or the bottom of the document. Typically, an address is rendered in italics and in smaller text than normal. The ADDRESS tags may be used as follows:

```
<HTML>
<HEAD>
<TITLE>McGraw-Hill Book Catalog</TITLE>
</HEAD>
<BODY>
<H3>The Web Developer's Guide to HTML</H3>
This book is a clear, concise reference for the development of
functional and attractive Web pages using the Hypertext Markup
Language (HTML). Among other things, you will learn the basics of
formatting text, building menus and lists, creating hypertext links,
and designing forms.
<P>
<ADDRESS>
by Nathan J. Muller<BR>
Consultant<BR>
Huntsville, AL<BR>
nmuller@ddx.com
</ADDRESS>
</BODY>
</HTML>
```

Notice the use of the <BR> tag, which breaks the line at the desired places. The last line of the address has no <BR> tag because the break is implied. The <BR> tag is not limited to use within the ADDRESS tags; it can be used whenever you want to break a line of text at a specific place.

Figure 1.5 shows how the address above is rendered by Netscape Navigator.

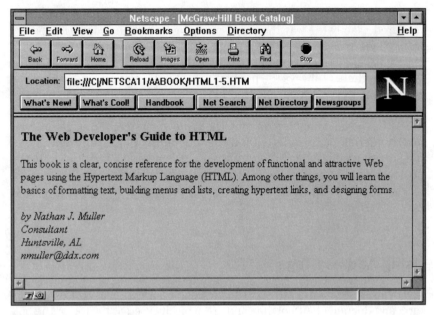

Figure 1.5

Using Blockquote Tags

The BLOCKQUOTE tags are used to encapsulate text quoted from another source. A typical rendering might include italic or smaller-than-normal text, which may be indented as well. It causes a paragraph break, providing space above and below the quote.

An example of how BLOCKQUOTE tags might be used is:

```
<HTML>
<HEAD>
<TITLE>The History of Particle Physics</TITLE>
</HEAD>
<BODY>
<H3>The Search Continues</H3>
Concerning the search for ever smaller subatomic particles, Werner
Heisenberg has observed,
<BLOCKQUOTE>
By getting to smaller and smaller units, we do not come to fundamental
units, or indivisible units, but we do come to a point where division
has no meaning.
</BLOCKQUOTE>
Moreover, reductionism fails to help us explain real-world events. As
Paul Davies, one of England's leading theoreticians, has noted,
<BLOCKQUOTE>
It would be ludicrous to try to understand consciousness, or a living
cell, or even an inanimate system such as a tornado, in terms of
quarks, for example.
</BLOCKQUOTE>
The difficulty of explaining what is made up of what at the subatomic
scale is illustrated by an aspect of the Heisenburg uncertainty
principle . . .
</BODY>
</HTML>
```

Figure 1.6 shows how this blockquote is rendered by Netscape Navigator.

The BLOCKQUOTE tags are especially useful for publishing academic and research papers on the Web. Such works often are laden with quotes from other sources.

Other Useful and Not-So-Useful Tags

HTML 2.0, which is supported by most browsers, offers several other tags to render text in different ways. These tags are summarized in Table 1.1.

New Tags

The draft HTML 3.0 specification proposes a number of additional ways to highlight text, but they are not yet widely supported. You might want to consider experimenting with these tags by viewing them with different browsers before committing to their use in all of your documents. These tags are summarized in Table 1.2.

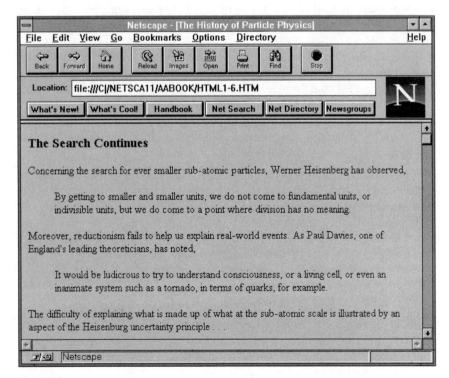

Figure 1.6

TABLE 1.1

Tags	Purpose
<CITE> . . . </CITE>	Indicates a citation, which is typically rendered as italics.
<CODE> . . . </CODE>	Indicates an example of code, which is typically rendered in a monospaced font.
<KBD> . . . </KBD>	Indicates that the encapsulated text should be rendered as an example of keyboard input, as might be used in an instruction manual. The text is typically rendered in a monospaced font.
<SAMP> . . .</SAMP >	Short for SAMPLE, indicates that the encapsulated text should be rendered as a sequence of literal characters, typically in a monospaced font.
<TT> . . </TT>	Indicates that the encapsulated text should be rendered in fixed-pitch teletypewriter font.
<U> . . . </U>	Indicates that the encapsulated text should be rendered as underlined. (This tag is not widely supported and should not be confused with hypertext links which also are underlined.)
<VAR> . . . </VAR>	Indicates that the encapsulated text should be rendered as a variable name, as might be used in an instruction manual. The text is typically rendered as italic.

If any of these tags would be useful to include in your documents, but you are not sure whether to use them because they are not yet widely supported, here are some general guidelines to help you make a decision:

- If you are operating under a tight deadline and all or most of your documents are already in electronic form, consider not using the new tags at all. Emphasis should be placed on adding the basic codes that will enable your documents to be published on the Web as soon as possible. You can speed the coding process by using an HTML converter that comes with (or can be integrated with) word processors such as Microsoft's Word for Windows and Novell's WordPerfect for Windows.

- If you have a lot of information to put on your Web server, and it is not already in electronic form, consider using the new tags. Because most of the information will have to be typed again anyway, or edited after being run through a scanner, it is very easy to add the new tags. Although you may not be able to reap the benefits of the new tags immediately, it can save you a lot of work adding them later. Meanwhile, no harm will occur to your documents because the new tags that are not supported by current browsers simply will be ignored.

- If you have a limited amount of information to make available on the Web, but it is expected to change frequently, you can hold off using the new codes until they become widely supported. Then, as part of your normal document update process, you can make use of newer HTML converters that include the new codes.

TABLE 1.2

Tags	Purpose
<ABBREV> . . . </ABBREV>	Indicates that the encapsulated text is an abbreviation.
<ACRONYM> . . . </ACRONYM>	Indicates that the encapsulated text is an acronym.
<AU> . . . </AU>	Indicates that the encapsulated text is the name of an author.
<BIG> . . . </BIG>	Indicates that a bigger font should be rendered for the encapsulated text versus the current font.
<DEL> . . . </DEL>	Indicates that the encapsulated text should be deleted, as might be used in a legal brief or a workgroup document to keep track of changes.
<DFN> . . . </DFN>	Indicates that the encapsulated text is the defining instance of a term.
<INS> . . . </INS>	Indicates that the encapsulated text is inserted text, as might be used in a legal brief or a workgroup document to keep track of changes.
<PERSON> . . . </PERSON>	Indicates that the encapsulated text is the name of a person. These tags allow names to be automatically extracted by indexing programs.
<Q> . . . </Q>	Indicates that the encapsulated text should be rendered as a short quotation. When nested, these tags alternate between matching double or single quotation marks.
<S> . . . </S>	Indicates strike through text, which is indicated by a horizontal line through the encapsulated text.
<SMALL> . . . </SMALL>	Indicates that a smaller font should be rendered for the encapsulated text versus the current font.
_{. . .}	Indicates that the encapsulated text should be rendered as a subscript using a smaller font compared with normal text.
^{. . .}	Indicates that the encapsulated text should be rendered as superscript text using a smaller font compared with normal text.

Inserting Comments in Documents

Within the body of a document, you can insert comments that will be ignored by the browser and will not show up on the screen when the document is viewed. Comments are especially useful for updating existing HTML documents, because they can remind the author of what needs attention the next time the document is updated.

An example of a comment and its format is:

```
<!--This document expires in six months-->
```

Each comment should be individually coded and no other HTML tags should appear within a comment. In addition, comments cannot be nested. An example of the coding for multiple comments is:

```
<!--This document expires in six months-->
<!--Check with Paul for possible document revisions-->
<!--Clear revisions with Norma before posting again on the Web server-->
```

Comments also can be used to call attention to particular sections of a document. They are especially useful when more than one person is involved in revising a document. An existing HTML-coded document can be mailed electronically to each person in turn, with the routing sequence and assignments embedded in the document itself, as in the following examples:

```
<!--Upon completion of your task, please route to the next person as
follows:-->
<!--Steve, rewrite this paragraph to include a statement about our
market share-->
<!--Marie, please insert a list of the product's new features here-->
<!--Amanda, can we link this to an e-mail form to make user feedback
easier?-->
<!--Tommy, when these items are added, post the document on the Web
server-->
```

The HTML coding for our document up to this point, adding paragraph and heading tags, as well as a few highlight tags and an embedded comment, looks like this:

```
<HTML>
<HEAD>
<TITLE>The Web Developer's Guide to HTML</TITLE>
</HEAD>
<BODY>
<H2>Introduction to the Web</H2>
The World Wide Web (WWW) is one of the fastest growing Internet
services. It is estimated that at the end of 1994, there were well
over 100,000 commercial sites on the Web.
<!--Bill can we get an updated figure for 1995?-->
<H3>Business Applications</H3>
According to a report issued by Strategic Information Resources,
<CITE>Business Applications of the World Wide Web</CITE>, this
Internet service can be an efficient and economical way to distribute
information globally. HTML-coded documents can comprise a vast
database—all or portions of which can be interconnected with
<B>hypertext links</B>.
<P>
In addition to distributing information to the public, companies can
use their Web servers for distributing information internally. A
<I>firewall</I> can be set up to prevent access by outside intruders
and passwords can be used to control access by employees.
</BODY>
</HTML>
```

Figure 1.7 is how the document looks as rendered by Netscape Navigator: There are several things to note in this rendering:

- As expected, the comment that is coded in the first paragraph is not rendered.

- Because the headings provide a line of space above and below, the use of a paragraph tag to separate the first two paragraphs is not needed.

- There is no appreciable difference between the rendering of text encapsulated between the ITALIC and CITE tags.

Although there is no difference in the way the CITE text and ITALIC text are rendered, the use of this tag can make it easier to update HTML documents. If you wanted to locate all citations in a document or a database, you could search on <CITE> to find them easily. If you use the ITALIC tags for citations, doing a search on <I> would find words and phrases in italics as well as citations.

This chapter has only scratched the surface of what can be done with the HyperText Markup Language. Already, you have become familiar with the power and simplicity of HTML. You also have become familiar with the inconsistent way browsers render various HTML-coded features. Finally, you should appreciate that just because the HTML tags are defined in various specifications does not mean that browsers available on the market today support them, or even that they will be useful enough for inclusion in your own documents.

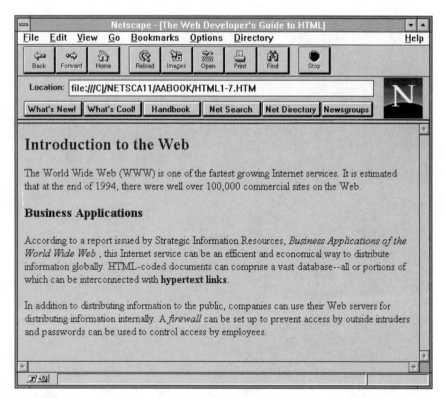

Figure 1.7

2

Creating HyperText Links

One of the key features of the World Wide Web is hypertext links. If you have ever accessed online help in Windows, you already are familiar with how hypertext links work. Instead of having to scroll down the length of a document to find the information, you just click on an underlined word or phrase in a list to get to the topic immediately. Using hypertext links, you can go from topic to topic in this fashion, obtaining the information you need in the least amount of time.

When used to find information in a large database, hypertext links are a powerful tool not only for finding information, but following numerous other links for related information. When hypertext links are applied to the tens of thousands of databases that make up the World Wide Web, the power of hypertext links is truly awesome. By clicking on a hypertext link located in a local database, you can quickly find yourself accessing information on servers that can be located anywhere in the world.

Hypertext links can take you to information in a variety of formats, not just text. There can be hypertext links to images, audio messages, and video clips. You can even link to other Internet services, such as a Usenet news server, a mail handler, an FTP server, or a Gopher site (Figure 2.1).

The hypertext link itself does not have to be text-based. An icon or button can be a hypertext link, as can an image or parts of an image. When selected, the hypertext link will bring the user to the selected information.

Anchors are used to implement hypertext links. There are pointer anchors and destination anchors. The pointer anchor, also known as the hypertext reference (HREF) anchor, is the text or graphical object the user clicks on to jump to another location. The destination anchor, also known as the named reference (NAME), marks the location at the other end of the hypertext link.

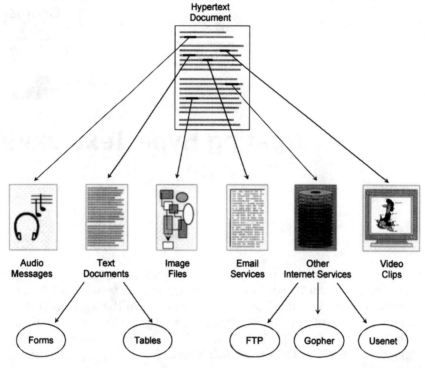

Figure 2.1

There are three types of hypertext links: internal, local, and remote. With an internal hypertext link, the destination anchor is somewhere within the same file as the pointer anchor. With a local hypertext link, the destination anchor is in another file in the same computer or network. With a remote hypertext link, the destination anchor is at another location on the Internet.

Link Components

In HTML, anchor tags are used to encapsulate a section of text that is the start and/or end destination of a hypertext link, as follows:

```
<A> . . . </A>
```

In the format above, the tags are not functional. However, the <A> tag can accept attributes that make it functional, one of which is known as the hypertext reference (HREF), which provides the destination address of the link. The following example illustrates its use:

```
<A HREF="filename.html"> . . . </A>
```

The destination (*filename*) must be enclosed in quotation marks, along with the file extension. While you are working with an HTML file in a word processor or text editor, it has the htm extension. After it is uploaded to your Web server, it must be renamed with the html extension. When referencing other HTML files within a hypertext link, they must use the html extension.

The text between the anchor tags is rendered as underlined, and as a different color than the surrounding text. This indicates to a user that the text is a hypertext link, which, when clicked on, will retrieve another document that contains related information.

Another common attribute of the anchor tag is known as the named reference (NAME), which is used to mark a specific location within a document at the other end of the hypertext link. This is the point the user will jump to when clicking on the hypertext link. Both ends of the hypertext link would be written as:

```
<A HREF="filename.html#wordtag"> . . . </A>
<A NAME="wordtag"> . . . </A>
```

The use of the HREF and NAME attributes within the anchor tags is illustrated in the following sections, which discuss the various applications of hypertext links.

Creating a Local Hypertext Link

Hypertext links can be used to tie together related documents that will reside in the same computer's database. These are called local hypertext links. The main document may consist of any number of references to other topics, with each hypertext reference providing a link to another document. When users click on these links, they are brought to the top of the appropriate document. In the following coding example, the paragraph has two references, each encapsulated in anchor tags:

```
<HTML>
<HEAD>
<TITLE>Creating a Business Presence on the Internet</TITLE>
</HEAD>
<BODY>
<H1>Approaches</H1>
There are several approaches for creating a business presence on the
Internet. One of the most popular is the <A HREF="filename.html">Yellow
Pages</A> approach, which relies on menus and links that point to other
sources of useful information as well as the company's products and
services. Another approach is the <A HREF="filename.html">Virtual
Storefront</A>, which is designed to showcase the company's products
and services, and may include order forms for online purchasing.
</BODY>
</HTML>
```

When specifying a hypertext link, do not underline the word or phrase. Whatever is encapsulated within the anchors will be rendered as underlined text by the browser, such as Netscape, as shown in Figure 2.2.

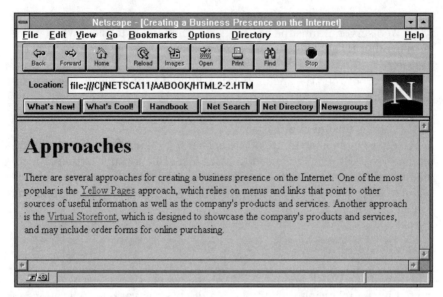

Figure 2.2

Creating an Internal Hypertext Link

When you want to create a link that brings the user to a specific place in the same document, such as a head or subhead, the HREF and NAME attributes are used within the anchor tags to specify the linkage. No file name is specified, because both ends of the hypertext link are in the same document.

A hypertext reference anchor that points to a specific place within the same document might be written as:

```
<HTML>
<HEAD>
<TITLE>Electronic Mail</TITLE>
<BODY>
<H1>Advantages of e-mail</H1>
e-mail has many advantages. It is fast, often delivered in minutes.
It is cheap, often costing considerably less than a postage stamp. It
is convenient, because it can be sent or received anytime, anywhere.
These advantages have made e-mail so popular that many people include
their <A HREF="#01">e-mail addresses</A> on their business cards and
letterheads.
<P>
```

Further down in the same document, the named reference (or destination anchor) is written as:

```
<H3><A NAME="01">E-mail Addresses</A></H3>
E-mail messages are routed on the Internet based on routing
information embedded in the e-mail address itself. A simple e-mail
address consists of the person's name, the computer that handles that
person's messages, and a three-letter designator that identifies the
type of Internet user. An example is nmuller@iquest.com, where nmuller
is the person's name, @iquest refers to the computer that handles
```

```
nmuller's messages, and .com identifies the computer as a commercial
entity on the Internet.
</BODY>
</HTML>
```

In this case, the internal link points to a Level 3 heading, which starts a new topic further down in the same document.

Creating a Link to a Specific Place in Another Document

Let's say that you have a document that contains a lot of technical terms. Instead of defining each term in the body of the document and interrupting the smooth flow of each topic, you could make each term a hypertext link to a glossary in a separate document. That way, users who are not familiar with the term can go to it, while those who are familiar can keep on reading without getting bogged down with unnecessary explanations.

For example, a technical term in the main document such as "spread spectrum" would be encapsulated with anchor tags as follows:

```
<H2>Spread Spectrum</H2>
A more reliable method of the wireless transmission is <A HREF=
"glossary.html#G218">spread spectrum</A>, which can be employed by
wireless bridges and routers, as well as in the transceivers attached
to each desktop computer.
<P>
```

Upon clicking on the term "spread spectrum," the user goes to a separate file containing the glossary. Because spread spectrum happens to be the 218th term in the glossary, it has been given the label G218. At the other end of the link, the term in the glossary must also be labeled as G218. The coding for the glossary entry looks like this:

```
<P>
<A NAME="G218">Spread Spectrum</A>
A digital coding technique in which the signal's power is spread over
a larger band of frequencies, making it appear as background noise.
Using the same spreading code as the transmitter, the receiver
correlates and collapses the spread signal back down to its original
form, making the information it carries intelligible only to the
addressee. The result is a more secure signal that also is less
susceptible to distortion than traditional RF signaling.
<P>
```

Creating Links to Images

Hypertext links not only are used for helping users navigate text, they can be used to bring up image files as well. Currently, two types of image file formats are handled by HTML: GIF and JPEG. Chapter 6 provides more information about these file formats. For now, this discussion is limited to creating links to these types of files.

When an image is displayed along with text, it is referred to as an inline image. When the images are small—such as bullets, bars, and icons—they can help organize text in a visually pleasing way. But when images are large, such as a picture of a network layout, they can cause the document to take a long time to load and impede the ability of users to quickly get at the information they want until all the image files that go along with the text are fully loaded.

This problem can be alleviated by using hypertext links to point to the image files. That way, if users want to view the images, they can use the hypertext links to call up the files. Users who would rather read text can do so without being slowed down by image loading.

The following coding example shows a section of text with a hypertext link to a GIF image:

```
<HTML>
<HEAD>
<TITLE>A Primer on Network Management</TITLE>
</HEAD>
<BODY>
<H1>
A network management system is an application that monitors the
performance of various devices and the links that interconnect them.
Among other things, it reports problems to a console so that
appropriate troubleshooting procedures can be initiated by the
operator. A typical network management system is shown in <A HREF=
"filename.gif">Figure 1.</A>
<P>
```

Notice that the hypertext link to an image file is written the same way as a hypertext link to a text file; only the file name and file extension are different. If the image file is JPEG instead of GIF, the file extension .jpg is used as follows:

```
<A HREF="filename.jpg"> . . . </A>
```

The same document can reference GIF files or JPEG files, or any mix of the two. And with each image contained in its own file, you can reference any number of image files without slowing down the loading of the main document.

Creating Links to Video Clips

The availability of video capture and editing products for PCs opens up new possibilities for using the Web to transfer video clips for offline playback. The two most common video file types found on the Web are QuickTime and MPEG (named after the Moving Pictures Experts Group, the international standards body that worked on it). QuickTime players are available for Macintosh and Windows computers, while MPEG players are available for UNIX (as well as Macintosh and Windows) computers. Decoding hardware also is available and is a virtual necessity for improving the performance of video playback.

A hypertext link to a QuickTime video file is written as:

```
<A HREF="filename.qt"> . . . </A>
```

while a hypertext link to an MPEG video file is written as:

```
<A HREF="filename.mpg"> . . . </A>
```

Because the video clips are contained in their own files, any number of hypertext links can be embedded in the main document, and in any mix of file formats.

Creating Links to Sound Files

Greetings, sound effects, and music clips can be included in hypertext documents for online or offline playback using an appropriate audio player. Keep in mind that users may also need a sound card to fully appreciate what is in these types of files.

The de facto standard for sound files on the Internet is .au, because it is compatible with most kinds of computers. There are several other sound file formats, including , .wav, .voc, .snd, and .mid. A hypertext link to a MIDI music format file, for example, is written as:

```
<A HREF="filename.mid"> . . . </A>
```

while a hypertext link to an audio format file is written as:

```
<A HREF="filename.au"> . . . </A>
```

Because the sound clips are contained in their own files, any number of hypertext links can be embedded in the main document, and in any mix of sound file formats. Although not all web browsers have audio support built in, nearly all can launch external "viewers" to handle audio files. These player programs are widely available as freeware or shareware for most architectures, if not already standard with your operating system. At any rate, most audio files need to be downloaded before they can be heard. Depending on the type of browser, the user may have to configure it for downloading before the link is activated. With some browsers, all the user has to do is click on the hypertext link to initiate the download.

New developments are making it possible to play back audio files as they are being downloaded.

Creating a Link to Another Home Page

On occasion, you may want to link your documents to other documents that reside on different Web servers. Let's say that your company has developed a new communications device that operates as a modem, but can be upgraded to operate over a basic ISDN line. Instead of explaining what ISDN is and how it can be used, you can link your product announcement to other pages on the Web that explain authoritatively the technology's advantages and applications. This saves space on your own server, and the links can add credibility to what you are saying about your product.

The format for a hypertext link to a specific file at another Web site on the Internet is:

```
<A HREF="http://www.iquest.com/~nmuller/isdn.html" > . . .</A>
```

Let's review the elements of this hypertext link:

`<A>  .  .  .  </A>`: these are the anchor tags that define the hypertext link.

`HREF`: hypertext reference, also known as the pointer anchor, indicates the destination of the link.

`HTTP`: refers to the HyperText Transfer Protocol used by Web servers to move HTML documents around the Internet.

`WWW`: World Wide Web.

`@iquest`: indicates the host computer or server where the file resides.

`com`: indicates a commercial site.

`~nmuller`: indicates the name of the Web page the link will bring you to.

`ISDN.HTML`: the name of the specific file that will be accessed.

Links to other Web sites and documents are very common. In fact, such links are the essence of the World Wide Web and other Internet services. Links are the main navigation tool.

Creating a Link to an FTP Site

Hypertext links can be created to bring the user to an FTP site. FTP stands for file transfer protocol. FTP sites usually contain documents, software, and other files that are contained in various directories and which can be downloaded using the file transfer protocol. The format for a hypertext link to a real FTP site is:

```
<A HREF="ftp://fwux.fedworld.gov/pub" > . . . </A>
```

This particular link will bring the user to a list of government publications offered by the National Technical Information Service (NTIS), which introduced FedWorld in November 1992 to help with the challenge of accessing U.S. government information online. The goal of NTIS FedWorld is to provide a one-stop location for the public to locate and order U.S. government information.

Creating a Link to a Gopher Site

The gopher system provides an extensive range of information, resources, and files. Every gopher session starts with a menu from which files, services, Internet tools, and other menus can be selected. These menus often lead to a series of submenus. The format for a hypertext link to a real gopher site is:

```
<A HREF="gopher://marvel.loc.gov" > . . . </A>
```

This particular gopher site is the home of the Library of Congress's (LoC) Machine-Assisted Realization of the Virtual Electronic Library (MARVEL), a campus-wide information system that combines the vast collection of information available about the Library with easy access to diverse electronic resources over the Internet. Its goal is to serve the staff of the Library of Congress, as well as the U.S. Congress and constituents throughout the world.

Creating a Link to a Usenet Newsgroup

Usenet is a distributed messaging interchange focused on topics. Each topic has its own newsgroup where people can exchange ideas, post requests for information, share experiences, or make announcements. Currently, there are over 4,500 newsgroups.

The format for a link to a real Usenet newsgroup is:

```
<A HREF="news:misc.book.technical"> . . . </A>
```

This Usenet newsgroup provides miscellaneous information on technical books, including announcements of new books and catalogs, reviews, and comments from readers. If you are looking for a technical book on a particular subject, including the Internet, or want a recommendation on which book to buy, you can post a question here and probably get an answer within a few hours.

Creating a Link to Internet E-mail

Many home pages on the Web include a hypertext link to e-mail for the convenience of users. Via this link, users can request more information about a product or service, ask a question, provide feedback, subscribe to an e-mail notification service, or report problems with the Web page. The format for a hypertext link to the Internet e-mail service is:

```
<A HREF="mailto:username@domainname.com"> . . .</A>
```

When the user clicks on the hypertext link, an e-mail form appears on the screen with all the necessary fields that should be filled in. There is plenty of space for free-form messages, and the user has the option of attaching a file or quoting a document (sending the current document or mail message), and sending or cancelling the message via radio buttons.

Figure 2.3 shows the e-mail form as rendered in Netscape.

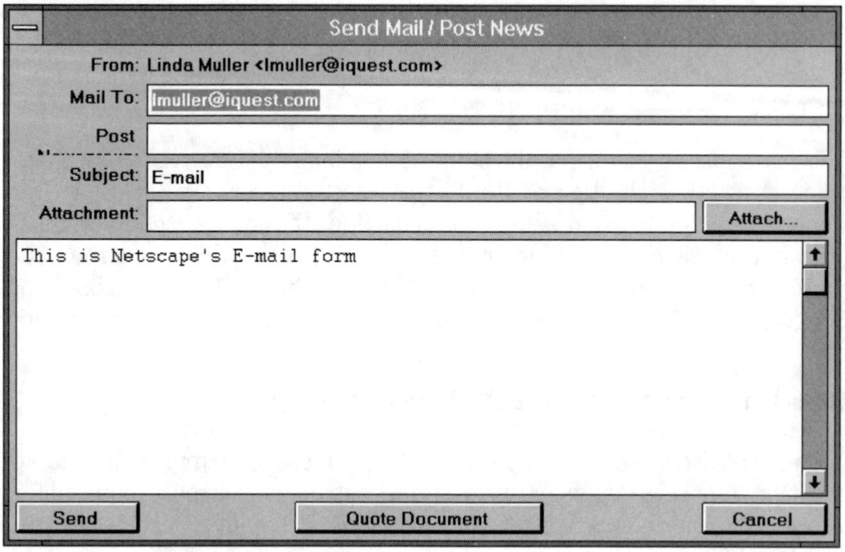

Figure 2.3

Hypertext links to e-mail forms can be placed anywhere in your database, not just the home page. For example, if the database contains academic research, technical reports, or white papers—anything in which authorship is important—a hypertext link to the author's e-mail address can be included at the beginning or end of the document, making it easier for readers to ask questions or provide feedback.

Table 2.1 shows how hypertext links to other popular e-mail services are formatted.

The formatting of addresses for CompuServe and MCI Mail merit particular attention. CompuServe addresses contain a comma, whereas MCI Mail addresses contain a hyphen. Internet e-mail does not recognize commas or hyphens in the address. In both cases, these should be replaced with periods.

TABLE 2.1

E-mail service	Hypertext link
AT&T Mail	<A HREF="username@attmail.com"> ... </A>
America Online	<A HREF="username@aol.com"> ... </A>
CompuServe	<A HREF="00000.0000@compuserve.com"> ... </A>
IBM Mail	<A HREF="username@ibmmail.com"> ... </A>
MCI Mail	<A HREF="000.0000@mcimail.com"> ... </A>
Prodigy	<A HREF="username@prodigy.com"> ... </A>

Creating Links to Forms

There are many different types of forms that can be designed for use on the Web, such as survey forms, purchase order forms, and subscription forms. Whatever the type of form, a hypertext link can be created to get the user there. Essentially, these forms are variations of the e-mail form discussed above, except that the user inputs may undergo some extra processing steps to arrange the collected information in a specified format.

In the case of a credit card purchase, user inputs may go through a third-party validation process before the transaction is considered complete. If there was a mistake in the credit card number or expiration date, for example, an appropriate notification is sent to the user, who usually is given another chance to enter the information.

Information that is input to forms also may go through extra processing steps so that it can be properly entered into an existing database format without having to be re-entered manually. When this information is included in the database in the right format, data extraction and report writing tools can be applied, such as those based on structured query language (SQL).

A hypertext link to a form looks exactly like that for any other document:

```
<A HREF="form.html"> . . . </A>
```

Creating Links to Telnet Sites

You can create hypertext links to host computers that can be accessed via telnet. The hosts contain such things as software archives, library catalogs, specialized databases, games, and other programs. They also provide access to other Internet resources such as e-mail, FTP, and gopher. Some telnet sites even support Internet Relay Chat (IRC), an interactive method of communicating with other online users. If you don't have, or can't get, an IRC client, you can try telneting to a host that supports this capability.

You can also use telnet to access remote bulletin board systems (BBSs) without incurring long-distance telephone charges. Because telnet relays your commands from computer to computer over the Internet, a remote host can provide local access to the BBS you want to reach. All you do is find a telnet host nearest to the location of the bulletin board you want to access. Once connected to that host, you can dial the local number of the BBS. A list of telnet sites can be obtained at http://honor.uc.wlu.edu/telnet.html, sorted by name, date, and geography. New telnet sites also are posted here.

Hypertext links can connect Web users to a company's host via a telnet session. For the link to work, the user's browser must be configured to find the directory and executable file of the telnet software program. In Netscape, this is done by selecting Options from the main menu bar, then Preferences, then Set Preferences On. From there, choose Applications and Directories to enter the location directory and file name of the telnet program.

The hypertext link to a telnet host is written as:

```
<A HREF="telnet://xxx.yyy.edu"> . . . </A>
```

If the Web page is private, then when the hypertext link is activated the user may be requested to enter a login ID and password for security purposes. If the link is intended for public use, the telnet host must be configured to allow access without a login ID and password. Typically, this is done by limiting access through a special port, in which case the user might be requested to enter "new" to display the main menu. The port may even be part of the link, as in the following example:

```
<A HREF="telnet://xxx.yyy.edu 1120"> . . . </A>
```

A special version of telnet is TN3270, which emulates an IBM 3270. The TN3270 program makes your computer act like a 3270 terminal, giving you access to the same functions and keys as a 3270 terminal. You can create a link to an IBM host that requires IBM 3270 terminal emulation by substituting tn3270 for telnet, as in the following example:

```
<A HREF="tn3270://xxx.yyy.edu"> . . . </A>
```

Another version of telnet is TNVT220, which is used to telnet to machines that use VT220 terminals. The link would be written as:

```
<A HREF="tnvt220://xxx.yyy.edu"> . . . </A>
```

Creating Links to Remote Login

The remote login (rlogin) program allows a user to log in to another host, much like telnet. The rlogin protocol is much simpler than telnet in that it does not use a protocol to effect the session. Every character the user types is sent to the other machine.

Links to rlogin are possible using the rlogin URL, as follows:

```
<A HREF="rlogin://username@xxx.yyy.edu"> . . . </A>
```

In this case, *username* is the account name for the rlogin. The user is prompted for a password, if one is required.

Creating Links to Internet Search Engines

In your Web pages you can create hypertext links to various search engines. There are several reasons why you might want to do this:

- It makes it convenient for users to find additional information about a topic covered in your Web pages, which enhances their value.

- It relieves you of having to keep updated on related topics.

- It saves you from having to duplicate information that can be found elsewhere on the Internet, an important consideration if you are paying a Web service provider for storage space.

Let's say, for example, that you have a Web page devoted to the telecommunications industry. Federal regulations play a key role in shaping this industry, but you might not want to follow the status of federal telecommunications reform efforts because you can't keep up with all the House and Senate bills and their status. Instead, you can provide the means for users to obtain the latest information themselves. This is done by linking to THOMAS, the legislative information service of the Library of Congress, which provides online copies of all House and Senate bills starting with the 103rd Congress. THOMAS includes a search engine that finds bills according to keyword, bill number, author, or title.

To write a hypertext link to a search engine, you need the Uniform Resource Locator (URL) of the service provider. The URL is something like an address that identifies the location of a particular resource on the Web. The URL for THOMAS is http://rs9.loc.gov. With this URL, the hypertext link is created as follows:

```
<A HREF="http://rs9.loc.gov"> . . . </A>
```

Of course, you could just as easily create a hypertext link to an Internet-wide search engine, such as Webcrawler. This would provide users with a convenient way of finding more information about any topic mentioned in your Web pages. The URL for the Webcrawler search engine is http://webcrawler.com, and the hypertext link would be written as:

```
<A HREF="http://webcrawler.com"> . . . </A>
```

Many companies have very extensive Web pages and provide search engines to help users locate specific information. You can provide hypertext links to these search engines in your own Web pages. For example, if you have a Web page that discusses different types of high-speed data communications services, you can provide links to the search engines of various service providers such as AT&T and MCI. That way, you would not have to keep updating your own Web page whenever these carriers make changes to their service offerings, but you can provide the means for users to check out the information themselves. To create links to the search engine of AT&T, for example, you need the URL for the company's page that accesses to the search engine, which is http://www.research.att.com/cgi-wald/db-access/68. The hypertext link to AT&T's search engine is written as follows:

```
<A HREF="http://www.research.att.com/cgi-wald/dbaccess/68"> . . .
</A>
```

The database is an online catalog for selecting and ordering a wide variety of documentation, including: AT&T practices, engineering drawings, product manuals, product specifications, books, international telephone directories, brochures, installation/service manuals, catalogs, training materials, product bulletins, technical bulletins and handbooks, administrative forms, employee benefit literature, and user guides. Subject areas include: data communications, telecommunications, terminal equipment, peripheral equipment, switching equipment, cabling, general business references, practices, operations reference tools, AT&T services, and software/programming documents.

You also could provide links to Veronica, a resource-discovery system providing access to the vast information resources of "gopherspace." Veronica provides "keyword-in-title" searches of information held on virtually all of the world's 5,000+ gopher servers.

The following hypertext links contain the URLs and names of several sites from which Veronica can be accessed:

```
<A HREF="gopher://info.psi.net:2347/7">PSINet</A>
<A HREF="gopher://empire.nysernet.org:2347/7">NYSERNet</A>
<A HREF="gopher://veronica.sunet.se:2347/7">SUNET</A>
```

An appropriate place to put hypertext links to any type of search engine is at the end of your documents. That way, users are more likely to finish reading your information before going somewhere else at the first opportunity.

Creating Links to Facsimile

It is possible to create links to a facsimile form such that clicking on the link will cause a fax form to appear. This would enable users to send documents via e-mail to non-Internet users, who would receive it on their fax machines. The concept is called remote-printing, but it is not available everywhere because it requires that the server at the destination end be equipped with fax spooling software.

To send a fax via e-mail entails the conversion of the recipient's fax number to an Internet domain name. This is done by inverting the fax number of the recipient, separating each number with a period, and adding tpc.int to the end (tpc is supposed to mean "the telephone company"), as in the following example for the phone number 1-202-555-1212:

```
remote-printer.Nathan_Muller/Consultant@2.1.2.1.5.5.5.2.0.2.1.tpc.int
```

A simpler way of writing the fax number is to write it normally (not inverted) and add iddd.tpc.int to the end. The iddd stands for international direct dialing designator.

A hypertext link to a facsimile form would be written just like a link to an e-mail form, except that you would specify the URL of the facsimile form. Your server does not have to be equipped with the fax spooling software—

only the destination server at the destination end must have that software. More information about remote printing can be found at the following URL:

```
http://town.hall.org/fax/faq.html
```

There are forms at these locations you can use to send faxes:

```
http://sable.ox.ac.uk/fax/faxsend-short.shtml
http://town.hall.org/fax/faxsend-short.html
```

Creating Graphical Hypertext Links

Up to this point, the discussion of hypertext links has been confined to text-based links—that is, turning keywords and phrases into pointers that bring users to other resources on the Internet. But a hypertext link can just as easily be a graphical object such as an icon.

When placed at the end of a document, for example, icons make useful navigation aids. Arrow icons can point the user back to the home page, up to the top of the current page, or forward to another document. The HTML disk includes a selection of icons that can be used for this purpose.

The following coding example shows how an icon is included with text as a clickable hypertext link:

```
<A HREF="http://rs9.loc.gov"> <IMG SRC="arrowr.gif"
ALIGN=MIDDLE>Go to Library of Congress</A>
```

The portion of the code IMG SRC means image source. In this case, the image source is arrowr.gif, which is an arrow icon pointing right. ALIGN= MIDDLE will cause the text "Go to Library of Congress" to line up at the middle of the icon. For the icon to show up next to the text, the file arrowr.gif must be located in the same directory as the text file it is being applied to. Thus, you will have a mix of text files and image files in the same directory.

If you do not want "Go to Library of Congress" to be included in the hypertext link, but just want the icon to be clickable as the link, you can revise the above coding example as follows, with the </A> tag placed in front of the text:

```
<A HREF="http://rs9.loc.gov"> <IMG SRC="arrowr.gif"
ALIGN=MIDDLE> </A>Go to Library of Congress
```

We can get quite sophisticated in the combination of text and images as hypertext links. In fact, it is becoming increasingly fashionable on the Web to have large images embedded with multiple hypertext links. This involves mapping an image containing so-called "hotspots" that can be clicked on to access other documents or resources. This method of creating hypertext links is covered in chapter 6.

Over the course of this chapter, it should have become apparent that there are many ways in which hypertext links can be used. Hypertext links are not limited to making connections between documents or even parts of the same document. They can be used to access information in other organizations' Web pages, provide access to different Internet services, remote hosts, other vendors' e-mail systems, and furnish users with ready access to a variety of search tools.

3

Creating Lists

Along with hypertext links, lists are a staple of the World Wide Web. Access to just about any kind of information on the Web starts with a list: a list of Web sites, a list of directories, a list of topics, or a list of subtopics. It goes without saying that lists are very useful organizing tools. With the Hyper-Text Markup Language (HTML), you can create several types of lists for your Web pages. The choice will depend on the purpose of the list. HTML enables you to create the following types of lists:

- Ordered list
- Unordered list
- Definition list

The early HTML standards mention two other lists: menu lists and directory lists. Menu lists are meant to be used for listing items consisting of only one line each, with the MENU tag causing each item to be indented. Directory lists are meant to be used for listing very short items vertically or horizontally. Not only is the utility of these lists questionable, but the draft HTML 3.0 specification does not mention them at all, an indication that they might be abandoned.

Creating Ordered Lists

An ordered list is a list of numbered items. This type of list is useful when the list items must appear in a specific sequence, as when conveying instructions or procedures or prioritizing tasks.

An ordered list is encapsulated with the `<OL>` . . . `</OL>` tags. Within the ordered list, each item is indicated with the `<LI>` tag.

The following is a coding example for an ordered list:

```
<HTML>
<HEAD>
<TITLE>Ordered List</TITLE>
</HEAD>
<BODY>
<H2>Defining the paragraph tag</H2>
ACME Publisher allows you to set the font for a paragraph tag. When
set, ACME will apply the same font to all characters in the selected
paragraph and to all paragraphs with the same tag. The font for a
paragraph tag is set as follows:
<OL>
<LI>Activate paragraph mode
<LI>Click on the paragraph
<LI>Drop the paragraph menu
<LI>Click on Font
<LI>Select a different typeface in the Face Box
<LI>Click on OK
</OL>
</BODY>
</HTML>
```

Figure 3.1 shows how the ordered list is rendered by Netscape.

The ordered list can be nested. In other words, for each item in the list there can be another set of lists. The following is a coding example of a nested list:

```
<HTML>
<HEAD>
<TITLE>Ordered List</TITLE>
</HEAD>
<BODY>
<H2>Defining the paragraph tag</H2>
ACME Publisher allows you to set the font for a paragraph tag. When
set, ACME will apply the same font to all characters in the selected
paragraph and to all paragraphs with the same tag. The font for a
paragraph tag is set as follows:
<OL>
<LI>>Activate paragraph mode
<LI>Click on the paragraph
<LI>Drop the paragraph menu
<LI>Click on Font
<LI>Select the following font attributes:
<OL>
<LI>Typeface
<LI>Size
<LI>Style
<LI>Color
</OL>
<LI>Click on OK
</OL>
</BODY>
</HTML>
```

Figure 3.2 shows how the ordered list is rendered by Netscape.

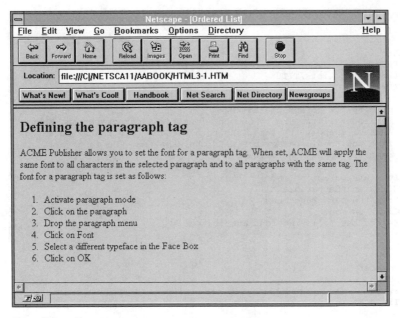

Figure 3.1

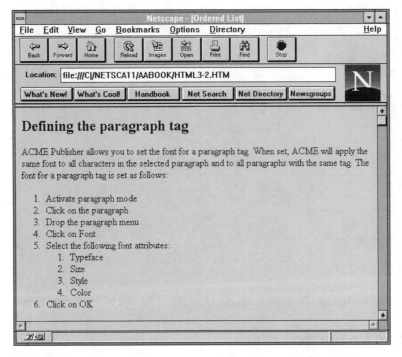

Figure 3.2

There can be several levels in the nested list, as the following coding example shows:

```
<HTML>
<HEAD>
<TITLE>Ordered List</TITLE>
</HEAD>
<BODY>
<H2>Defining the paragraph tag</H2>
ACME Publisher allows you to set the font for a paragraph tag. When
set, ACME will apply the same font to all characters in the selected
paragraph and to all paragraphs with the same tag. The font for a
paragraph tag is set as follows:
<OL>
<LI>Activate paragraph mode
<LI>Click on the paragraph
<LI>Drop the paragraph menu
<LI>Click on Font
<LI>Select the following font attributes:
<OL>
<LI>Typeface
<OL>
<LI>Courier
<LI>Dutch
<LI>Swiss
<LI>Times Roman
</OL>
<LI>Point Size
<OL>
<LI>6
<LI>8
<LI>10
<LI>12
<LI>14
</OL>
<LI>Style
<OL>
<LI>Light
<LI>Normal
<LI>Bold
<LI>Italic
</OL>
<LI>Color
<OL>
<LI>White
<LI>Black
<LI>Red
<LI>Green
</OL>
</OL>
<LI>Click on OK
</OL>
</BODY>
</HTML>
```

Figure 3.3 shows how the multilevel ordered list is rendered by Netscape.

Creating Unordered Lists

An unordered list, as you might guess, is one in which the items appear in no particular order. An ordered list is encapsulated with the <UL> . . . </UL>

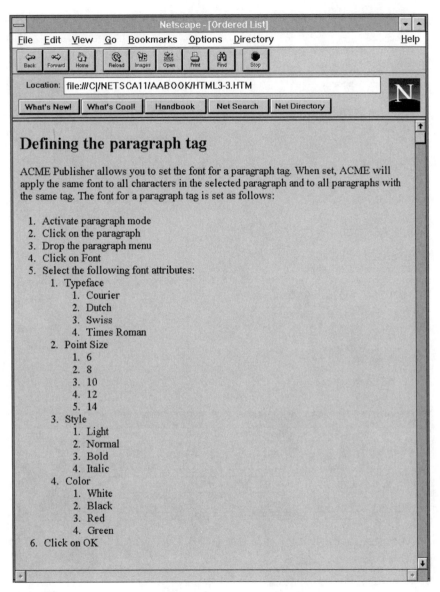

Figure 3.3

tags. Within the unordered list, each item is indicated with the <LI> tag.
When used within the <UL> . . . </UL> tags, the <LI> tag indicates bullets.
   The following is a coding example for an unordered list:

```
<HTML>
<HEAD>
<TITLE>Unordered List</TITLE>
</HEAD>
<BODY>
```

```
<H2>Multimedia Features of Windows 3.1</H2>
Windows supports several multimedia capabilities, including sound,
graphics, animation, and video. Among the new multimedia features
offered by Windows version 3.1 are:
<UL>
<LI>Media Player
<LI>Sound Recorder
<LI>Control Panel Enhancements
</UL>
For more information about these and other multimedia features, refer
to your Windows 3.1 manual.
</BODY>
</HTML>
```

Figure 3.4 shows how the unordered list is rendered by Netscape.

The unordered list can be nested. The following is a coding example of a nested list:

```
<HEAD>
<TITLE>Unordered List</TITLE>
</HEAD>
<BODY>
<H2>Enhanced Multimedia Control</H2>
Among the new multimedia control features offered by Windows version
3.1 are:
<UL>
<LI>Media Player, for control of
<UL>
<LI>Sound cards
<LI>CD-ROM drives
<LI>Videodisc players
</UL>
<LI>Sound Recorder, for
```

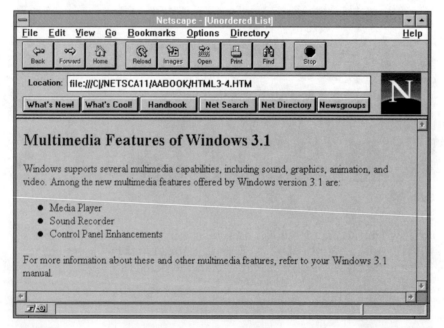

Figure 3.4

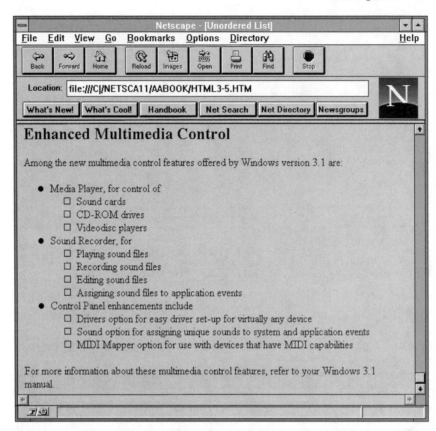

Figure 3.5

```
<UL>
<LI>Playing sound files
<LI>Recording sound files
<LI>Editing sound files
<LI>Assigning sound files to application events
</UL>
<LI>Control Panel enhancements include
<UL>
<LI>Drivers option for easy driver set-up for virtually any device
<LI>Sound option for assigning unique sounds to system and application
events
<LI>MIDI Mapper option for use with devices that have MIDI capabilities
</UL>
</UL>
For more information about these multimedia control features, refer
to your Windows 3.1 manual.
</BODY>
</HTML>
```

Figure 3.5 shows how the unordered nested list is rendered by Netscape.

Notice the difference in the way bullets are handled from one level to the next.

The following is a coding example of a three-level nested list:

```
<HEAD>
<TITLE>Unordered List</TITLE>
</HEAD>
<BODY>
<H2>Impact on Network Load</H2>
Document image files are often quite large and, when passed from
workstation to workstation in a workflow process, can slow down the
network to an intolerable level. Software-based compression is easy and
economical to implement and can greatly improve network performance:
<UL>
<LI>Compression
<UL>
<LI>Lossless
<UL>
<LI>Compression ratios vary between 1.5-to-1 and 8-to-1
<LI>Upon decompression, completely restores image without pixel loss
</UL>
<LI>Lossy
<UL>
<LI>Compression ratios can be as high as 300-to-1
<LI>Upon decompression, restores image with some pixel loss
</UL>
</UL>
</BODY>
</HTML>
```

Figure 3.6 shows how the multilevel nested list is rendered by Netscape.

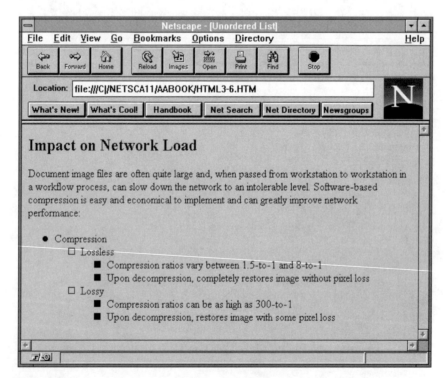

Figure 3.6

Creating Definition Lists

A definition list is a list of terms and corresponding definitions. Definition lists are usually formatted with the term flush left and the definition, formatted in paragraph style, indented after the term. A good use of the definition list is for glossaries.

A definition list is encapsulated with the <DL> . . . </DL> tags. Within the definition list, terms are indicated with the <DT> tag and definitions are indicated with the <DD> tag.

The following is a coding example for three glossary terms using all of these tags:

```
<HTML>
<HEAD>
<TITLE>Glossary</TITLE>
</HEAD>
<BODY>
<DL>
<DT>Michael Faraday
<DD>
An English chemist and physicist, Michael Faraday (1791-1867)
discovered the principle of electromagnetic induction in 1831. By
moving a magnet through a coil of copper wire, he found that it
caused an electric current to flow through the wire. The electric
motor and electric generator are based on this principle.
<DT>Guglielmo Marconi
<DD>An Italian inventor and electrical engineer, Guglielmo Marconi
(1874-1937) pioneered the use of wireless telegraphy. Telegraph
signals had previously been sent through electrical wires. In 1895,
Marconi demonstrated that telegraph signals could also be sent
through the air.
<DT>James Clerk Maxwell
<DD>A British scientist, James Clerk Maxwell (1831-1879) is best
known for his research on electricity and magnetism and for his
kinetic theory of gases. In 1864, Maxwell combined his ideas with
those of Michael Faraday and others to form a theory describing the
relationship between electric and magnetic fields. He theorized that
waves in the combined fields, called electromagnetic waves, travel at
the speed of light.
</DL>
</BODY>
</HTML>
```

Figure 3.7 shows how the definition list is rendered by Netscape.

To make the glossary easier to read, you can add boldface to the terms using the <B> . . . </B> tags and separate each item with a paragraph <P> tag. With these simple changes, the results can be quite dramatic, as shown in Figure 3.8.

The definition list can be nested. In other words, within each definition there can be subdefinitions, unordered lists, or notes. These can even have hypertext links. The following is a coding example of how all of these elements can be embedded within a single definition list:

```
<HTML>
<HEAD>
<TITLE>Glossary</TITLE>
```

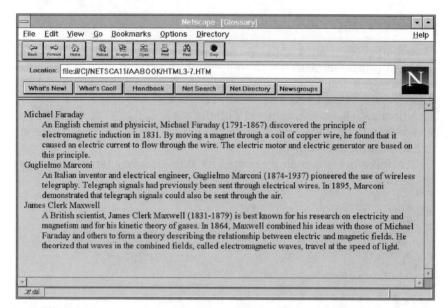

Figure 3.7

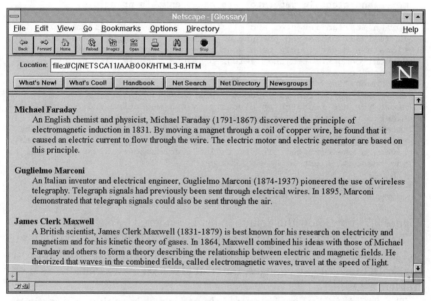

Figure 3.8

```
</HEAD>
<BODY>
<DL>
<DT><B>Michael Faraday</B>
<DD>
An English chemist and physicist, Michael Faraday (1791-1867)
```

```
discovered the principle of electromagnetic induction in 1831. By
moving a magnet through a coil of copper wire, he found that it
caused an electric current to flow through the wire. The electric
motor and electric generator are based on this principle.
<P>
<DT> <B>Guglielmo Marconi</B>
<DD>An Italian inventor and electrical engineer, Guglielmo Marconi
(1874-1937) pioneered the use of wireless telegraphy. Telegraph
signals had previously been sent through electrical wires. In 1895,
Marconi demonstrated that telegraph signals could also be sent
through the air.
<P>
<DL> <DT> <DD>See also: <A HREF="glossary.html#M1">Microwave</A> and
<A HREF="glossary.html#SW1">Short Wave</A> </DL>
<P>
<DT> <B>James Clerk Maxwell</B>
<DD>A British scientist, James Clerk Maxwell (1831-1879) is best
known for his research on electricity and magnetism and for his
kinetic theory of gases. In 1864, Maxwell combined his ideas with
those of Michael Faraday and others to form a theory describing the
relationship between electric and magnetic fields. He theorized that
waves in the combined fields, called electromagnetic waves, travel at
the speed of light. This theory was confirmed in the late 1880s by
the German physicist Heinrich R. Hertz.
<P>
<DL> <DT> <DD>Hertz used a rapidly oscillating electric spark to
produce ultrahigh frequency waves. These waves caused similar
electrical oscillations in a distant wire loop. This discovery paved
the way for the development of radio, television broadcast, and radar.
<P>
<DL> <DT> <DD>See also:
<UL> <LI> <A HREF="glossary.html#R1">Radio</A> <LI> <A
HREF="glossary.html#T1">Television</A> <LI> <A
HREF="glossary.html#R2">Radar</A> </UL> </DL> </DL>
<P>
<DT> <B>Nathan J. Muller</B>
<DD>Author of McGraw-Hill's <I>The Web Developer's Guide to HTML</I>,
Nathan Muller is known in some circles as "The Hemingway of High-Tech"
for his ability to write complex technical books on short notice,
employing the economical prose style of Ernest Hemingway.
</DL>
</BODY>
</HTML>
```

Notice how each nested item is encapsulated within its own <DL> and
</DL> tags. Also notice the use of double </DL> tags in the nested list. The
use of double </DL> tags is necessary to start the next term—Nathan J.
Muller—flush left. If only one </DL> tag is used here, the next term would
be indented instead of flush left.

Figure 3.9 shows how this nested definition list is rendered by Netscape.

Using Lists for Menus

As a Web page developer, your first occasion to use a list will come very early
in the creation of a new Web page. The first page, or "home page," usually will
contain a list of topics that are coded as hypertext links. These links will take
users to other documents in your database. Typically, the home page's menu

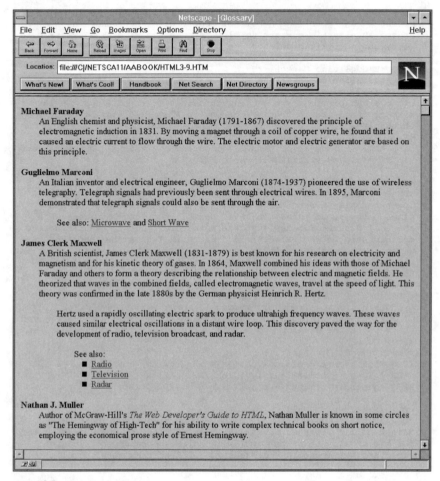

Figure 3.9

will be in the form of an unordered list. The following coding example of an unordered list also provides hypertext links, making it suitable as a menu:

```
<HTML>
<HEAD>
<TITLE>Telecommunications</TITLE>
</HEAD>
<BODY>
<CENTER> <H2>Main Menu</H2> </CENTER>
<P>
<HR>
<UL>
<LI> <A HREF="netserve.html">Network Services</A>
<LI> <A HREF="netapps.html">Network Applications</A>
<LI> <A HREF="netman.html">Network Management</A>
<LI> <A HREF="netadmin.html">Network Administration</A>
<LI> <A HREF="netsup.html">Network Support</A>
</UL>
</BODY>
</HTML>
```

The menu can be expanded with subtopics, each with hypertext links, as follows:

```
<HTML>
<HEAD>
<TITLE>Telecommunications</TITLE>
</HEAD>
<BODY>
<CENTER> <H2>Main Menu</H2> </CENTER>
<P>
<HR>
<UL>
<LI> <A HREF="netserve.html">Network Services</A>
<UL>
<LI> <A HREF="t1.html">"T1</A>
<LI> <A HREF="isdn.html">ISDN</A>
<LI> <A HREF="f-relay.html">Frame Relay</A>
</UL>
<LI> <A HREF="netapps.html">Network Applications</A>
<UL>
<LI> <A HREF="data.html">High-speed Data Transfer</A>
<LI> <A HREF="video.html">Videoconferencing</A>
<LI> <A HREF="workflow.html">Workflow Processing</A>
</UL>
<LI> <A HREF="netman.html">Network Management</A>
<UL>
<LI> <A HREF="stats.html">Statistics Gathering</A>
<LI> <A HREF="events.html">Event Reporting</A>
<LI> <A HREF="mantools.html">Management Tools</A>
</UL>
<LI> <A HREF="netadmin.html">Network Administration</A>
```

Figure 3.10 shows how this unordered list appears as a menu, as rendered by Netscape.

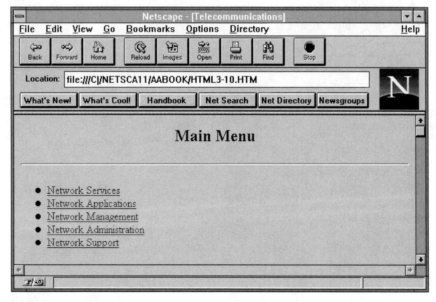

Figure 3.10

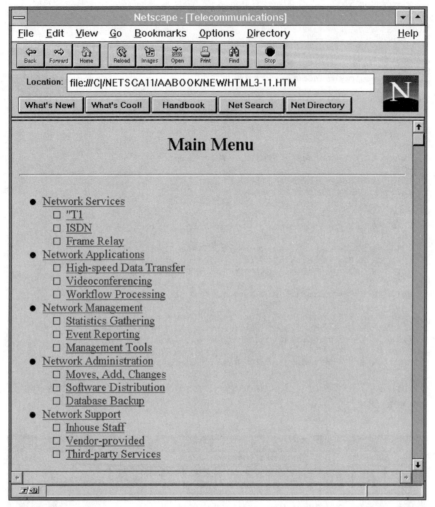

Figure 3.11

```
<UL>
<LI> <A HREF="macs.html">Moves, Add, Changes</A>
<LI> <A HREF="soft.html">Software Distribution</A>
<LI> <A HREF="backup.html">Database Backup</A>
</UL>
<LI> <A HREF="netsup.html">Network Support</A>
<UL>
<LI> <A HREF="inhouse.html">Inhouse Staff</A>
<LI> <A HREF="vendors.html">Vendor-provided</A>
<LI> <A HREF="party.html">Third-party Services</A>
</UL>
</UL>
</BODY>
</HTML>
```

Figure 3.11 above shows how this expanded unordered list appears as a menu, as rendered by Netscape.

Although lists can contain any number of levels, you might want to consider limiting yourself to only three or four levels. After that, the list tends to confuse rather than help the reader. If you've ever accessed a busy newsgroup in Usenet, you are probably familiar with this situation.

4

Enhancing Text Pages

The purpose of the World Wide Web is to distribute information. Most of this information is in text form and, fortunately, there are a number of navigational aids that make it easier for users to find what they need. Examples include WWW search engines such as Webcrawler (`http://webcrawler.com`) and Lycos (`http://lycos.cs.cmu.edu`) and the tens of thousands of page-specific search engines. All of the information on the Web ultimately is woven together with hypertext links, allowing users to jump from topic to topic as their needs and interests change from moment to moment.

Despite the ease of navigation, we are still left with the cold, stark reality that most business information on the Web is conveyed in text form. For the Web developer, this has several ramifications:

- Pages that consist mainly of text do not compete well with pages that make extensive use of color and images, if for no other reason than that text is harder to read on a computer screen than text on a printed page.

- Despite useful content, text-laden pages can convey the wrong image: that the company lacks energy and creativity. For certain companies, like advertising and public relations firms, consultants, publishers, catalog companies, and countless other information-oriented service organizations, this kind of image must be avoided.

- With so many visually exciting places to go on the Web, it is unlikely that any user will want to stay on a text page long enough to fully appreciate the message.

You could limit the amount of text and make more extensive use of graphics, but for certain types of businesses and applications, text avoidance is not an option, especially if they involve offering information as a commercial service on the Web. Publishers of books, encyclopedias, research reports, and manuals, for example, cannot hope to survive by limiting the amount of information they offer to subscribers. Yet they must package the information in a visually compelling way to ensure subscription renewal.

This chapter focuses on the use of HTML tags and tag attributes to give text pages more visual impact. In fact, this chapter assumes that the Web developer has no special image editing programs or artistic skills—only reams of information that must be converted to HTML. The use of graphical objects and images is covered in chapters 5 and 6.

Using Horizontal Rules

Large text documents can be broken up to make them easier to read and understand. There are two ways to partition documents: physically and logically. The physical approach entails breaking the document up into multiple smaller files and interconnecting them with hypertext links. The logical approach entails the use of HTML tags and tag attributes to visually break a single large document into multiple sections.

There are two problems with the physical approach: First, it does not add visual impact to the pages, except for the hypertext links. Second, the use of multiple files can actually slow down performance, especially if the files are located on different Web servers. The reason for slow performance is that the file request and retrieval process activated by a hypertext link takes some time while the following procedures are carried out:

- Request initiated
- Connect: looking up host
- Host contacted
- Waiting for reply
- Transferring data
- Document received

Every time a hypertext link to another file is activated, this process is put into play. It is actually more complicated than this; in fact, there is a formal handshaking process that goes on behind the scenes to get any intervening computers linked up and communicating before a file is even transferred across the Internet. If all the documents reside on the same Web server, the delay is minimal. But because companies often have multiple servers with distributed databases, Web developers cannot always count on all the links pointing to local documents.

With the logical approach, unnecessary delays can be avoided. Instead of partitioning one large document into several smaller files, you can make the one large text file easier to read by employing a number of visual aids. While the large file will take longer to load initially, the amount of delay is often less than the cumulative delay resulting from multiple loads of smaller files.

This brings us to the actual method of logically partitioning a large file. One way of doing this is accomplished with HTML's horizontal rule tag <HR>. As its name implies, the <HR> tag causes a horizontal rule to be rendered across the screen. It can be used as a separator between sections of text or topics, thus logically breaking up large documents and adding some visual impact.

When used with the SIZE attribute, the thickness of the horizontal line can be specified with different values. For example, <HR SIZE=5> provides a horizontal rule that is five times thicker than the horizontal rule specified by <HR>, while <HR SIZE=10> provides a horizontal rule 10 times thicker than <HR>.

Figure 4.1 compares the different Netscape renderings of the <HR> tag when used with the SIZE attribute and different values.

If you do not want the horizontal rule to be rendered as spanning the entire width of the screen, you can specify the percentage of the screen it should span by adding the WIDTH attribute as follows:

```
<HR SIZE=5 WIDTH=50%>
```

In this case, the horizontal rule will span only half the available screen space, instead of spanning the entire width.

You can also specify that the horizontal rule be rendered as centered on the page. This can be done in either of two ways. The first way is by encapsulating the <HR> tag and its attributes with the Netscape-specific CENTER tags as follows:

```
<CENTER>
<HR SIZE=5 WIDTH=50%>
</CENTER>
```

The second way is to use HTML' s ALIGN=CENTER attribute as follows:

```
<ALIGN=CENTER>
<HR SIZE=5 WIDTH=50%>
```

When there is a choice between Netscape-specific tags and HTML, you should choose HTML, because many more browsers will be able to render your documents the way you intended them to be rendered. Of course, if there are no HTML alternatives to Netscape-specific tags, you must decide whether to push the envelope or cater to the lowest common denominator.

While horizontal rules can be used to add visual impact to Web documents, they should not be overly used (Figure 4.1). For example, it would not be a good idea to separate every paragraph with a horizontal rule. One effective use of horizontal rules would be to use them in conjunction with the heading tags—perhaps leading a head tag with an appropriately sized horizontal rule. For example, if you have an HTML document that makes

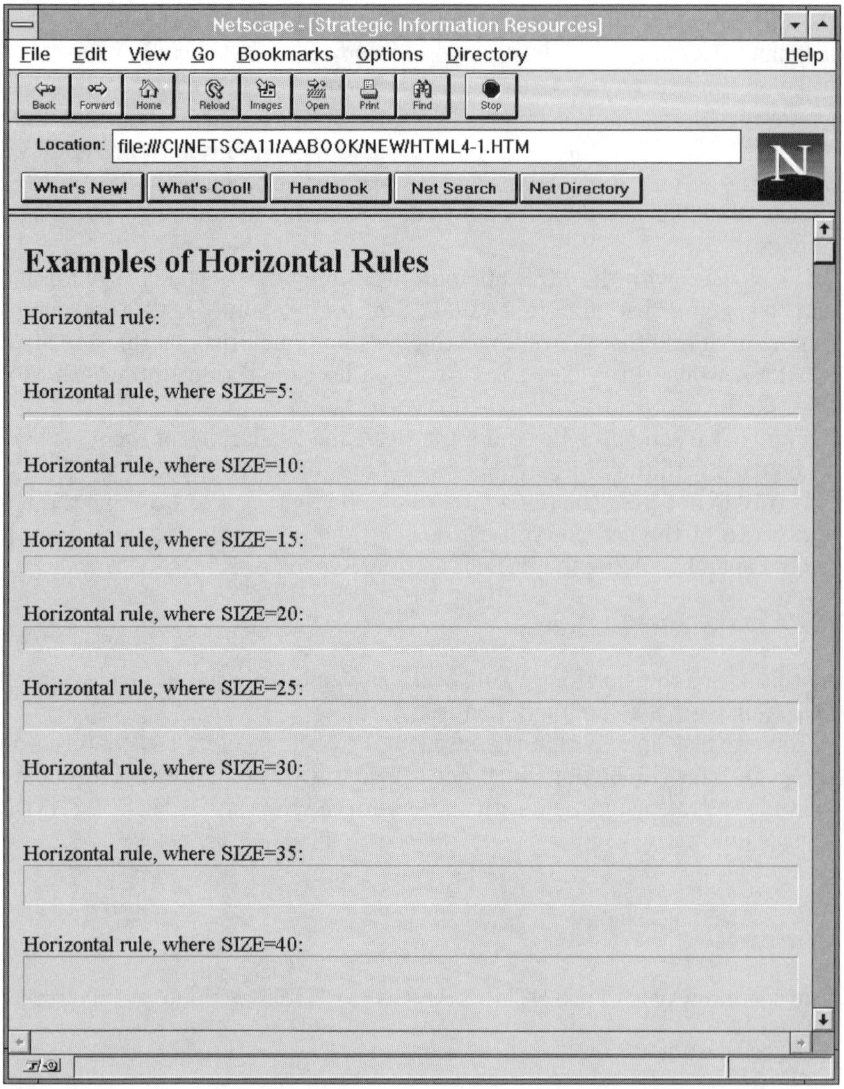

```
┌─────────────────────────────────────────────────────────────────┐
│ ─          Netscape - [Strategic Information Resources]    ▼  ▲   │
├─────────────────────────────────────────────────────────────────┤
│ File   Edit   View   Go   Bookmarks   Options   Directory   Help │
├─────────────────────────────────────────────────────────────────┤
│  ⇦⇨    ∞    ⌂     ⟳     ▥     ▦     ▤     ⋔      ●                │
│ Back Forward Home Reload Images Open  Print  Find    Stop         │
├─────────────────────────────────────────────────────────────────┤
│ Location: file:///C|/NETSCA11/AABOOK/NEW/HTML4-1.HTM      ┌────┐ │
│                                                           │ N  │ │
├───────────────────────────────────────────────────────────┴────┤ │
│ │What's New!│ │What's Cool!│ │ Handbook │ │Net Search│ │Net Directory│ │
└─────────────────────────────────────────────────────────────────┘
```

Examples of Horizontal Rules

Horizontal rule:

Horizontal rule, where SIZE=5:

Horizontal rule, where SIZE=10:

Horizontal rule, where SIZE=15:

Horizontal rule, where SIZE=20:

Horizontal rule, where SIZE=25:

Horizontal rule, where SIZE=30:

Horizontal rule, where SIZE=35:

Horizontal rule, where SIZE=40:

Figure 4.1

use of three heading levels, you can associate a different sized horizontal rule with each of them, as follows:

```
<HR SIZE=5>
<H1>Paragraph Heading Level 1</H1>
<HR SIZE=3>
<H2>Paragraph Heading Level 2</H2>
<HR>
<H3>Paragraph Heading Level 3</H3>
```

You should experiment with a style and consider applying it to all of your HTML documents to achieve a consistent look and feel that will become an identifying feature of your Web page. This consistency also will result in faster HTML coding, because you will not have to waste time trying to think of a style for every document.

Specifying Font Sizes

The HTML heading tags are fine for specifying the font size of various heads in the document, but they tend to be rendered in boldface by most browsers. Additional flexibility is offered by the Netscape-specific FONT tag and the SIZE attribute, which are written as follows:

```
<FONT SIZE=7> . . . </FONT>
```

In this example, the encapsulated text is rendered in the largest font size available, and in normal face rather than boldface. Figure 4.2 contrasts the use of HEAD and FONT tags.

The BOLD and ITALIC tags can be used within the FONT tags to highlight the encapsulated text as follows:

```
<FONT SIZE=6> <B>This is an example of boldface</B> </FONT>
<FONT SIZE=6> <I>This is an example of italic</I> </FONT>
<FONT SIZE=6> <B><I>This is an example of bold italic</I> </B>
</FONT>
```

Figure 4.3 shows how these HTML tags and attributes are rendered in Netscape Navigator.

Among the many possible uses of the FONT tag is to render the starting character of an opening paragraph in a larger font size than the rest of the word. This is used when you want to delineate the start of a new section of text. It also can be used for highlighting a document's title and subtitles. Here is the coding for a title and paragraph that makes use of this convention, in conjunction with the Netscape-specific CENTER tags:

```
<CENTER>
<FONT SIZE=+2>A</FONT>sset <FONT SIZE=+2>M</FONT>anagement
</CENTER>
<P>
<FONT SIZE=+2>A</FONT>sset management services differ greatly in
their general capabilities. All offer some degree of automated data
collection in the environments they address and all offer some degree
of help desk support. However, only a few vendors offer the means to
integrate asset management information gathered by other network
management platforms.
<P>
```

Figure 4.4 shows how the paragraph is rendered by Netscape Navigator.

Using Preformatted Text

The PRE tags are used to enclose text to be rendered in a fixed-width type-writerlike font. The HTML coding structure for the PRE tags is:

```
<PRE> . . . </PRE>
```

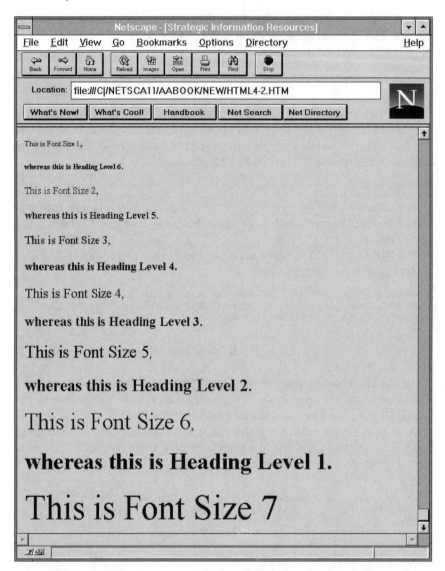

Figure 4.2

One of the main uses for these tags has been for building text tables, because the use of a fixed-width font permits tables to be rendered pretty similar to the way they are laid out between the tags, including the horizontal and vertical spaces between text elements. As mentioned in chapter 1, however, such factors as video drivers and screen resolutions may cause the text between PRE tags to be rendered differently from one user to the next. So it may not be a good idea to put too much time in very elaborate text formats, especially for tables. The proposed HTML 3.0 specification includes tags and attributes for building very sophisticated tables that go far beyond

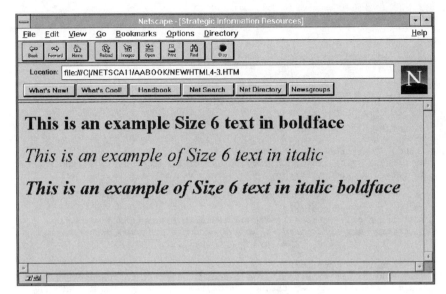

Figure 4.3

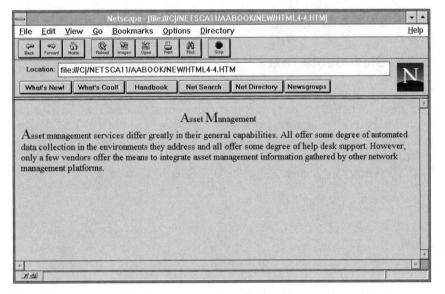

Figure 4.4

what can be rendered with the PRE tags. Nevertheless, the PRE tags have many uses, such as providing some visual interest to text pages, as in the following HTML coding example:

```
<HTML>
<HEAD>
<TITLE>Welcome to B&G on the Web</TITLE>
```

```
</HEAD>
<BODY>
<CENTER>
<P>
<H1>B&G Enterprises</H1>
<P>
<PRE>
Y O U R C E N T R A L S O U R C E F O R M A C I N T O S H P R O D U C T S
</PRE>
<HR SIZE=10 WIDTH=60%>
</CENTER>
<P>
<H3>Our Guarantee</H3>
We offer a 30-day return policy to all of our customers. If you need
to return a product for any reason, our returns specialists will be
happy to help.
<P>
<H3>Quality Products</H3>
B&G offers only nationally-recognized name brand products to our
customers. Our goal is to bring you products that represent the best
in value, technology, quality, functionality, and innovation.
<P>
<H3>Technical Support</H3>
B&G provides lifetime toll-free technical support to customers from
9 a.m. to 9 p.m. Monday through Friday and 9 a.m. to 5 p.m. Saturday.
All of our technicians are trained by our vendors.
</BODY>
</HTML>
```

Figure 4.5 shows how the page is rendered by Netscape Navigator.

Using Blockquote Text

The BLOCKQUOTE tags are most often used for encapsulating extended quotations. When these tags are used, the encapsulated text will be indented from the surrounding paragraphs. However, the BLOCKQUOTE tags can be used in other ways as well, such as to add some visual interest to HTML text documents.

The HTML coding structure for the BLOCKQUOTE tags is:

```
<BLOCKQUOTE> . . . </BLOCKQUOTE>
```

The BLOCKQUOTE tags can be nested, as in the following HTML coding example:

```
<HTML>
<HEAD>
<TITLE>Welcome to B&G on the Web</TITLE>
</HEAD>
<BODY>
<CENTER>
<P>
<H1>B&G Enterprises</H1>
<P>
<PRE>
Y O U R C E N T R A L S O U R C E F O R M A C I N T O S H P R O D U C T S
</PRE>
<HR SIZE=10 WIDTH=60%>
```

Figure 4.5

```
</CENTER>
<P>
<BLOCKQUOTE>
<P>
<H3>Quality Products</H3>
<BLOCKQUOTE>B&G offers only nationally-recognized name brand products
to our customers. Our goal is to bring you products that represent
the best in value, technology, quality, functionality, and
innovation.<P>
</BLOCKQUOTE>
<H3>Easy Returns</H3>
<BLOCKQUOTE>We offer a 30-day return policy to all of our customers.
If you need to return a product for any reason, our returns
specialists will be happy to help.</BLOCKQUOTE>
<H3>Technical Support</H3>
<BLOCKQUOTE>B&G provides lifetime toll-free technical support to
customers from 9 a.m. to 9 p.m. Monday through Friday and 9 a.m. to
5 p.m. Saturday. All of our technicians are trained by our
vendors.</BLOCKQUOTE>
<H3>Customer Service</H3>
<BLOCKQUOTE>Our trained customer service staff will help you pick out
the right hardware and software for your needs. We can even build a
computer to your specifications, preload the software, and test the
entire system before it ships.</BLOCKQUOTE>
```

```
</BLOCKQUOTE>
</BODY>
</HTML>
```

The outer BLOCKQUOTE tags are used to indent the entire body of text, while the inner BLOCKQUOTE tags are used to indent the specific paragraphs from their headings. If you don't like the idea of using BLOCK-QUOTE tags for this purpose, you can substitute the much shorter `<UL>` and `</UL>` tags instead.

Figure 4.6 shows how the page is rendered by Netscape Navigator, using either the BLOCKQUOTE or UL tags.

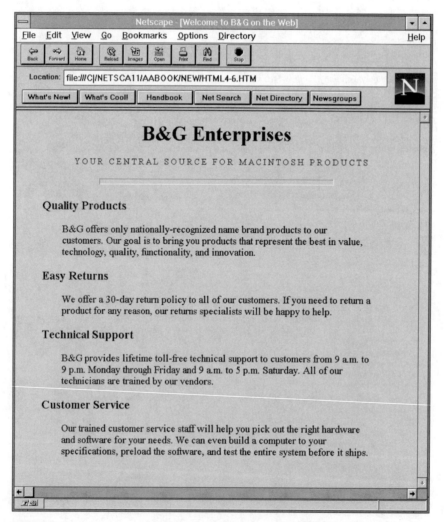

Figure 4.6

Using Blinking Text

Sometimes you may want to highlight an important word or phrase to convey a sense of urgency. Instead of bold or italic, you can flash the text on and off by encapsulating it within the Netscape-specific BLINK tags, as in the following coding example:

```
<BLINK>News Flash!</BLINK>
```

In this example, the phrase News Flash! will turn on and off every second or so. The thing to keep in mind is that inline GIF or JPEG images (warning symbols, for example) cannot be encapsulated between the BLINK tags; the blinking effect will not work at all. The BLINK tags only work with text. Not even horizontal rules can be made to blink. You can encapsulate different words in the same document with the BLINK tags, but they will blink in unison and not at staggered intervals. Obviously, the BLINK tags should not be used often or they will lose impact, possibly even branding the Web developer as a "hot-dog."

Specifying Menu Structure

Most menu pages on the Web have lists of hypertext links arranged flush left, with a bullet for each item. This is achieved using an <LI> tag for each list item, with the entire list encapsulated with the <UL> and </UL> tags. Many times this is unavoidable, but other times a classier look can be achieved by centering the list of hypertext links and dispensing with the bullets entirely, as shown in Figure 4.7. In this case, the Netscape-specific CENTER tags are used to encapsulate the list.

Specifying Text Color

By default, the text of Web pages is rendered as black. Another way to dress up your Web pages is to use HTML tags and attributes to specify how the text should be rendered in terms of color. To do this, you must use the BODY tag, which is normally omissible, with the TEXT attribute and specify a color value. Color values take the form of hexadecimal red-green-blue (RGB) triplets, as in 0000FF (for blue).

An example of the HTML code for rendering the text of a document as blue is:

```
<BODY TEXT="#0000FF">
```

Only one color code for text can be used in the same file; you cannot associate colors with different heading levels, for example, or alternate the colors of words or paragraphs. Once a color value is specified for the TEXT attribute (or any other attribute), it is applied throughout the doc-

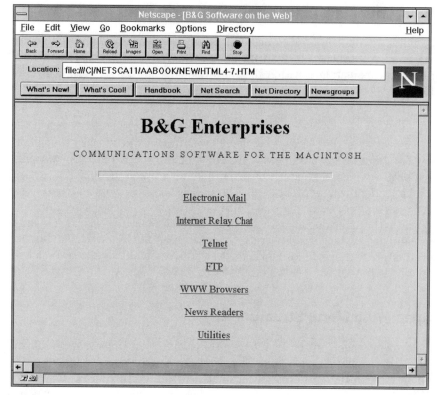

Figure 4.7

ument. While browsing through other Web pages, you might notice that some clever Webmeisters have managed to use many different colors for text in the same document. This is accomplished by using image editing programs that turn text into GIF files, which are referenced in the HTML-coded document and fetched by the browser. This method results in much slower document retrieval, because multiple files must be retrieved to fully render a Web page.

For purposes of discussion, the following colors and RGB codes are listed below. More colors and RGB codes are listed in appendix A.

Color	RGB#
White	FFFFFF
Blue	0000FF
Magenta	FF00FF
Scarlet	8C1717
Violet	CC3299

Specifying Background Color

If you are going to use colored text, it may be helpful to vary the background color as well to obtain better contrast. For example, blue shows up better against a white background than a browser's default gray background. To specify background color, the Netscape-specific BGCOLOR attribute is used within the BODY tag. This attribute is used to specify the background color without having to specify a separate image file that requires another network access to load.

The Netscape-specific coding for rendering the background of a document as white and the text as blue is:

```
<BODY BGCOLOR="#FFFFFF" TEXT="#0000FF">
```

If you like the idea of selecting your own colors for your Web pages, particularly for both background and text, you should experiment with various color combinations. Some combinations, like white text over a black background, are very difficult for many people to read and may cause the reader to go elsewhere on the Web.

Specifying Link Color

In the same way that the colors for text and screen background can be specified, the color for hypertext links can be specified as well. The default color of a link might be blue, but if you want the text of an entire document to be rendered as blue, the link will not stand out the way it should and the reader may mistake it for underlined text. The following Netscape-specific coding example specifies a white background, blue text, and magenta links.

```
<BODY BGCOLOR="#FFFFFF" TEXT="#0000FF" LINK="#FF00FF">
```

Specifying Visited Link Color

The color of visited links can be specified with the VLINK attribute within the BODY tag. A visited link, or VLINK, is one that a user has already visited and which is indicated with a different color than a link that has not been visited. The color differences allow users to keep track of their hypertext jump activity without inadvertently repeating visits to documents and resources they have already accessed. The default coloring of the VLINK might be purple.

The following Netscape-specific coding example specifies a white background, blue text, magenta links, and scarlet visited links.

```
<BODY BGCOLOR="#FFFFFF" TEXT="#0000FF" LINK="#FF00FF"
VLINK="#8C1717">
```

Specifying Active Link Color

When the user clicks on a link, it becomes the active link (ALINK). The default color for an active link might be red, but can be changed with the ALINK attribute in the BODY tag.

The following Netscape-specific coding example specifies a white background, blue text, magenta links, scarlet visited links, and a violet red active link.

```
<BODY BGCOLOR="#FFFFFF" TEXT="#0000FF" LINK="#FF00FF"
VLINK="#8C1717" ALINK="CC3299">
```

Implementing Fade-In/Fade-Out Screens

There is an interesting effect that can be produced with the RGB color codes that causes a Web page to fade in when opened and fade out when closed. This is achieved by listing the RGB codes for various color gradients within the BODY start tag. Below is an example of what this might look like:

```
                 <body bgcolor=#010002> <body bgcolor=#030206> <body
  bgcolor=#05040a> <body bgcolor=#07060e> <body bgcolor=#090812> <body
  bgcolor=#0b0a16> <body bgcolor=#0d0c1a> <body bgcolor=#0f0e1e> <body
  bgcolor=#111022> <body bgcolor=#131226> <body bgcolor=#15142a> <body
  bgcolor=#17162e> <body bgcolor=#191832> <body bgcolor=#1b1a36> <body
  bgcolor=#1d1c3a> <body bgcolor=#1f1e3e> <body bgcolor=#212042> <body
  bgcolor=#232446> <body bgcolor=#25244a> <body bgcolor=#27264e> <body
  bgcolor=#292852> <body bgcolor=#2b2a56> <body bgcolor=#2d2c5a> <body
  bgcolor=#2f2e5e> <body bgcolor=#313062> <body bgcolor=#333266> <body
  bgcolor=#35346a> <body bgcolor=#37366e> <body bgcolor=#393872> <body
  bgcolor=#3b3a76> <body bgcolor=#3d3c7a> <body bgcolor=#3f3e7e> <body
  bgcolor=#414082> <body bgcolor=#434286> <body bgcolor=#45448a> <body
  bgcolor=#47468e> <body bgcolor=#494892> <body bgcolor=#4b4a96> <body
  bgcolor=#4d4c9a> <body bgcolor=#4f4e9e> <body bgcolor=#5150a2> <body
  bgcolor=#5352a6> <body bgcolor=#5554aa> <body bgcolor=#5756ae> <body
  bgcolor=#5958b2> <body bgcolor=#5b5ab6> <body bgcolor=#5d5cba> <body
  bgcolor=#5f5ebe> <body bgcolor=#6160c2> <body bgcolor=#6362c6> <body
  bgcolor=#6564ca> <body bgcolor=#6766ce> <body bgcolor=#6968d2> <body
  bgcolor=#6b6ad6> <body bgcolor=#6d6cda> <body bgcolor=#6f6ede> <body
  bgcolor=#7170e2> <body bgcolor=#7372e6> <body bgcolor=#7574ea> <body
  bgcolor=#7776ee> <body bgcolor=#7978ee> <body bgcolor=#7b7aee> <body
  bgcolor=#7d7cee> <body bgcolor=#7f7eee> <body bgcolor=#8180ee> <body
  bgcolor=#8382ee> <body bgcolor=#8584ee> <body bgcolor=#8786ee> <body
  bgcolor=#8988ee> <body bgcolor=#8b8aee> <body bgcolor=#8d8cee> <body
  bgcolor=#8f8eee> <body bgcolor=#9190ee> <body bgcolor=#9392ee> <body
  bgcolor=#9594ee> <body bgcolor=#9796ee> <body bgcolor=#9998ee> <body
  bgcolor=#9b9aee> <body bgcolor=#9d9cee> <body bgcolor=#9f9eee> <body
  bgcolor=#a1a0ee> <body bgcolor=#a3a2ee> <body bgcolor=#a5a4ee> <body
  bgcolor=#a7a6ee> <body bgcolor=#a9a8ee> <body bgcolor=#abaaee> <body
  bgcolor=#adacee> <body bgcolor=#afaeee> <body bgcolor=#b1b0ee> <body
  bgcolor=#b3b2ee> <body bgcolor=#b5b4ee> <body bgcolor=#b7b6ee> <body
  bgcolor=#b9b8ee> <body bgcolor=#bbbaee> <body bgcolor=#bdbcee> <body
  bgcolor=#bfbeee> <body bgcolor=#c1c0ee> <body bgcolor=#c3c2ee> <body
  bgcolor=#c5c4ee> <body bgcolor=#c7c6ee> <body bgcolor=#c9c8ee> <body
  bgcolor=#cbcaee> <body bgcolor=#cdccee> <body bgcolor=#cfceee> <body
  bgcolor=#d1d0ee> <body bgcolor=#d3d2ee> <body bgcolor=#d5d4ee>
```

In this example, when the document is accessed, the screen goes to black and fades to a light blue. A copy of this example is included on HTMLdisk so you can try it out. You can do this with different colors with the aid of a utility called Color Ramper, which can be found on the Web (http://www.net-creations.com/ramper/index.html). Color Ramper takes your start color and end color, and provides you with the intervening color codes that will produce the fade-in/fade-out effect.

Creating Two-Column Text

Two-column text is accomplished by building a transparent table with two columns and specifying the text that will go into each column. Because the table's border is transparent, the text will appear as arranged in two columns when rendered by the browser.

Here is an HTML coding example that will cause the text to be rendered in a format similar to a computer magazine editorial:

```
<HTML>
<BODY>
<TABLE CELLPADDING=15 WIDTH="90%">
<TR><TH COLSPAN=2 ALIGN=LEFT><H1>Companies Can Gain With Asset
Management</H1> </TH></TR>
<TR> <TD COLSPAN=2> <I>by Nathan J. Muller</I> </TD> </TR>
<TR>
<TD>Today's large corporate networks consist of a vast assemblage of
hardware and software. Thousands of different computer models, cards,
peripherals, and software packages may be in use—most of it purchased
from different vendors to suit the varying needs and preferences of
employees.<P>
Asset management is essential for controlling costs—most of which are
"hidden costs" that drain IT budgets and divert scarce resources.
Industry analysts say the cost of operating and supporting a single
workstation can reach $40,000 over five years. About 90 percent of
this amount consists of hidden support costs which remain unmanaged
and unaccountable. A hidden cost is anything a LAN administrator or
systems manager does not know about, such as having too many software
licenses or too</TD>
<TD> many overconfigured workstations that have more disk capacity or
memory than is really needed.<P>While various software programs are
available to inventory assets and track changes, the major computer
makers are entering this emerging market in a big way. Among those
offering asset management services are IBM, Unisys, Sun and HP. All
offer some degree of automated data collection and all offer some
degree of help desk support. Some even provide the means to integrate
asset management information gathered by other network management
platforms and share the data.<P> Industry experts say companies can
trim network operating costs by 10 percent in the first six months of
implementing an asset management program—compelling enough reason to
get started right away!
</TD></TR>
</TABLE>
</BODY>
</HTML>
```

The <TABLE> and </TABLE> tags encapsulate the entire two-column table. Within the <TABLE> tag are two attributes: CELLPADDING and WIDTH. The CELLPADDING attribute with a value of 15 specifies the amount of point space between the two columns of text. Without it, the text of the two columns will bump up against each other. The WIDTH attribute with a value of 90% specifies the amount of available space the table will span across the screen when rendered by the browser.

The <TR> and </TR> tags are used to define a table row. Within these tags are the <TH> and </TH> tags, which define a table head. Normally, these tags cause the text to be rendered in bold and centered across the available row space. However, this coding example uses the <H1> and </H1> heading level 1 tags to cause the editorial's headline to be rendered in a larger point size than that rendered by the <TH> and </TH> tags.

The COLSPAN attribute within the <TH> tag specifies that the headline, when rendered, be allowed to span the entire two columns of the table. The ALIGN attribute specifies that the headline be rendered as flush left.

The next row is again defined by the <TR> and </TR> tags. The author's name is encapsulated with two sets of tags. The <I> and </I> tags cause the name to be rendered in italics, and the <TD> and </TD> tags indicate that the author's name is table data. The COLSPAN attribute with a value of two specifies that the author's name, when rendered, be allowed to span the entire two columns of the table, if needed.

The first column of text is encapsulated by the <TD> and </TD> tags, indicating that it be rendered as table data. The text fills up as much space as needed. The rest of the text also is encapsulated by the <TD> and </TD> tags. All of this information, in turn, is encapsulated with the <TR> and </TR> tags.

The result, as rendered by Netscape Navigator, is shown in Figure 4.8.

Creating Three-Column Text

Three-column text is accomplished in a similar manner as two-column text, except that there will be an extra set of <TD> and </TD> tags to rearrange the same amount of text so that it will be rendered as three columns by the browser.

Here is the HTML coding for the exact same article which, when rendered, will appear as three-column text:

```
<HTML>
<BODY>
<TABLE CELLPADDING=15 WIDTH="90%">
<TR><TH COLSPAN=3 ALIGN=LEFT><H1>Companies Can Gain With Asset
Management</H1></TH> </TR>
<TR><TD COLSPAN=3> <I>by Nathan J. Muller</I> </TD> </TR>
<TR>
<TD>Today's large corporate networks consist of a vast assemblage of
hardware and software. Thousands of different computer models, cards,
peripherals, and software packages may be in use—most of it purchased
from different vendors to suit the varying needs and preferences of
employees.<P>
Asset management is essential for controlling costs—most of which are
"hidden costs" that drain IT budgets and divert scarce
resources.</TD>
<TD>Industry analysts say the cost of operating and supporting a
```

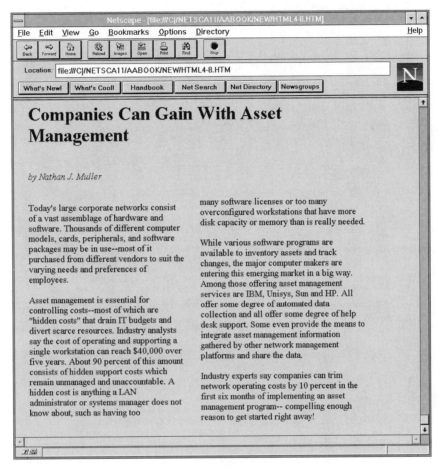

Figure 4.8

single workstation can reach $40,000 over five years. About 90
percent of this amount consists of hidden support costs which remain
unmanaged and unaccountable. A hidden cost is anything a LAN
administrator or systems manager does not know about, such as having
too many software licenses or overconfigured workstations that have
more disk capacity or memory than is really needed.<P>
While various software programs are available to inventory assets and
</TD>
<TD>track changes, the major computer makers are entering this
emerging market in a big way. Among those offering asset management
services are IBM, Unisys, Sun and HP. All offer some degree of
automated data collection and all offer some degree of help desk
support. Some even provide the means to integrate asset management
information gathered by other network management platforms and share
the data.<P> Industry experts say companies can trim network operating
costs by 10 percent in the first six months of implementing an asset
management program—compelling enough reason to get started right away!
</TD></TR>
</TABLE>
</BODY>
</HTML>

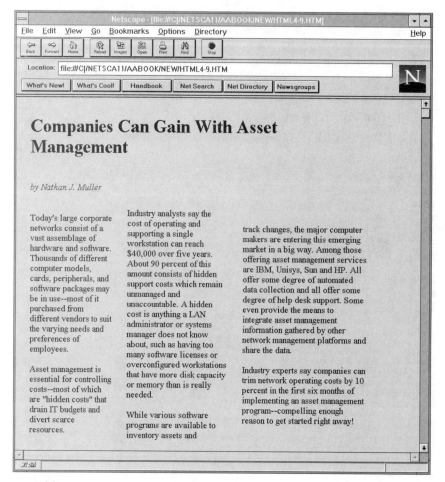

Figure 4.9

The result, as rendered by Netscape Navigator, is shown in Figure 4.9.

Before coding all of your documents as either two-column or three-column text, you should be aware of some limitations.

First, the amount of text should not exceed 250 words. If the text is longer, the user has to scroll down, up, and down again to read an entire two-column document. With three-column text, the user has to scroll down, up, down, up and down again to read the whole document. This can drive users batty! If the text can be displayed on a single screen without too much scrolling, it can be a nice enhancement to your Web pages.

An effective use of two- or three-column text documents would be to use them as short summaries for larger documents that can be accessed with a hypertext link embedded at the end of the summary document. You can also use two- or three-column text on each page, linking them together with a "turn page" link at the end of the last column. This technique would come closest to mimicking a newspaper or magazine.

Creating Multiple-Column Menus

The menus of most Web pages use single-column lists that are either rendered as centered on the screen or flush left. Another application of two- and three-column text is lists, both ordered and unordered, such as the home page's main menu.

Here is the HTML coding for a two-column unordered list with hypertext links that is used as a main menu on a home page:

```
<HTML>
<HEAD>
<TITLE>Welcome to B&G on the Web</TITLE>
</HEAD>
<BODY>
<CENTER>
<P>
<H1>B&G Enterprises</H1>
<P>
<PRE>
Y O U R  C E N T R A L  S O U R C E  F O R  M A C I N T O S H  P R O D U C T S
</PRE>
<HR SIZE=10 WIDTH=60%>
<P>
<H1>Main Menu</H1>
<P>
<TABLE CELLPADDING=15 WIDTH="90%">
<TR>
<TD><UL><UL><UL><LI><A HREF="books.html">Books</A><LI><A HREF=
"software.html">Software</A><LI><A HREF="drives.html">Hard Drives</A>
<LI><A HREF="video.html">QuickTime</A><LI><A HREF="camera.html">
Digital Cameras</A><LI><A HREF="printers.html">Printers</A><LI><A
HREF="media. html">Multimedia</A><LI><A HREF="lans.html">Local Area
Networking </A></UL></UL></UL></TD> <TD><UL><UL> <LI><A HREF=
"isdn.html">ISDN </A><LI><A HREF="emulate.html">PC Emulators</A>
<LI><A HREF="mobile. html">Communications Software</A><LI><A HREF=
"graphics.html">Graphics Packages </A><LI><A HREF="cdrom.html">CD-ROM
Drives </A><LI> <A HREF= "modems.html">Modems </A><LI><A HREF=
"internet.html">Internet Tools</A><LI><A HREF="monitors.html">
Monitors</A>
</UL></UL></UL></TD>
</TR>
</TABLE>
</CENTER>
</BODY>
</HTML>
```

The square bullets are achieved by using nested <UL> and </UL> tags, which also are used to better position the two lists under Main Menu. Because the Netscape-specific CENTER tag does not work in other browsers, and in this case even works inconsistently when rendered by the same versions of Netscape, you might be better off using spaces within the <PRE> and </PRE> tags to achieve a centered look. The extra work is worth it for a short menu page, especially if you have nothing else going for you in the way of visual elements.

The result, as rendered by Netscape Navigator, is shown in Figure 4.10.

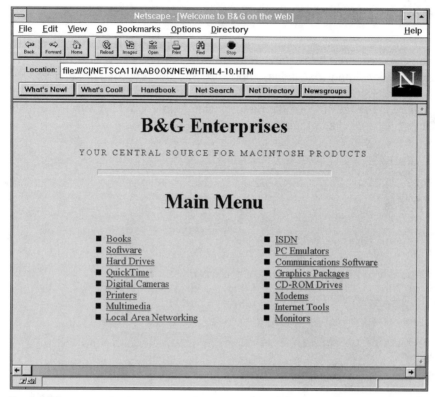

Figure 4.10

Specifying Column Width and Position of Text

Text-laden Web documents are difficult to read because the lines of text span the entire width of the screen. This is a lot of text to take in all at once, and if the reader's attention lapses even for a moment, it is not all that easy to quickly find one's place and resume. The user could easily size the browser's window by grabbing a corner and pulling it in, but this can result in some unacceptable distortion, especially if inline images are included among the text.

An alternative would be to specify the width of the document's text so that it spans only 50 or 60 percent of the available screen space, making it easier for users to read long documents. This is accomplished by encapsulating the entire document with the <TABLE> and </TABLE> tags, which provides you with the opportunity to take advantage of the <TABLE> tag's WIDTH attribute to specify a value of 50 percent, for example. The first and last paragraphs in the document are encapsulated with the <TD> and </TD> tags.

In the following coding example, the text spans only half the available screen space:

```
<HTML>
<BODY>
<TABLE WIDTH="50%">
<H1>Companies Can Gain With Asset Management</H1>
<I>by Nathan J. Muller</I>
<P>
<TD>Today's large corporate networks consist of a vast assemblage of
hardware and software. Thousands of different computer models, cards,
peripherals, and software packages may be in use—most of it purchased
from different vendors to suit the varying needs and preferences of
employees.
<P>
Asset management is essential for controlling costs—most of which are
"hidden costs" that drain IT budgets and divert scarce resources.
Industry analysts say the cost of operating and supporting a single
workstation can reach $40,000 over five years. About 90 percent of
this amount consists of hidden support costs which remain unmanaged
and unaccountable. A hidden cost is anything a LAN administrator or
systems manager does not know about, such as having too many software
licenses or overconfigured workstations that have more disk capacity
or memory than is really needed.
</TD>
</TABLE>
</BODY>
</HTML>
```

The result, as rendered by Netscape Navigator, is shown in Figure 4.11.

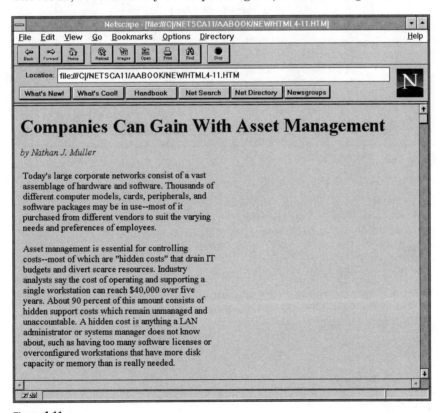

Figure 4.11

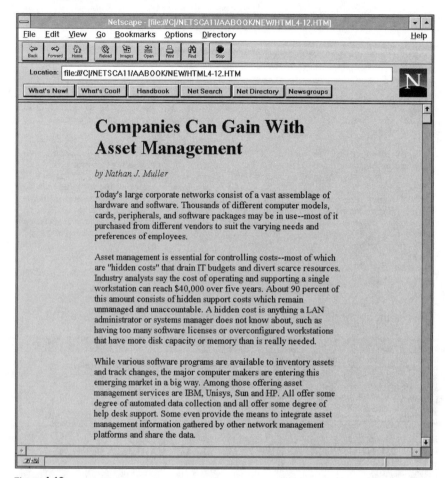

Figure 4.12

You can go a step further by encapsulating the table tags with the <CEN­TER> and </CENTER> tags to achieve the result shown in Figure 4.12. If you are worried that the page will be viewed by non-Netscape browsers that cannot render the <CENTER> tag, don't be; the page will be rendered flush left by default.

This chapter has focused on the different ways to enhance text-based Web pages without the use of image editing programs and artistic skills. Of course, the biggest part of Web page enhancement involves coming up with something worthwhile to say.

Graphical Elements

This chapter discusses the use of various graphical objects that can be used to dress your Web pages, making them more attractive to readers. As used in this discussion, the term "objects" refers to any graphical item such as icons, bullets, logos, and backgrounds that are created using such image editing products as Adobe Photoshop, CorelDRAW!, or Micrografx Picture Publisher. These objects are contained in their own files in GIF or JPEG format and called up for display whenever they are referenced in the HTML document. Used judiciously, some of these objects can even be used to lead the reader through voluminous text that otherwise would not hold their attention very long.

A graphical object that is called up for rendering in an HTML document is referred to as an inline image, which is specified using the IMG tag and its associated attributes:

- The SRC attribute indicates the file name, in quotation marks, of the image that will be called up for display when the document is rendered by a browser.

- The ALT attribute indicates a text-only alternative to the image for readers who are using text-only browsers.

- The ALIGN attribute specifies how the text next to the image is aligned in relationship to the image: TOP, MIDDLE, or BOTTOM.

To specify an inline GIF or JPEG image, the HTML coding is as follows:

```
<IMG SRC="filename.gif">
```

or

```
<IMG SRC="filename.jpg">
```

To specify a GIF or JPEG image with a text alternative, the following HTML coding format is used:

```
<IMG SRC="filename.gif" ALT="(company logo)">
```

or

```
<IMG SRC="filename.jpg" ALT="(company logo)">
```

To specifiy a GIF or JPEG image with a text alternative and text alignment, the following HTML coding format is used:

```
<IMG SRC="filename.gif" ALT="(company logo)" ALIGN=MIDDLE>
```

or

```
<IMG SRC="filename.jpg" ALT="(company logo)" ALIGN=MIDDLE>
```

Any number of inline images may be specified within a single HTML document, and in any mix of GIF and JPEG image formats. There may even be multiple places within the document where the same image will be rendered repeatedly, as in the case of custom bullets. However, the size of the images will determine the speed at which the document loads when it is accessed. Later in this chapter there is a discussion of some methods for handling inline images to make them load faster.

Specifying Image Backgrounds

In the previous chapter, we discussed how to specify the background color of Web pages using RGB color codes. It is also possible to specify a GIF or JPEG image as the background for your Web pages. Backgrounds can be created using image editing products such as Adobe Photoshop, Corel-DRAW!, and Micrografx Picture Publisher, or shareware programs like Paint Shop Pro, which can be downloaded from the Internet.

The following example provides the HTML coding for a GIF image, included on HTMLdisk, that will cause the background to be rendered as a leather texture.

```
<BODY BACKGROUND="leather.gif">
```

GIFs or JPEGs can be used to specify various textures, grains, patterns, and color gradients for your backgrounds. However, you might also have to specify the color of the text, links, visited links, and active links to make these visible against the selected background. You might want to review the previous chapter for the HTML coding format for specifying the color of these elements.

Several background files are included on the enclosed HTMLdisk, but if you want more of a selection, there are numerous background archives on the Web. One of them is part of Kai's Power Tips and Tricks for Photoshop, and has the URL `http://the-tech.mit.edu/cgi-bin/KPT_bgs.pl`. Another background archive is maintained by the Netscape Hall of Shame, which has the URL `http://www.europa.com/~yyz/textures/textures.html`.

Using Tiled Image Backgrounds

A tiled image is one that repeats itself as a series of separate but seamless tiles. When used as the background of a document, it can produce some very dramatic effects. Tiling is used most often for corporate logos, but it can be used with any image to liven up otherwise bland text pages. From an HTML coding perspective, there is nothing special to do. The following HTML coding example is much the same as that used in the previous example, except that it specifies a logo as the GIF:

```
<BODY BACKGROUND="logo.gif">
```

What is different, and not apparent by the HTML coding, is the size of the image. The smaller the image (such as thumbnail size), the faster it will load and the more frequently it will be repeated (or tiled). The larger the image, the longer it will take to load and the less frequently it will be tiled. Achieving exactly the right balance will entail some experimentation with image sizing using your favorite image editor. You also must adjust the lightness of the image to increase the contrast between the background and the various foreground elements such as the text and links, making them easier to read.

Figures 5.1a through 5.1c show an image of a square whose size varies from thumbnail to large, to illustrate the impact of image size on the tiling effect (as rendered by Netscape Navigator).

(a)

(b)

Figure 5.1

(c)

Notice that the smaller the image, the more tiles are rendered; the larger the image, the fewer the tiles. Again, the frequency and size of the tiles rendered in the background are a function of image size and not HTML coding.

Specifying Image Bullets

As described in chapter 3, unordered lists are encapsulated with the <UL> and </UL> tags. When the <LI> tag is used with these tags, each list item starts with a bullet. There may be occasions when you want something a bit more elaborate for your lists than the default black, round bullet. You can use any GIF or JPEG image as a bullet, provided it is small enough. Instead of the <UL> and </UL> tags, you would encapsulate the list using the definition list tags <DL> and </DL>. And instead of the <LI> tag for each list item, you would specify an inline image preceded by the <DD> or definitions tag, as in the following HTML coding example:

```
<HTML>
<BODY>
<TITLE>B&G Product Catalog</TITLE>
<H2>Catalog Menu</H2>
<DL>
<DD><IMG SRC="star.gif" ALIGN=TOP> Hardware
<P>
<DD><IMG SRC="star.gif" ALIGN=TOP> Software
<P>
<DD><IMG SRC="star.gif" ALIGN=TOP> Customer Service
<P>
<DD><IMG SRC="star.gif" ALIGN=TOP> Technical Support
</DL>
</BODY>
</HTML>
```

Notice that the ALIGN attribute specifies TOP as the relationship between the text labels and the images, whereas in the Netscape Navigator rendering in Figure 5.2, the labels are positioned at the middle of the stars. Because a GIF is being used as a bullet, it can distort the usual alignment between text and image as specified by the ALIGN attribute. With some experimentation, the desired alignment can be achieved.

Specifying Buttons and Icons

Although any graphical object can be rendered as a hypertext link, buttons and icons are typically rendered as such. The difference between a button and icon is that the former is usually much smaller than the latter. However, there is no difference between the two as far as coding them as hypertext links in HTML. To accomplish this, the reference to the inline image must be encapsulated within the hypertext reference anchors as in the following example:

```
<A HREF="index.html"><IMG SRC="arrow.gif"
ALIGN=MIDDLE></A><EM> Go back to Main Menu</EM>
```

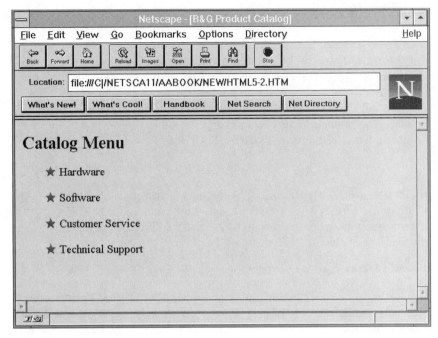

Figure 5.2

In this example, "index.html" is the name of the file containing the Web page's Main Menu. The image source is "arrow.gif," which is a button or icon of an arrow pointing left, indicating to the user that he or she can go back to the Main Menu simply by clicking on it. The `ALIGN=MIDDLE` attribute indicates that the label, "Go back to Main Menu," should be positioned next to the button or icon; specifically, the middle of the object. The `<EM>` and `</EM>` tags cause the text to be rendered as emphasized. Notice that the end anchor `</A>` is not used to enclose the label. This is because we want only the object to activate the hypertext link, not the text beside it. If we wanted the text to be included as the hypertext link, we would move the end anchor as follows:

```
<A HREF="index.html"><IMG SRC="arrow.gif" ALIGN=MIDDLE><EM>
Go back to Main Menu</EM></A>
```

The enclosed HTMLdisk contains an assortment of buttons and icons to get you started with your Web pages. Many more can be downloaded from various archives on the Internet at Gopher sites, as well as Web sites. One image browser is located at URL http://www.cli.di.unipi.it/iconbrowser/icons.html. There also is an image finder that allows you to select an image category and the type of file (GIF, JPEG, or both) so you can launch a search for appropriate images. The URL of this image finder is http://arachnid.cm.cf.ac.uk/Misc/wustl.html.

Specifying Bars

Bars are customized versions of HTML's horizontal rule <HR> in a GIF or JPEG format. They can be created using various image editors or grabbed from various image libraries on the Web. Bars can be used to logically partition a large document or add visual interest to a home page. HTMLdisk includes a selection of bars that can be used for these purposes. The HTML coding is the same as for any other image. The following coding example references a bar GIF that is included in HTMLdisk:

```
<IMG SRC="bluebar.gif">
```

Unlike the <HR> tag, GIF and JPEG images of bars do not span the entire width of the screen when rendered by the browser. To make GIF and JPEG bar images span the entire screen width, the WIDTH attribute must be specified with the value of 100% as follows:

```
<IMG SRC="bluebar.gif" WIDTH=100%>
```

By altering the WIDTH value, you can specify that the bar be rendered to span any percentage of the available screen space. A bar whose WIDTH value is less than 100% also can be centered on the page by encapsulating the image tag with the Netscape-specific CENTER tags as follows:

```
<CENTER>
<IMG SRC="bluebar.gif" WIDTH=50%>
</CENTER>
```

Using Vertical Rules

As described in chapter 4, HTML provides for the rendering of horizontal rules via the <HR> tag, whose width can be specified using the SIZE attribute. The HTML specifications do not provide for vertical rules, yet there may be times when a vertical rule can add just the right touch to a Web page. This can be done with a GIF or JPEG image file of a vertical bar.

To position the vertical rule (or bar) down the left side of the Web page, for example, the TABLE tags are used in the same way they were used in chapter 4 to achieve two-column text within a transparent table. But instead of two columns of text, we have one column containing the vertical rule and the other column containing the text.

The following is an example of the HTML coding for a two-column transparent table which contains a graduated vertical rule down the left-side column. The key line of HTML code is highlighted in bold:

```
<HTML>
<BODY>
<TABLE CELLPADDING=15 WIDTH="90%">
<TR><TH COLSPAN=2 ALIGN=LEFT><H1>Companies Can Gain With Asset
Management</H1></TH></TR>
```

```
<TR><TD COLSPAN=2> <I>by Nathan J. Muller</I></TD> </TR>
<TD><IMG<P><B>SRC="rulev.gif"></TD>
<TD>Today's large corporate networks consist of a vast assemblage of
hardware and software. Thousands of different computer models, cards,
peripherals, and software packages may be in use—most of it purchased
from different vendors to suit the varying needs and preferences of
employees.
<P>
Asset management is essential for controlling costs—most of which are
"hidden costs" that drain IT budgets and divert scarce resources.<P>
Industry analysts say the cost of operating and supporting a single
workstation can reach $40,000 over five years. About 90 percent of
this amount consists of hidden support costs which remain unmanaged
and unaccountable. A hidden cost is anything a LAN administrator or
systems manager does not know about, such as having too many software
licenses or overconfigured workstations that have more disk capacity
or memory than is really needed.
<P>
While various software programs are available to inventory assets and
track changes, the major computer makers are entering the service
segment of this market in a big way.
<P>
Among those offering asset management services are IBM, Unisys, Sun
and HP. All offer some degree of automated data collection and all
offer some degree of help desk support. Some even provide the means
to integrate asset management information gathered by other network
management platforms and share the data.
<P>
<B>Why Delay?</B>
<P> Industry experts say companies can trim network operating costs by
10 percent in the first six months of implementing an asset management
program—compelling enough reason to get started right away!
<P>
<I>For more information . . .</I><P><A HREF="asset1.html"><IMG SRC=
"sheet.gif" ALIGN=LEFT></A></TD></TR>
</TABLE>
</BODY>
</HTML>
```

Figure 5.3 shows how this example is rendered in Netscape Navigator.

Placing Images in Page Margins

With a transparent table, a photo can be rendered along with the text to give the document a magazinelike appearance. This is accomplished using the TABLE tag and associated attributes and values. An example of the HTML code that will provide such a rendering is:

```
<HTML>
<BODY>
<TABLE CELLPADDING=15 WIDTH="90%">
<TR><TH COLSPAN=2 ALIGN=LEFT><H1>Companies Can Gain With Asset
Management</H1></TH></TR>
<TD VALIGN=TOP><IMG SRC="nate1.jpg"><P><I>by Nathan J.
Muller</I></TD>
<P>
<TD>Today's large corporate networks consist of a vast assemblage of
hardware and software. Thousands of different computer models, cards,
peripherals, and software packages may be in use—most of it purchased
from different vendors to suit the varying needs and preferences of
employees.
```

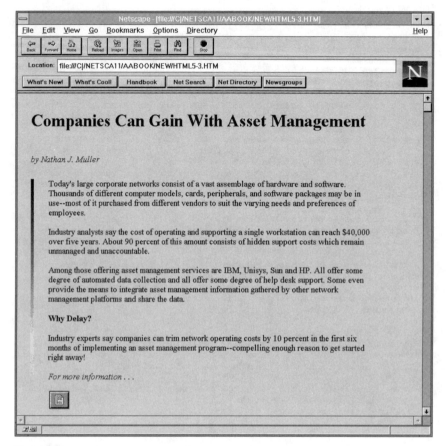

Figure 5.3

```
Asset management is essential for controlling costs—most of which are
"hidden costs" that drain IT budgets and divert scarce resources.<P>
Industry analysts say the cost of operating and supporting a single
workstation can reach $40,000 over five years. About 90 percent of
this amount consists of hidden support costs which remain unmanaged
and unaccountable. A hidden cost is anything a LAN administrator or
systems manager does not know about, such as having too many software
licenses or overconfigured workstations that have more disk capacity
or memory than is really needed.
</TD></TR>
</TABLE>
</BODY>
</HTML>
```

Notice the use of the VALIGN attribute within the <TD> tag on the line of
code that includes the inline image tag. (This line is highlighted in bold.)
Since the position of the photo will default to the middle of the column, the
vertical align, or VALIGN, attribute must be used to specify that the table
data (in this case, the photo) appear at the TOP of the column. By specify-

ing VALIGN=TOP, the photo is positioned directly across from the first line of text in the other column. If you fail to use the VALIGN attribute, the photo will default to the middle of the column, which can be quite long in some documents. When you think about it, allowing the author's photo to appear halfway down a long column would not make too much design sense, especially because the user may choose not to read that far.

Figure 5.4 shows how this HTML coded example is rendered by Netscape Navigator.

Placing Images and Callouts in Page Margins

In the same way that a photo can be placed in a page margin, a callout can be placed in the page margin as well. A callout is a short phrase that tells the reader what to expect in the adjacent body of text. Callouts typically are used to pull the reader from one idea or page to another.

The following HTML code adds a callout (highlighted in bold) to the previous example:

```
<HTML>
<BODY>
<TABLE CELLPADDING=15 WIDTH="90%">
<TR><TH COLSPAN=2 ALIGN=LEFT><H1>Companies Can Gain With Asset
Management</H1></TH></TR>
<TD VALIGN=TOP><IMG SRC="nate1.jpg"><P><I>by Nathan J. Muller</I>
<PRE>
```

Figure 5.4

```
</PRE>
<STRONG>Support costs can add up to $40,000 per workstation over five
years.</STRONG>
</TD>
<TD>Today's large corporate networks consist of a vast assemblage of
hardware and software. Thousands of different computer models, cards,
peripherals, and software packages may be in use—most of it purchased
from different vendors to suit the varying needs and preferences of
employees.<P>
Asset management is essential for controlling costs—most of which are
"hidden costs" that drain IT budgets and divert scarce resources.<P>
Industry analysts say the cost of operating and supporting a single
workstation can reach $40,000 over five years. About 90 percent of
this amount consists of hidden support costs which remain unmanaged
and unaccountable. A hidden cost is anything a LAN administrator or
systems manager does not know about, such as having too many software
licenses or overconfigured workstations that have more disk capacity
or memory than is really needed.
</TD></TR>
</TABLE>
</BODY>
</HTML>
```

Notice the use of the <STRONG> and </STRONG> tags to highlight the callout. Also note the use of the <PRE> and </PRE> tags to move the callout down to the desired position. If an image or callout has to appear midway down the column or at the bottom of the column, you can use VALIGN=MIDDLE or VALIGN=BOTTOM attribute, respectively.

Figure 5.5 shows how this HTML coded example is rendered by Netscape Navigator.

Placing Multiple Images and Callouts in Page Margins

The technique of using a transparent table to put images and callouts alongside of the main text works well with relatively short documents, especially when there are only one or two such items. The question is how do you specify any number of images and callouts in documents that might be rather long? It should have become apparent in the previous example that you can only use the VALIGN attribute and associated elements once per cell (or column, in this case)—either to render the object at the TOP, MIDDLE, or BOTTOM of the column. In the previous example, this was overcome by using the <PRE> and </PRE> tags to put some white space between the image and the callout. But as the length of the document increases, the usefulness of this technique quickly diminishes. It not only greatly inflates the byte count, but all you have to show for it is a lot of white space between objects!

This awkward situation can be overcome by specifying an additional table row wherever you want to place an image or callout. This is done with the <TR> and </TR> tags, which allows you to create new columns or cells for images or callouts with the <TD> and </TD> tags. Because the entire table is transparent, it really does not matter how many times you break up the main text with additional rows; nobody will ever know that what they are viewing is really a table unless they view the source code.

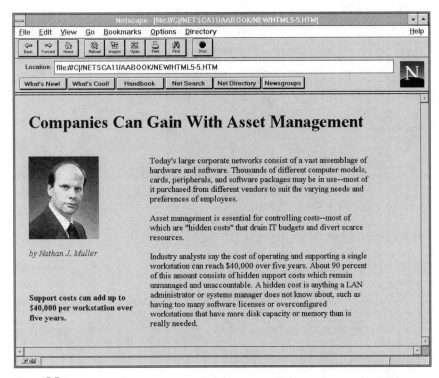

Figure 5.5

To illustrate the use of table rows in this way, the following HTML coding is for the last paragraph of the same document used in the previous example. Instead of a callout or photo, arrow icons with labels are rendered beside the main text. The key HTML tags are in bold.

```
<HR>
<TR></TR>
<TD VALIGN=BOTTOM><A HREF="infomgmt.html"><IMG
SRC="al03.gif"></A><BR>
<P><I>Go to Topics List</I>
<PRE>

</PRE>
<A HREF="index.html"><IMG SRC="al03.gif"></A><BR><P><I>Go to Main
Menu
</I>
</TD>
<TD>
<H2>Conclusion</H2>
One of the key principles of asset management is that things cannot be
managed and costs cannot be controlled if there is no indication that
they exist. IS managers and LAN administrators can choose from among a
variety of asset management packages to easily and economically obtain
the competencies they need for inventory tracking. Alternatively,
asset management can be outsourced, leaving the service provider to
worry about such matters.
<P>
```

```
Regardless of the method of implementation, companies are advised
to implement an asset management program right away. Desktop asset
management can go a long way toward trimming operational costs and
free up scarce dollars for more pressing IS needs. Tangible results
can be achieved in a very short time. Some industry analysts estimate
that organizations implementing asset management can expect to reduce
the total cost of system and network ownership by 10 percent in only
six months. </TD>
<P>
</TR></TD>
</TABLE>
</BODY>
</HTML>
```

Notice the use of the <PRE> and </PRE> tags to put some distance between the arrow icons. Figure 5.6 shows how this HTML coded example is rendered by Netscape Navigator.

Wrapping Text Around an Object

One of the most dramatic effects you can achieve in your HTML documents is wrapping text around objects, especially because it is rarely seen on the Web. Wrapping text around an object can be achieved simply by encapsu-

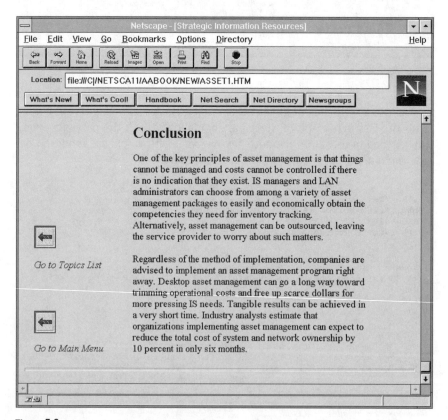

Figure 5.6

lating the inline image source tag with the <BLOCKQUOTE> and </BLOCK-QUOTE> tags, as in the following HTML coding example:

```
<HTML>
<HEAD>
<TITLE>B&G on the Web</TITLE>
</HEAD>
<BODY>
<CENTER>
<P>
<H1>B&G Enterprises</H1>
<P>
<PRE>
Y O U R C E N T R A L S O U R C E F O R M A C I N T O S H P R O D U C T S
</PRE>
<HR SIZE=10 WIDTH=60%>
</CENTER>
<P>
<B>Our Guarantee:</B> We offer a 30-day return policy to all of our
customers. If you need to return a product for any reason, our returns
specialists will be happy to help.<P>
<B>Quality Products:</B> B&G offers only nationally-recognized name
brand products to our customers. Our goal is to bring you products
that represent the best in value, technology, quality, functionality,
and innovation.
<P>
<BLOCKQUOTE>
<IMG SRC="support.gif" ALIGN=LEFT>
</BLOCKQUOTE>
<B>Easy Returns:</B> We offer a 30-day return policy to all of our
customers. If you need to return a product for any reason, our returns
specialists will be happy to help.<P>
<B>Technical Support: </B>B&G provides lifetime toll-free technical
support to customers from 9 a.m. to 9 p.m. Monday through Friday and
9 a.m. to 5 p.m. Saturday. All of our technicians are trained by our
vendors.<P>
<B>Customer Service: </B>Our trained customer service staff will help
you pick out the right hardware and software for your needs. We can
even build a computer to your specifications, preload the software,
and test the entire system before it ships.
</BODY>
</HTML>
```

If you do not like the idea of using the cumbersome BLOCKQUOTE, you can use the shorter alternative, which is BQ. Notice the use of the ALIGN=LEFT attribute and element in the inline image source tag. If you leave this out, the text on the right side of the object will position itself at the bottom right of the image when rendered, instead of alongside the image where it is supposed to be.

Figure 5.7 shows how this HTML coding example is rendered in Netscape Navigator.

Wrapping Text Within and Around Multiple Objects

As easily as text can be wrapped around one object, it can be wrapped around two objects. An example of the HTML coding that will achieve this is as follows:

```
<HTML>
<HEAD>
```

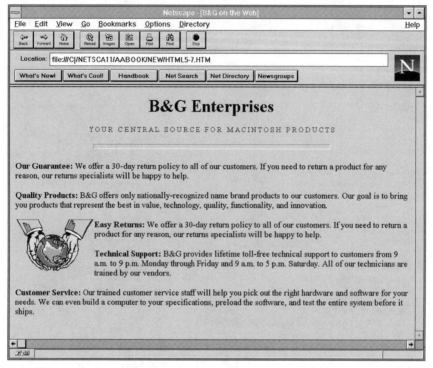

Figure 5.7

```
<TITLE>B&G on the Web</TITLE>
</HEAD>
<BODY>
<CENTER>
<P>
<H1>B&G Enterprises</H1>
<P>
<PRE>
Y O U R   C E N T R A L   S O U R C E   F O R   M A C I N T O S H   P R O D U C T S
</PRE>
<HR SIZE=10 WIDTH=60%>
</CENTER>
<P>
<B>Our Guarantee:</B> We offer a 30-day return policy to all of our
customers. If you need to return a product for any reason, our returns
specialists will be happy to help.<P>
<B>Quality Products:</B> B&G offers only nationally-recognized name
brand products to our customers. Our goal is to bring you products
that represent the best in value, technology, quality, functionality,
and innovation.<P>
<BQ>
<IMG SRC="support.gif" ALIGN=LEFT></BQ><B>Easy Returns:</B> We offer
a 30-day return policy to all of our customers. If you need to return
a product for any reason, our returns specialists will be happy to
help.
<BQ>
<IMG SRC="macos.gif" ALIGN=RIGHT>
</BQ>
<P>
```

```
<B>Technical Support: </B>B&G provides lifetime toll-free technical
support to customers from 9 a.m. to 9 p.m. Monday through Friday and
9 a.m. to 5 p.m. Saturday. All of our technicians are trained by our
vendors.<P>
<B>Customer Service: </B>Our trained customer service staff will help
you pick out the right hardware and software for your needs. We can
even build a computer to your specifications, preload the software,
and test the entire system before it ships.
</BODY>
</HTML>
```

The key lines of HTML code are highlighted in bold. Notice that instead of ALIGN=LEFT, the second inline image tag uses the attribute and element ALIGN=RIGHT. The BLOCKQUOTE tags that encapsulate the inline image tag cause the text to go around the image when rendered.

Figure 5.8 shows how this HTML coding example is rendered in Netscape Navigator.

Borrowing Images from Other Locations

When using standard graphical objects such as icons, bullets, buttons, and bars, you do not have to keep the actual files in your own HTML directory. The Web site administrator can set up a directory just for these kinds of files. Each person connected to the server can use the URLs of these image

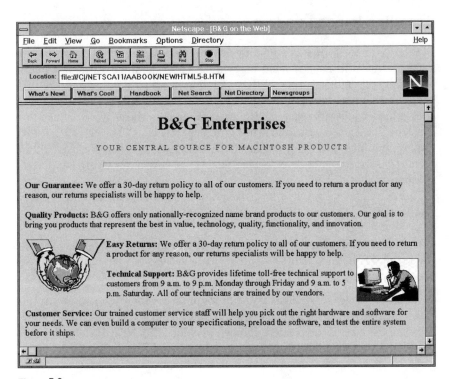

Figure 5.8

files in their own documents instead of wasting space in their own HTML directories. As new objects are collected from the Web, or designed to meet specific applications, they can be added to the pool of objects and used by everyone. A special index can even be set up to display each object, along with its name. If the object files are named with a descriptive keyword, a search program can be written to find exactly the kind of object a user is looking for without having to waste time looking through every item in the archive.

You can also reference objects at other Web sites to make them appear in your own documents. However, this is not recommended. The most immediate impact of this practice is that it causes delays in document loading, while images are collected from other servers. Over the long term, sites can occasionally go offline or cease operating altogether, and the locations of directories and files may change over time, leaving your document without the specified objects. When an object is not available for a document, browsers use different means of letting the reader know. Netscape Navigator displays an icon with a question mark where the image should be and continues to render the rest of the page. Other browsers, such as AIR Mosaic, use a dialog box that notifies the reader that it could not find the file, upon which the user must click OK before continuing. This disruptive procedure is repeated for every object that cannot be found.

Speeding Image Loading

Of the two image formats commonly used in Web pages, JPEG does a better job with realistic images such as scanned photographs. Although many browsers still cannot handle JPEGs as inline images, they have no trouble handling them as external files when referenced by a hypertext link. GIF does a better job with crisp, sharp images, such as those typically used to construct buttons, charts, and other graphical objects. All browsers that can display graphics at all can display GIFs inline. Of the two formats, there seems to be no agreement as to which loads faster when both are supported as inline images by the browser.

There are several ways of preparing and using image files to make them load faster:

- As alluded to above, the most obvious way to increase performance is to keep all HTML documents and image files on the same server to minimize loading delay.

- Keep the images as small as you can to minimize their byte count. In the case of simple graphical objects, such as rules or bars, you can often increase the size of the rendered image by specifying HEIGHT and WIDTH values within the inline image source tag.

- You can reduce the byte count and increase loading performance by using grayscale images whenever possible. In some situations, grayscale images can provide your Web pages with a subdued, but very classy look.

- Finally, you can reduce the byte count by creating images in 16 colors rather than the usual 256 colors. This is particularly effective for small images. When used with large images, the dither becomes a problem; that is, the smooth transition from color to color is absent and is instead represented by very noticeable dots.

Interlacing is a technique for preparing GIF files to make it appear as though the image is loading faster than it really is. Interlaced GIFs appear initially with poor resolution and then progressively improve in resolution until the entire image has loaded, as opposed to loading linearly from the top row of pixels to the bottom row, and making the user wait until it has completely loaded before the text can be read and scrolled. Interlacing is covered in more detail in the next chapter.

6

Working with Image Files

The World Wide Web is capable of handling graphic images in a number of sophisticated ways: They can be interlaced, sized, mapped, and animated. Interlacing and image sizing are features that can speed the loading of HTML documents. Image maps and animations add a lot of visual interest to Web pages, but also cause them to load much more slowly. In addition, the backgrounds of graphical objects can be made transparent, so that they appear to float on the screen. The backgrounds of documents can be images, either a solid color or a design. These techniques add a nice touch to Web pages and, if done properly, will not significantly impact loading performance.

When preparing images for use in your Web pages, you should choose 256 colors or less. Preferably, 100 colors or less should be the goal. A smaller number of colors is preferable, because you cannot assume that most people have high-resolution monitors. At 256 colors, the image will look good on a VGA monitor and great on an SVGA monitor, which supports higher resolutions. The higher the number of colors used, the more likely images will appear dithered on VGA monitors. Dithering refers to how the spacing of dots (or pixels) appears on the monitor. These dots are used to produce colors in the image. The goal is to have a smooth transition from one color to another. When the dots are spaced far enough apart to become noticeable, it is because the monitor does not support as many colors as the image requires to provide a smooth transition between the colors.

For example, in a gradient that goes from white to black (Figure 6.1a), there is a big difference between the two colors, so there will be a lot of dithering. Going from white to gray (Figure 6.1b), however, results in much less dithering.

Figure 6.1 (a) above; (b) below

Image Formats

As noted in the previous chapter, the two most widely supported image formats used on the Web are GIF and JPEG. The JPEG image format offers much higher compression ratios than other image formats, particularly for photographic images. JPEG is also a "lossy" compression method, meaning that some of the image data is lost upon decoding. However, during the encoding process, you can generally specify the compression amount. In Micrografx Picture Publisher, for example, the choices are: high quality/low compression, good quality/good compression, and low quality/high compression. The lower the quality value, the higher the compression ratio and the faster the image will load.

Images can be made to appear inline along with the text or in a separate window accessed by a hypertext link. Most graphical browsers support both GIF and JPEG for external images. Some graphical browsers support only GIF for inline images, while others such as Netscape and Mosaic support both GIF and JPEG formats for inline images. In the case of JPEG, you have to specify a JPEG-format image as the SRC value for an IMG tag, and the browser will decode and display the image in the same way as a GIF image.

The tag format for inlined GIF and JPEG images is as follows:

```
<IMG SRC="image.gif">
```

and

```
<IMG SRC="image.jpg">
```

JPEG is the preferred format for photographic images and provides a smooth transition of color, which is especially important for portraits and landscapes. GIFs are better suited for graphics that contain text and for images where sharp lines are important, such as maps or engineering drawings.

You will have to decide what image format to use in your Web pages. You cannot specify JPEG as the preferred format and GIF as the default format. Unfortunately, today's Web servers lack the intelligence to send JPEG images only to Netscape browsers and GIF images to non-Netscape browsers. The HyperText Transfer Protocol (HTTP) generally does not give the server enough information to decide whether to send GIF or JPEG images to the client. The situation is further complicated by the fact that many browsers tell the servers that they support the JPEG format, but without making a distinction between internal and external support.

Transparent Background Images

The rendering of some images might be more effective if their background color matches the browser window, making the image appear to float in the window. You cannot do this by setting the background color of the image, because you cannot control how people will configure their browsers. You can control this by using GIF89 images, which have the ability to mark a single color in the colormap as transparent, forcing the browser to use its background color for those pixels in the image. A safe color to choose for your background is a light gray. If a browser does not support transparent images, you will at least have a color that is close to the one used in most browser windows.

Create (or capture) the initial image

You can create or capture the initial image with a variety of tools, including the shareware program Paint Shop Pro, which has a snapshot feature that enables you to grab windows and regions of your screen. You can also obtain an image from an online image archive or draw it using any of a number of paint or drawing tools.

Once the image is captured or created, it must be saved in GIF format. CorelDRAW! and Micrografx Designer are two popular commercial packages that allow you to save or export images in GIF format. In addition some shareware programs do the same thing, such as Paint Shop Pro, Graphics Workshop for Windows, and LView Pro.

Touch up the background

If the image does not have a single background color, you will need to touch it up with a paint program. The goal is to make sure that the background of the image is a single color that is not used anywhere else in the image. This is important, because any pixel in the picture using that color will disappear when it is finally displayed in a browser window—unless, of course, this is the effect you want to achieve.

If possible, make the background color light gray (you can try RGB values 207, 207, 207) so that the image will still look somewhat transparent when viewed with a browser that does not support transparent images.

Make the background transparent

There are two ways to create a transparent background, depending on the colors used in the image. If your image has elements that are white and you do not want them to become transparent along with the background, you will have to create a background of a different color.

White is the default background color of any image created or captured in a paint program. When white is selected as the background color, all white elements in the image will become transparent. Figure 6.2a shows an image with white elements. Figure 6.2b shows the same image as rendered by Netscape Navigator when white is chosen as the transparent color. As you can see, the background as well as the white elements in the image are transparent.

What follows is a procedure for creating a transparent background when white is not used in the original image:

1. Create an image and size it appropriately using any popular graphics or paint program.

2. Save (or export) the image as a GIF.

3. Open the image in LView Pro.

4. In the Options menu, choose "Background Color," which opens a palette entry screen (Figure 6.3).

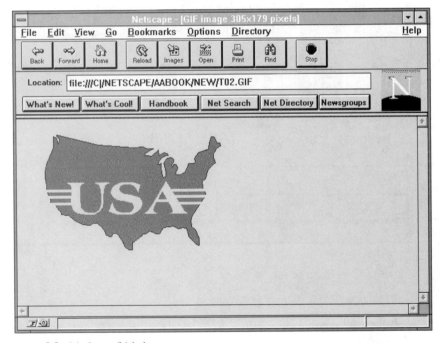

Figure 6.2 (a) above; (b) below

5. Choose the button labeled "dropper." The screen will close and the cursor changes to an eye-dropper shape.

6. With the cursor, click on the background color of the image (Figure 6.4). The cursor will change back to the cross-hairs shape.

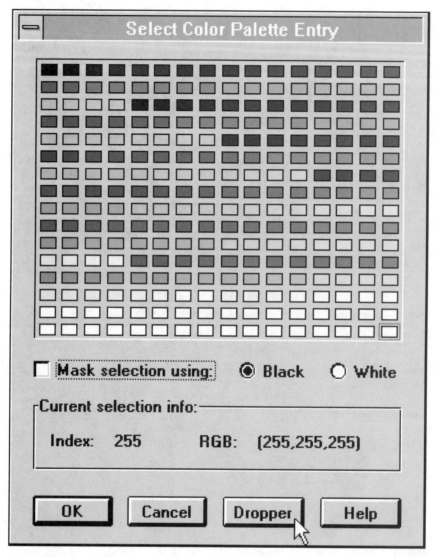

Figure 6.3

7. From the File menu, choose "Save As ..."

8. In the "Save Image As" window, choose GIF89a as the file type and click OK (Figure 6.5).

When you open the resulting image in Netscape Navigator, it will have a transparent background, as well as transparent image elements. Figure 6.6a shows the map as it would be rendered without the transparent background, while Figure 6.6b shows the map as it would be rendered with a transparent background.

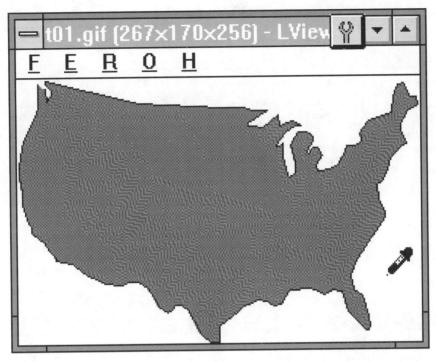

Figure 6.4

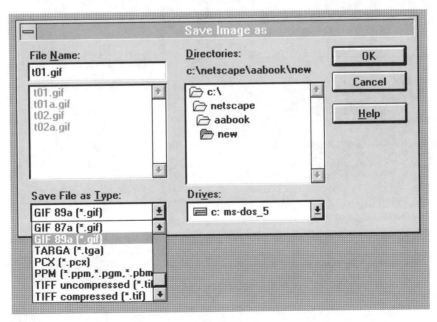

Figure 6.5

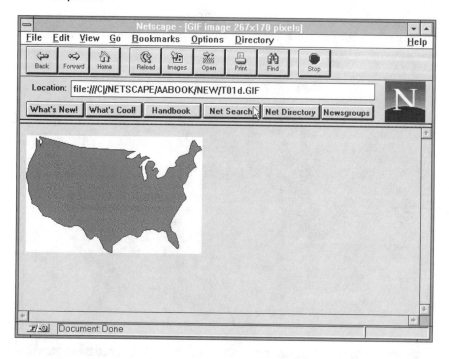

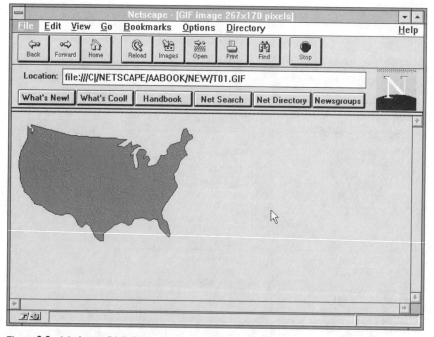

Figure 6.6 (a) above; (b) below

When you have an image with white elements that you do not want to become transparent, a different procedure must be used to create a transparent background. This procedure is as follows:

1. Create an image and size it appropriately using any popular graphics or paint program.

2. Draw a separate rectangle or square, and fill it with a color that is not used in the image. (Try a light shade of gray, but any color can be used if it is not in the image.)

3. Place the rectangle or square behind the image.

4. Size the rectangle or square so that it is larger than your image.

5. Save (or export) the image as a GIF.

6. In LView Pro, open the image. The cursor appears in the shape of crosshairs.

7. Using the crosshairs, draw a bounding box around the original image. As you do this, keep only a small border around the image, as in Figure 6.7.

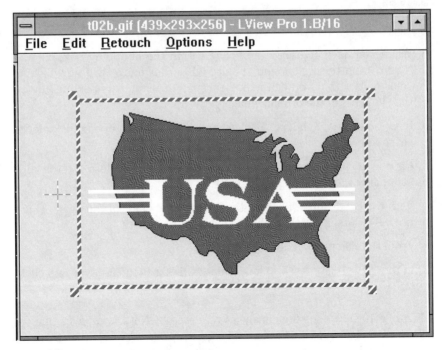

Figure 6.7

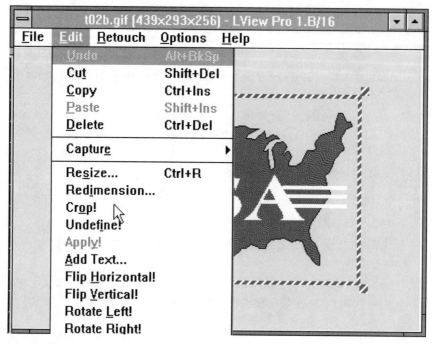

Figure 6.8

8. When you have centered the image within the bounding box, choose "Crop" from the Edit menu (Figure 6.8). Your image will now have a color border that you can make transparent without impacting any of the elements in the original image.

9. In Options menu, choose "Background Color," which opens the palette entry screen.

10. Choose the button labeled "dropper." The screen will close and the cursor changes to an eyedropper shape.

11. With the eyedropper, click on the background color of the image (Figure 6.9). Cursor will then change back to cross-hairs.

12. From the File menu, choose "Save As ..."

13. In the "Save Image As" window, choose GIF89a as the file type and click OK.

Figure 6.10 shows the final image as rendered by Netscape Navigator.

The reason for cropping the image in this way using LView Pro is to eliminate a white halo that would normally result if you had used your drawing program to size the image. This white halo would have been visible around your image when viewed through a browser.

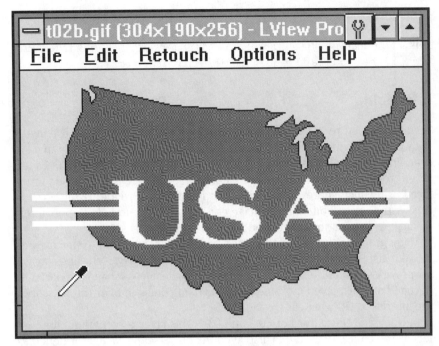

Figure 6.9

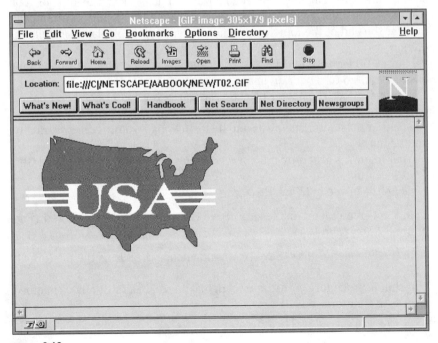

Figure 6.10

Although these procedures have focused on the use of LView Pro, a readily available shareware program, other programs may be used as well. Among the many good sources of graphics shareware, including LView Pro, is `ftp://oak.oakland.edu/SimTel/win3/graphics/`

Interlacing

A standard feature of the GIF image format is the option to store the image data in the GIF file in an interlaced fashion: Instead of storing the image's scan lines in exact sequence, equally spaced nonadjacent sets of lines are stored together, and these sets are stored in sequence. GIFs can be interlaced using such shareware products as Paint Shop Pro and LView Pro. At this writing, most commercial image editing products do not support interlacing, but the vendors plan to add it in their next releases.

Many graphical browsers that support GIF files, including Netscape and Mosaic, display both normal and interlaced GIFs properly. Netscape Navigator provides an additional feature: Because images in Netscape are normally decoded and displayed incrementally (as data comes in over the network), the interlaced GIFs appear to "fade in."

In Netscape Navigator beta 0.9 and 0.91, this gives a "venetian blind" effect as the data arrives and is displayed. As of Netscape Navigator beta 0.92 and beyond, the code has been changed to replicate available lines of the image during the first three (of four) decoding stages. In this way, the user sees a complete, but not fully recognizable, image after the first of four passes. Subsequent passes progressively enhance the quality of the image until, at the end of the fourth pass, the entire image is displayed at full resolution.

Figures 6.11 a through d show an image at the end of each of the four passes required to render an image in Netscape Navigator.

If the user does not have Netscape Navigator, both interlaced and noninterlaced images will be displayed anyway. You can convert any GIF image on your server to be interlaced without at all affecting how other browsers render the image.

What follows is a step-by-step procedure for producing an interlaced GIF:

1. Open the image in LView Pro.

2. In the Option menu, make sure "Save GIFs Interlaced" is checked (Figure 6.12 on page 105).

3. In the File menu, click "Save As..." and choose GIF89a as the file format.

This simple procedure converts the original image, in almost any bitmapped format, to an interlaced GIF.

Figure 6.11a

Image Reduction

To reduce the amount of time to load your images, you can take steps to reduce the byte count. This can be done in a number of ways using commercial and shareware graphics products. Some of the ways to reduce the byte count of images include reducing the number of colors, lowering the resolution, and physically reducing the size of the image.

For example, you might start with a 24-bit CMYK-color TIFF file of 64,000 to 1.7 million colors, with a high resolution (in pixels per inch, or ppi). To illustrate the impact of reducing only the resolution, consider an image with a resolution of 600 ppi with a byte count of 1.9MB. The same image reduced to 100 ppi becomes 54.1KB, which indicates a reduction of the original file

Figure 6.11b

length by a factor of 35 times. This kind of savings will speed image loading substantially.

You can reduce the number of colors, preferably to 256 or less. This not only reduces the byte count of the image to make it load faster, but reduces dither on low-resolution monitors. To illustrate the impact of reducing the number of colors in an image, consider an image with 1.6 million colors with a byte count of 4.4MB. The same image reduced to 256 colors becomes 1.5MB, which is a reduction of almost 3 times the original.

You can also reduce the physical size of the image to reduce the byte count. For example, consider an image that is 1.5MB and measures 1109 pixels in width by 1374 pixels in height. You can reduce it by 50 percent to achieve an image that is 373KB and measures 555 pixels in width by 687 pixels in height, which is a reduction of about 4 times the original.

You can choose one or all of these variables for reduction to speed image loading. Of course, there may be instances where you do not want to apply

Figure 6.11c

any image reduction techniques at all, such as when fine detail is important to convey quality.

Image Sizing

Image sizing is different than image reduction. The latter refers to the actual physical dimensions of an image, whereas the former has to do with the logical dimensions of an image—the size of the image as presented by the browser. The logical dimensions of an inlined image can be specified in the IMG tag, as follows:

```
<IMG SRC="sample.gif" WIDTH=197 HEIGHT=292 BORDER=1>
```

In this case, the inline image will be presented by Netscape Navigator within a border that is 197 pixels wide and 292 pixels high. If you want to preserve

Figure 6.11d

the exact dimensions of your images, most general-purpose image utility programs will give you the exact size of an image in pixels.

Specifying the height and width of an inline image is another technique for speeding image loading. This is because as Netscape Navigator is laying out a new document, it must pause at each inline image and return to the network to discover the height and width of the image before it can continue laying out the document. This information is needed so that a properly sized bounding box for each image can be put into place within the document. However, if there is significant delay on the network link while the height and width information is being retrieved, there will be a corresponding delay in the browser's ability to lay out the document. This delay could be minimized if the browser knew the height and width of each inline image from the start. Then with the bounding boxes in place (Figure 6.13a), the rest of the document can be laid out properly while the actual images are still loading (Figure 6.13b and Figure 13c).

Figure 6.12

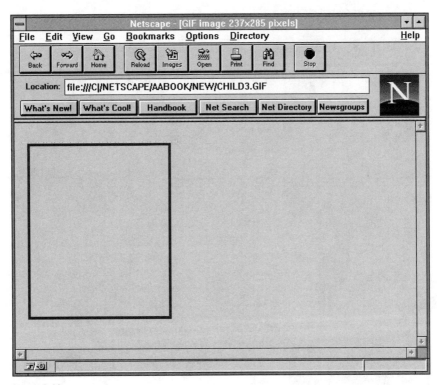

Figure 6.13a

Figure 6.13 (b) above; (c) below

Browsers that do not support the WIDTH and HEIGHT attributes of the IMG tag will simply ignore them and lay out the document normally. Netscape Navigator, on the other hand, will use the height and width information to pop in place a properly-sized bounding box upon encountering the IMG tag and will continue laying out the document text, with no performance delay that would usually result from having to go back to the network to discover the width and height of each inline image.

Autoscaling

If you specify WIDTH and/or HEIGHT values in an IMG tag that differ from the actual width and/or height of the image, Netscape Navigator will use the width and height values specified in the IMG tag and scale the actual image to fit. This is called autoscaling.

For example, if you have an image that is actually 297 pixels wide and 392 pixels high (Figure 6.14a), but you create a document that inlines the image as follows:

```
<IMG SRC="sample.gif" WIDTH=97 HEIGHT=150>
```

Figure 6.14a

The image will be scaled to fit the dimensions 97 by 150 pixels (Figure 6.14b). This means you can deliberately cause any image (GIF or JPEG) to be scaled by Netscape Navigator to a larger size or a smaller size on the fly. Browsers that do not support autoscaling will ignore any WIDTH and HEIGHT attributes and will render the inline image at the normal, unscaled size.

Autoscaling can also be done based on the percentage of available space rather than pixels. For example, you can give an image a WIDTH value of 80% and a HEIGHT value of 200 (pixels), as follows:

```
<IMG SRC="sample.gif" WIDTH="80%" HEIGHT=200>
```

This will render the image as shown in Figure 6.15a.

Or, the same image with a width of 100 and a height of 75% can be written as:

```
<IMG SRC="sample.gif" WIDTH=100 HEIGHT="75%">
```

Figure 6.15b shows how this image is rendered by Netscape Navigator.

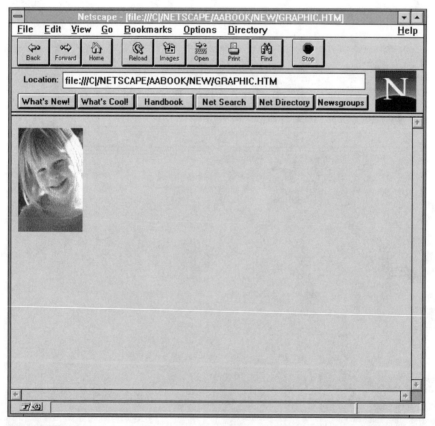

Figure 6.14b

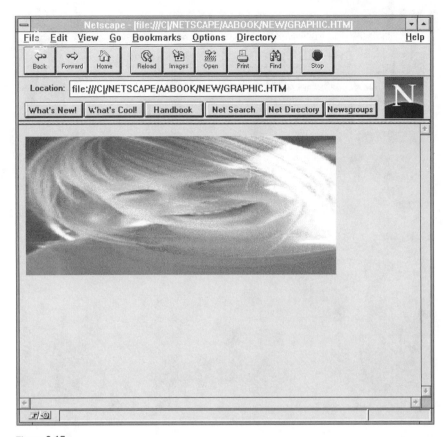

Figure 6.15a

Specifying width in percentage is generally much more useful than specifying height in percentage. If you specify only one dimension as a percentage and leave the other dimension unspecified, the image's aspect ratio will be maintained. For example, the following image is specified as width 35%:

```
<IMG SRC="image.gif" WIDTH="35%">
```

Figure 6.16 shows how this image is rendered by Netscape Navigator.

Specifying Alternate Image Resolution

Netscape Navigator supports an IMG tag attribute called LOWSRC, which allows a very low-resolution version of an image to load initially. If the user stays on the page after the initial layout phase, a higher-resolution (and presumably bigger) version of the same image can "fade in" and replace it.

Figure 6.15b

To accomplish this, the IMG tag is written as:

```
<IMG SRC="highres.jpg" LOWSRC="lowres.gif">
```

Netscape Navigator will load the image called "lowres.gif" on its first layout pass through the document (Figure 6.17). Then, when the document and all of its images are fully loaded, the Netscape Navigator will do a second pass through and load the image called "highres.jpg" in its place (Figure 6.18). Browsers that do not recognize the LOWSRC attribute will ignore it and simply load the first image as specified in the IMG tag.

You can freely mix and match GIF (both normal and interlaced) and JPEG images using this method. You can also specify width and/or height values in the IMG tag, and both the high-res and low-res versions of the image will be appropriately scaled to match.

If the images are of different sizes and a fixed height and width are not specified in the IMG tag, the second image (the image specified by the SRC attribute) will be scaled to the dimensions of the first (LOWSRC) image. The reason is, by the time the Netscape Navigator knows the dimensions of the second image, the first image has already been displayed in the document at its dimensions.

Image Maps

Image maps are a feature of NCSA and CERN HTTP servers. They allow you to turn a graphic in GIF format (not JPEG) into a clickable image. Each type of server handles image maps slightly differently. However, there are shareware and freeware utilities available on the Web, such as MapEdit and Map THIS!, that support both.

Although a clickable image map can be made from any GIF image, a good clickable image map is a planned effort. It contains "hotspots"—shapes that are drawn on top of an image—that are associated with particular URLs. Hotspots are the graphical equivalents of hypertext links. A well-planned clickable image map makes it apparent to users—via text labels or image details—what kind of resources await them at the other end of the link.

Figure 6.16

Figure 6.17

For example, if you had an image of a computer setup, you could define hotspots for the different system components, such as the monitor, disk drive, modem, and printer. Upon clicking on each system component, the user would get detailed specifications on each item.

In addition to these localized hotspots, the image map can have a default or "background" URL that provides an overview of the entire system if the user clicks on an area of the image that is external to any of the hotspots. It is not mandatory to have a background URL. In such cases, most browsers are intelligent enough to return to the current URL.

Clickable image maps are built with the aid of map editors. Regardless of which product is used, there are three basic shapes that can be drawn over an image to define the hotspots:

- Circle: defined as x, y, and r where the intersection of x and y define the center and r specifies the radius.

- Rectangle: defined as x, y, w, h where x and y define the upper-left corner and w and h define the width and height, respectively.

- Polygon (an irregularly shaped area): defined as n pairs of coordinates: $x_1, y_1; x_2, y_2; x_3, y_3 \ldots$ The polygon is closed by a line linking the last point to the first. This means the first and last pairs of coordinates will be the same.

A typical image map editor allows you to load a GIF image into a scrollable, resizable window and then draw circles, rectangles, and polygons on top of it, specifying a URL for each. Some image map editors support the ellipse as well. An ellipse can be thought of as a circle squeezed into a rectangle. The choice of shape will be determined by the shapes of the areas in the image that will be designated as hotspots. The shapes that can be mapped are shown in Figure 6.19.

To specify a polygon, you typically select "polygon" from the image map editor's toolbar. A polygon is started by positioning the mouse pointer at some point on the edge of an element in the image and then clicking on it. By repeating this process so that a rubber-band line follows along from point to point, you can trace the outline of the image element. Upon completing the outline, you are prompted for the URL to which the polygon should link.

Figure 6.18

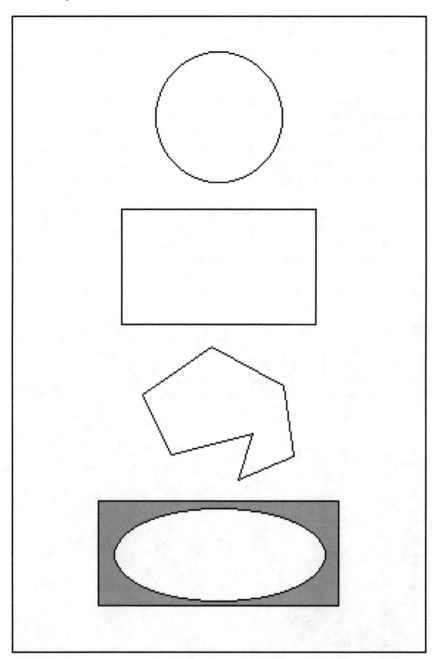

Figure 6.19

To specify a rectangle, you select "rectangle" from the image map editor's toolbar. Next, you position the mouse pointer at one corner of a rectangular element in the image, click and move the mouse pointer to the opposite corner. This traces out a rectangle.

Circles are as easy to specify as rectangles. In this case, you select "circle" from the image map editor's toolbar. Wherever you position the mouse pointer and click becomes the center of the circle. When you move the mouse pointer to the edge of the selected image element and click again, this constitutes the radius from which a circle is defined.

Some image map editors support the ellipse, which is an oval that is created in the same way as a rectangle. To define an ellipse, you select "ellipse" from the toolbar. You then position the mouse pointer at a corner of the imaginary rectangle, click, and move the mouse pointer to the opposite corner.

Regardless of shape, you have the option of canceling it while you are tracing or accepting it. After accepting the shape, you can adjust it, copy it, move it, or delete it. In addition, you can edit the hotspot's URL. Some image map editors even allow you to cut and paste the hotspots and edit the colors of hotspots.

Here is what the coordinates of the three basic shapes might look like when you are finished:

- rect: 83,284 180,383

- circle: 382,193 383,200

- poly: 175,320 227,383 347,268 345,166

In the first of these lines, the rectangle is specified by the coordinates 83,284 and 180,383. The first coordinate is the upper-left corner (in pixels) and the second coordinate is the lower-right corner.

The circle is specified by the coordinates 382,193 and 383,200. The first coordinate is the center of the circle and the second coordinate is the edge of the circle (radius).

The polygon is specified by four coordinates, which indicate the outline of the shape. Notice that the path is not closed as you would expect (i.e., the first and last coordinate pairs are not the same). In this case, the first and last coordinate pairs are assumed to be connected.

The coordinates for the shapes can be found in most commercial graphics packages and some shareware image file editors, such as LView Pro. With the right map program, the coordinates of each shape are automatically determined for you.

Figure 6.20a shows a map of the United States that has been imported into the MapEdit program. A circle shape has been drawn to define a particular area of the eastern central states (Figure 6.20b). Figure 6.20c shows the same map with a polygon defining select states. Also shown in this figure is the Object URL screen, where you would enter the URL of

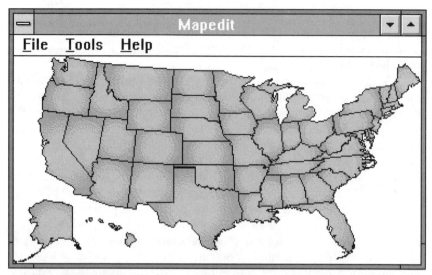

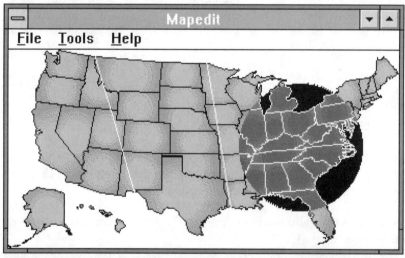

Figure 6.20 (a) top; (b) middle; (c) below

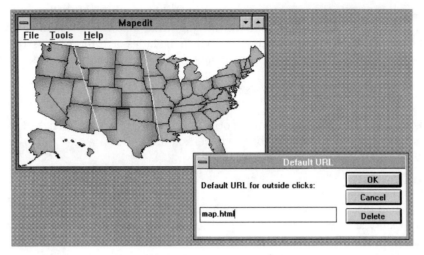

Figure 6.20d

that polygon. Figure 6.20d shows the map with a Default URL box for defining a URL that is not covered by a polygon or circle.

Finally, each clickable image has to be fully described in an image map file. The coordinates of each hotspot must be entered into your image map file, and this file must then be added to the server's collection of image maps. To do this you will have to find out how the system administrator named the server's image map configuration file, which contains an alias list of where each image map is stored on the server. The image map configuration file might have a name like:

```
conf/imagemap.conf
```

After you (or the system administrator) load the image map into the appropriate directory, the server's image map program—a cgi script—is what actually makes your image map work.

Here is what your completed image map file might look like:

```
default /public_html/index.html
rect http://iquest.com/~nmuller/file1.html 83,284 180,383
circle gopher://loc.gov/11/global 382,193 383,200
poly http://iquest.com/~nmuller/file2.html 175,320 227,383 347,268
345,166
```

The first line defines the default URL. This URL is used if the user happens to click on any area of the image that is not defined specifically as a hotspot by one of the shapes you created. In this case, the default URL is the index page. If the clickable map is on the index page, the user will stay on the index page and be forced to make another selection. The second, third, and fourth lines of the image map file give the URLs associated with each shape. The file itself is assigned a name with .map as the extension. In this case (and in the HTML coding example below), the file is named example.map.

In your HTML document, the resulting clickable map is identified as such by adding the ISMAP attribute to the IMG tag. What follows is an example of the entire HTML coding sequence, which includes a reference to the server's cgi-bin directory where the image map program resides.

```
<A HREF="/cgi-bin/imagemap/~username/example.map"><IMG
SRC="image.gif" ISMAP></A>
```

When the user clicks on any hotspot in the image, the location clicked is sent to the server designated by the hypertext link.

Animation

Although discussions of specialty topics such as animation, video, and virtual reality are beyond the scope of this book, there are certain animations that are quite easy to implement in your Web pages without the aid of multimedia authoring tools. Animations are implemented using a special capability supported by Netscape Navigator (starting with version 1.1), called server-push. (See the end of chapter 9 for examples of applications that make use of a complementary capability called client-pull.)

With server-push, the server sends data to the browser and leaves the HTTP connection open for an indefinite time. With this open connection, the server can continue to send data at specified intervals and the browser will display it. The connection stays open until the server knows (from a program) that it is done sending data, or until the client interrupts the connection.

Typically, an HTTP response consists of only a single piece of data. However, MIME has a standard facility for representing many pieces of data in a single message (or HTTP response). This facility uses a standard MIME type called "multipart/mixed," but for server-push a variant called "multipart/x-mixed-replace" is used instead. The "x-" indicates this type is experimental. The "replace" indicates that each new data block will replace the old data block.

This technique can be used to implement simple animations. This is done by having the SRC attribute of the IMG tag point to a URL for which the server pushes a series of images in succession. The image will get replaced inside the document each time a new image is pushed; the document itself is not affected. The result is "poor man's animation."

What follows are the directions for preparing a simple animation that displays the welcome message: "Welcome to my home page." Within a table border, each word of the message will be flashed in turn. The animation ends when the complete message is displayed.

You will have to prepare the following items to implement this animation:

- Each word of the message must be rendered in a graphics program, and saved as a GIF89a with a transparent background. Each image must be the same size, including the last GIF, which contains the entire message.

- You must list the names of the GIF files in an ASCII file.

- You must have a Perl script to implement the animation, and it must be stored in your cgi-bin directory along with the GIF images and the list of GIF files.

- You must reference the cgi-bin directory, Perl script, and list of GIF files within the IMG tag in your HTML document, where the animation will appear.

The transparent GIFs, ASCII file, and Perl script for this animation are included on HTMLdisk. What follows is the HTML coding for the document in which the animation will appear. Items for discussion are highlighted in bold.

```
<HTML>
<CENTER>
<P>
<TABLE BORDER=5>
<TR><TH ROWSPAN=4><IMG SRC="/nmullerbin/
nph-home.pl?giflist.txt"></TH>
</TR>
</TABLE>
<P>
<FONT SIZE=6>Main Menu</FONT>
</CENTER>
<HR>
<P>
<UL>
<LI><A HREF="file1.html">Who am I?</A><P>
<LI><A HREF="file2.html">All about me.</A><P>
<LI><A HREF="file3.html">More about me.</A><P>
<LI><A HREF="file4.html">Why everyone should be like me.</A><P>
<LI><A HREF="file5.html">Why I'm divorced.</A>
</UL>
</HTML>
```

The IMG tag refers to /nmullerbin/nph-home.pl?giflist.txt, which is the key information required to make the animation work. nmullerbin is my "bin alias" for my cgi-bin directory. You should substitute your own bin alias here. The next item in the IMG tag is nph-home.pl, which is the name of the demonstration Perl script that will tell the server what to do and when to do it. The question mark separates the Perl script from the next item, which is the name of the ASCII file containing the list of GIF files, giflist.txt.

The ASCII file contains the list of GIFs and no other information, as follows:

```
a_1.gif
a_2.gif
a_3.gif
a_4.gif
a_5.gif
a_6.gif
```

The Perl script that gives the server its instructions is as follows:

```
#! /usr/bin/perl

$ | = 1;
print "HTTP/1.0 200 \n";
print "Content-Type: multipart/x-mixed-replace;boundary=plaintext\n";

print "\n- -plaintext\n";

open(imagelist,@ARGV[0]) || die "Cannot open @ARGV[0]: $!";
while (<imagelist>)
{
chop $_;
print "Content-Type: image/gif\n";
print "\n";
open (sendgif, $_);
print (<sendgif>);
close sendgif;
print "\n- -plaintext\n";
}
close(imagelist);
```

In the Perl script above, `#!/usr/bin/perl` sends the script to Perl for processing. The next line is intentionally left blank, as is required by the Perl syntax. The next line, `$ | = 1`, unbuffers your I/O, enabling the animation to run. The rest of the script tells the server to send the GIFs to the client. The GIFs are sent to the client in the order that they appear in the list, one right after another. There is very little delay, because the HTTP connection between the client and the server remains open while the GIFs are being delivered. Figures 6.21a through 6.21c show some of the frames in the "Welcome to my home page" animation.

Although crude, this Perl script demonstrates how simple animations can add visual interest to your Web pages. You can experiment with these items by substituting your own GIFs in any number or sequence you wish. They need not be words; they can be pictures, abstract designs, or numbers. You can even mimic motion—such as a person running or cycling—by capturing each stage of motion in its own GIF. When the animation runs, it provides the illusion of motion without affecting the rest of the document.

The extensive use of images is one of the most compelling features of the Web and the reason the Web has become so popular in recent years. You should not feel obligated to dummy down your Web pages just because there may be people with slow network connections, antiquated computers, and text-only browsers. If we had to cater to the lowest common denominator, television would never have supplanted radio as the preferred entertainment medium. Imagine if the developers of the earliest television shows gave up what they were doing out of the sudden realization that not too many people owned televisions! On the flip side, if there were no shows to watch, why would anyone want to buy a television?

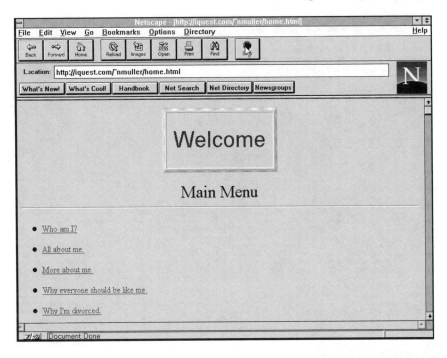

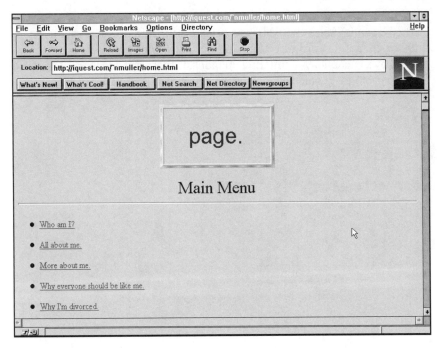

Figure 6.21   (a) above; (b) below

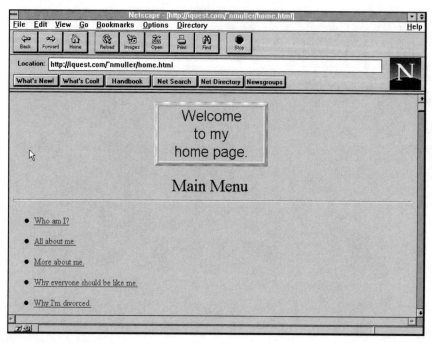

Figure 6.21c

The lesson is that if the Web is to progress further, developers must continue to go in a forward direction, and not allow themselves to become distracted by a cacaphony of differing opinions. If there is value in what the Web developer offers, people will make the necessary adjustments to access it.

7

Forms Development
and Processing

One of the most powerful features associated with the Web is the ability to request information from users via online forms, to manipulate the input via Common Gateway Interface (CGI) programs, and to receive it in the proper format via e-mail. Such programs can even supply you with information about the user's connections, add up the prices of items on order forms, and send acknowledgments back to the sender that include verifications of various form inputs.

The forms are developed using HTML's form tags, attributes, and values. However, HTML is only good for designing the forms; it has no means of doing anything with the information entered into the forms. All HTML can do is provide the fields in which users enter information, and then pass that information to another program that actually does the processing.

The facility that gathers the form input and calls other programs to process it is the CGI. There are several terms that are used to describe these programs, such as CGI programs or scripts, gateways, and virtual document programs. The last term is the most descriptive; it refers to a document that does not exist until it is put together on the fly based on form inputs.

The forms processing program can be written in any language, but is usually written in a UNIX-based scripting language such as Perl, TCL, the C Shell, or the Bourne Shell. These programs also can be written in C or C+. Of these, Perl—Practical Extraction and Report Language—is among the more popular. It is used for all kinds of processing tasks on the Web and is fairly easy to learn.

There are many ways to write a Perl script for processing the same form. This book offers a very simple script template that can be modified to meet basic forms processing requirements. The resulting scripts do not include a lot of bells and whistles, but they do get the job done—and with a reasonable degree of sophistication. After experimenting with the HTML forms and Perl scripts, you may have more incentive to learn Perl so you can add the bells and whistles yourself.

Using the HTML Forms and Perl Scripts

This chapter provides the HTML coding for a variety of forms, as well as for the CGI programs that process the input of the forms. The CGI programs are written in Perl. It is not the purpose of this chapter to teach Perl; in fact, this chapter assumes you do not know or even wish to learn Perl. The HTML forms and Perl scripts discussed in this chapter are included in HTMLdisk and (with slight modifications) can be used as is. They also are somewhat modular, so they can be easily modified to suit your personal preferences and application needs. Before changing anything, you should view each of these HTML forms with your browser to get an idea of what you would like to change or add.

To use the Perl scripts (or ones that you have modified), they must be put into a cgi-bin subdirectory on the server. If you do not already have a cgi-bin directory, you must either establish a telnet session with the server to create one, or request that the system administrator create it for you. The HTML-coded forms can be located in any directory, preferably with your other HTML documents. Typically, HTML documents and programs are loaded into their respective directories via FTP.

Once the Perl scripts are placed in the cgi-bin directory in ASCII form (never save them in binary form), they must be initialized so they will be executable. You can have the system administrator do this for you, or you can do it yourself via a telnet session. After loading the Perl script to the cgi-bin directory via FTP, just access the directory via telnet and perform the following function (assuming a UNIX server) the first time a Perl script is loaded:

```
chmod a+rx formname.pl
```

This determines who gets to use the file for processing forms. Essentially, chmod means change mode, which makes the script executable and sets the permissions. In this case, the permissions are set as a+rx, which allows formname.pl to read (r) and execute (x) for everyone (a+). Formname.pl is the name you assign for the particular script, and .pl is the extension for the Perl script. You only have to do this procedure the first time you load a Perl script. You can modify and reload a script any number of times via FTP, and the permissions will hold unless specifically changed. Any time you modify and reload the Perl script via FTP, it must be as an ASCII file and not binary. Uploading the file as binary will introduce hard returns into the Perl script, which will render the script unusable.

This chapter provides the HTML coding and Perl script for the following types of common forms:

- Evaluation form
- Guest book form
- Catalog request form
- Single-product order form
- Multiproduct order form
- Subscription form
- Seminar registration form
- Help request form

For each type of form, the following items are provided:

- HTML coding for the form
- A Netscape rendering of the form
- Perl script to process the form
- E-mail output of the form
- A Netscape rendering of the acknowledgment message sent to the user after the form is submitted

The first form discussed in this chapter—the evaluation form—will include a detailed description of each element used in the HTML-coded form and will provide only the essential information about the Perl program. In subsequent forms, the discussions will focus only on the changed elements of the HTML-coded form and Perl program. As you will notice, a great variety of forms of any length can be produced using essentially the same HTML and Perl elements in different combinations. All of the HTML forms and Perl scripts are on HTMLdisk.

If you do not have experience with HTML forms or Perl programs that process the forms, you should read the next section on writing and processing an evaluation form. This section provides the essential information concerning what can and should be changed in the HTML form and Perl program to get them working properly on the Web. For example, you will have to add your own e-mail address to the beginning of each Perl program, as well as an appropriate hypertext link at the end of each Perl program. You may even want to rename the HTML and Perl files to something more appropriate to your needs. It is advisable not to change the forms and programs in any other way until you have them running as is. As you get more comfortable working with the forms and programs, you can easily modify or expand them, or mix-and-match elements from each to meet the most common information gathering and form processing requirements.

Creating an Evaluation Form

You may want to include an evaluation form in your Web pages to get an idea of what users like and dislike about your publishing efforts. An evaluation form can be a good method of collecting these kinds of inputs. The comments can point out deficiencies you overlooked and even stimulate your creativity when you are making improvements.

A short form is best for this purpose, if only because more people will fill out a small form than a big one. A simple evaluation form would ask for the person's name and e-mail address, as well as the most useful and least useful topics in your Web pages. You also can ask them to rate the content and the organization of your Web pages, and invite them to add any other comments.

HTML coding for an evaluation form

What follows is the HTML coding for a simple evaluation form. Note the items highlighted in bold. These are discussed later.

```
<HTML>
<HEAD>
<TITLE>The Webmaster's Workshop</TITLE></HEAD>
<BODY>
<CENTER>
<H1>Evaluation Form</H1>
</CENTER>
<P>
We are interested in your suggestions for improving <B>The Webmaster's
Workshop</B>. We would also like to hear about who visits our site,
why, and if they found the service informative and easy to use.
<P>
<FORM METHOD="POST" ACTION="/nmullerbin/evalform.pl">
<HR SIZE=5>
<B>Please enter your name: <input name="name" size=30></B>
<P>
<B>Please enter your e-mail address: <input name="e-mail"
size=30></B>
<P>
<B>Which topic on the Main Menu interested you the most? </B>
<SELECT NAME="most">
<option selected> I have no opinion
<option value="Introduction_to_Forms"> Introduction to Forms
<option value="Elements_of_Forms"> Elements of Forms
<option value="Designing _Forms"> Designing Forms
<option value="The_Role_of_CGI"> The Role of CGI
<option value="Programming_in_Perl"> Programming in Perl
<option value="Debugging_Your_Programs"> Debugging Your Programs
<option value="Internet_Sources"> Internet Sources
</SELECT>
<P>
<B>Which topic on the Main Menu interested you the least? </B>
<SELECT NAME="least"><option selected> I have no opinion
<option value="Introduction_to_Forms"> Introduction to Forms
```

```
<option value="Elements_of_Forms"> Elements of Forms
<option value="Designing _Forms"> Designing Forms
<option value="The_Role_of_CGI"> The Role of CGI
<option value="Programming_in_Perl"> Programming in Perl
<option value="Debugging_Your_Programs"> Debugging Your Programs
<option value="Internet_Sources"> Internet Sources
</SELECT>
<P>
<B>How would you rate the content of these pages?</B>
<P>
<MENU>
<input name="rate1" value="Poor" TYPE="radio"> Poor<BR>
<input name="rate1" value="Fair" TYPE="radio"> Fair<BR>
<input name="rate1" value="Good" TYPE="radio"> Good<BR>
<input name="rate1" value="Excellent" TYPE="radio"> Excellent<BR>
<input name="rate1" value="Outstanding" TYPE="radio"> Outstanding<BR>
</MENU>
<B>How would you rate the organization of these pages?</B>
<P>
<MENU>
<input name="rate2" value="Poor" TYPE="radio"> Poor<BR>
<input name="rate2" value="Fair" TYPE="radio"> Fair<BR>
<input name="rate2" value="Good" TYPE="radio"> Good<BR>
<input name="rate2" value="Excellent" TYPE="radio"> Excellent<BR>
<input name="rate2" value="Outstanding" TYPE="radio"> Outstanding<BR>
</MENU>
<P>
<B>Please feel free to add any other comments:</B>
<P>
<TEXTAREA NAME="comments" ROWS=8 COLS=50></TEXTAREA>
<P>
Thanks for taking the time to let us know what you think.
<P>
Press <INPUT TYPE="submit" VALUE="Send"> to submit this form, or
<INPUT TYPE="reset" VALUE="Clear"> to start over.
</FORM>
</BODY>
</HTML>
```

Figure 7.1 shows how this evaluation form is rendered by Netscape Navigator.

Every form must be encapsulated within the <FORM> and </FORM> tags. The beginning of the HTML-coded form makes reference to METHOD, POST, and ACTION, which are attributes of the FORM tag. These refer to how forms are processed by the common gateway script. METHOD specifies the HTTP method to be used to submit the form information to the server. METHOD can have either of two arguments:

- GET (the default): The form contents are appended to the URL.

- POST (recommended): The form contents are sent to the server in the body of the message. To take advantage of POST, the local HTTP server must support the POST method.

Throughout this chapter, the forms will be coded for the POST method. The ACTION specifies the URL of the Perl program to which the form inputs will

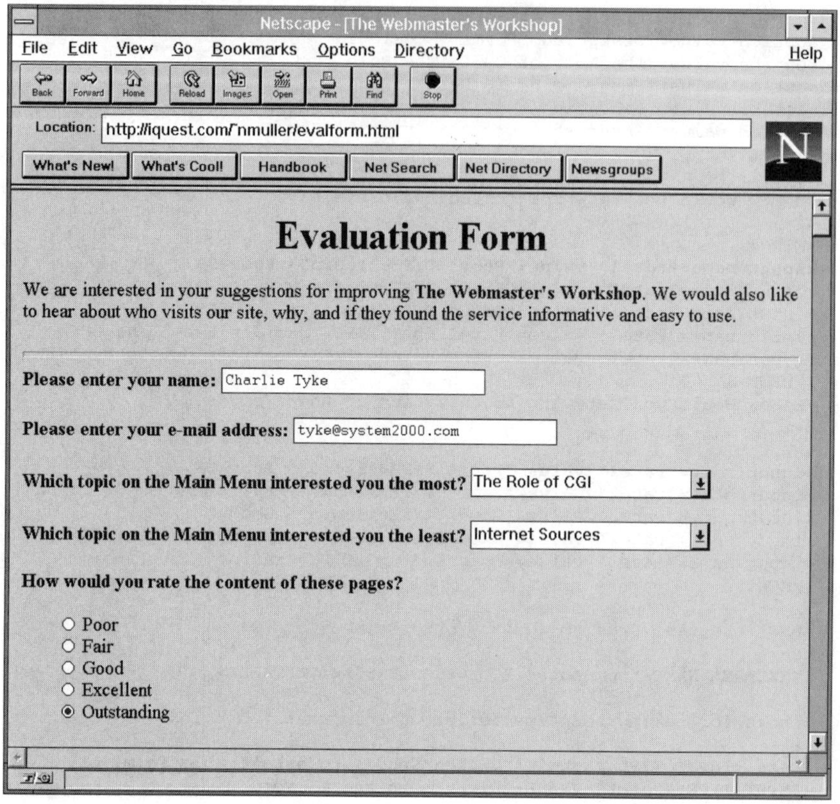

Figure 7.1

be sent. The program should reside in the cgi-bin directory. In this example, the location and name of the Perl file is simply "/nmullerbin/evalform.pl." The reference nmullerbin is a "bin alias" that is set up at the Web server. It is merely shorthand for a much longer directory/subdirectory name that identifies the exact location of the Perl file on the server. On a shared Web server, directory/subdirectory names can be quite long. For example, using nmullerbin saves me from having to type this whenever I want to create a new form:

```
/home/users/nmuller/public_html/cgi-bin/
```

If you create a lot of forms, you will appreciate having your own bin alias. It takes only a few seconds for your system administrator to set you up with one.

The next items in the HTML-coded form that merit explanation are the input fields for the name and e-mail address. In both cases, the INPUT tag is used to indicate a single-line text field. The NAME attribute is used to identify the particular field when the form's contents are processed by the Perl script. The SIZE attribute specifies the visible width of the field in characters.

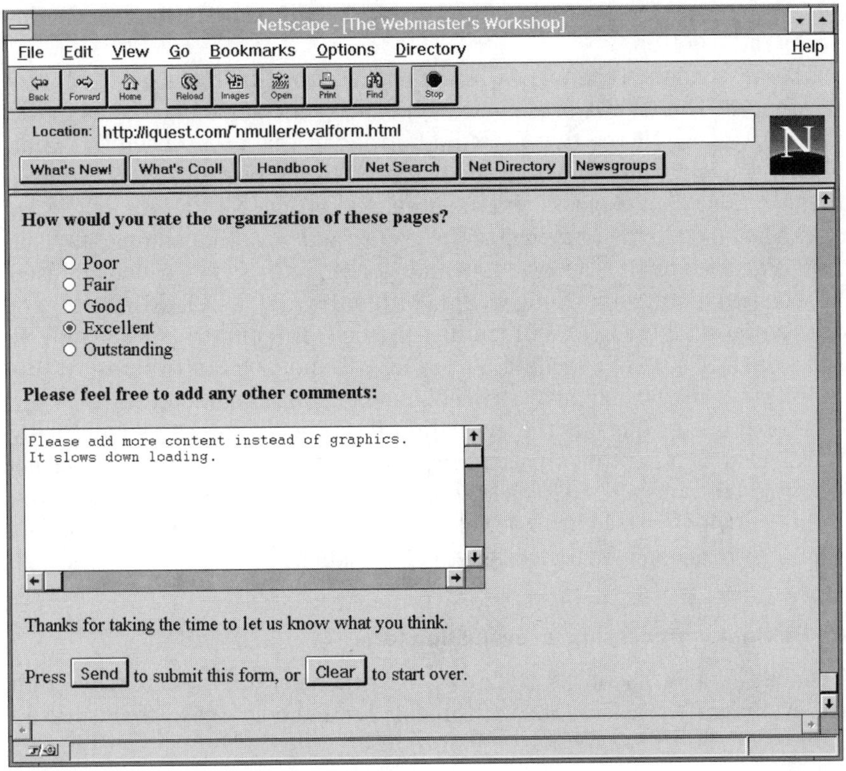

Figure 7.1 *(Continued)*

Further down in the form there is a single choice menu from which the user can select the topic that he or she found the most interesting. Generally, this menu is rendered as a pop-up or drop-down menu, and offers a more compact alternative to multiple choice radio buttons or checkboxes. The list of choices is encapsulated with the <SELECT> and </SELECT> tags. Associated with the SELECT tag is a NAME attribute that is used to identify the particular menu when the form's contents are processed by the Perl script. The two menus in our example are referred to as "most" and "least."

Each choice that appears in the menus is identified as an OPTION, with the first option always referred to as the SELECTED (or default) option. This option will be output if the user does not select any other option. Subsequent options have associated values that identify a particular choice the user can select. For each menu, the item the user selects will be processed and output by the Perl script.

The next menu of the form asks the user to rate the content of your Web pages. The user can select a desired rating from a list of items, each of which has a radio button. The INPUT tag has three attributes: NAME, VALUE, and TYPE. All radio buttons in the same group have the same NAME, in this case "rate1." All the choices have an appropriate VALUE, which should coincide with the choice the user sees on the form. TYPE refers to "radio," which renders a radio button.

The next menu of the form asks the user to rate the organization of your Web pages. The user is presented with exactly the same choices as in the previous menu. Notice that all radio buttons in this group have the same NAME, which is different from the one used in the previous menu. To distinguish this set of choices from the previous set, the NAME is "rate2."

The last field in the form invites the user to add any other comments. This field is defined by the <TEXTAREA> and </TEXTAREA> tags, which are used to specify a multiline text entry field. Within the first TEXTAREA tag there are several attributes. NAME identifies the field as "comments." The dimensions of the field are specified by the ROWS and COLS attributes, in this case 8 rows and 50 columns (each column is a single character wide).

After the user fills out the evaluation form, he or she can submit it by clicking the Send button or reset it by clicking the Clear button. The labels on these buttons can be changed to anything you want. Simply change the VALUE attributes. When rendered, the size of the button will expand (or contract) to accommodate the length of the label.

Perl script for processing an evaluation form

The following Perl script is used to process the user information entered in the evaluation form. Note the items highlighted in bold; these are discussed later.

```perl
#!/usr/local/bin/perl

$mailprog = '/usr/bin/mail';
$recipient = 'yourname@ddx.com';

print "Content-type: text/html\n\n";
print "<Head><Title>The Webmaster's Workshop</Title></Head>";
print "<Body><H1>Thanks for your assistance!</H1></Body>";

read(STDIN, $buffer, $ENV{'CONTENT_LENGTH'});


foreach $pair (@pairs)
{
  ($name, $value) = split(/=/, $pair);
  $value =~ tr/+/ /;
  $value =~ s/%([a-fA-F0-9][a-fA-F0-9])/pack("C", hex($1))/eg;

 $FORM{$name} = $value;
}

open (MAIL, "|$mailprog $recipient $FORM{'e-mail'} $FORM{'NAME'}") ||
die "Can't open $mailprog!\n";
print MAIL "This is a Web page evaluation from $FORM{'name'} who is
reachable at: $FORM{'e-mail'}\n";
print MAIL "\n";
print MAIL "I would say the most useful item on the Main Menu is:
$FORM{'most'}\n";
print MAIL "\n";
```

```
print MAIL "I would say the least useful item on the Main Menu is:
$FORM{'least'}\ n";
print MAIL "\n";
print MAIL "I give the content of these pages a rating of: $FORM
{'rate1'}\n";
print MAIL "\n";
print MAIL "I give the organization of these pages a rating of: $FORM
{'rate2'}\n";
print MAIL "\n";
print MAIL "---------------------------------------------\n";
print MAIL "Here is what else $FORM{'name'} had to say:\n";
print MAIL "\n";
print MAIL "$FORM{'comments'}\n";
print MAIL "\n";
print MAIL "---------------------------------------------\n";
print MAIL "\n";
print MAIL "The browser used to access my Web page: $ENV{'HTTP_USER
_AGENT'}\n";
close (MAIL);

print "Your comments will help improve The Webmaster's Workshop.
<P>
\n";
print MAIL "\n";
print "Return to the <A HREF=\"http://iquest.com/~nmuller/
index.shtml\">Main Menu</a>\n";
```

The Perl script begins with a line that says:

```
#!/usr/local/bin/perl
```

This line tells the machine to run the script through Perl. The program will not work without this line. In addition, this line must be followed by a blank line.

Next comes $mailprog, which references the server's mail program. This may differ according to the way your server is set up. Some choices include:

```
$mailprog = '/usr/bin/mail';
$mailprog = '/usr/lib/sendmail';
```

You should check with your system administrator to find out the preferred reference. Sometimes these references are called "mail aliases." The first reference above is used in all the Perl scripts in this chapter and should work for you until you have time to do some fine-tuning.

The next line, $recipient, is your e-mail address. However, if you would like the form's output to go to another e-mail address as well, just add another address and separate them with a comma, as in the following example:

```
$recipient = 'hisname@ddx.com, hername@ddx.com';
```

The next section of the script specifies the content type; in this case, text and/or html-coded text. The next two lines refer to parts of the acknowledgment message that will appear to the user after he or she submits the completed form. After that, the next lines in the program establish the relationships of name and value pairs. These lines are the same for all the Perl programs in this chapter and should not be changed.

The part of the program that actually causes the form's contents to be output as e-mail, and in the format you specify, is encapsulated with the open MAIL and close MAIL commands. Wherever $FORM appears, with a label in parentheses, the HTML form's inputs will be printed.

For example, $FORM{'name'} refers back to the field in the HTML-coded form that asked for the user's name. That field was given the input name of "name," which is referenced in the Perl script as 'name'. The only difference is that in the HTML version double quotation marks are used, and in the Perl version single quotation marks are used. The same convention is used for the e-mail address. On the HTML-coded form this field is labelled "e-mail." Wherever $FORM{'e-mail'} appears in this portion of the Perl program, the user's e-mail address will be output.

In the first menu of the HTML-coded form, the user is asked to select a topic from the Main Menu that he or she found the most interesting. That menu was given the label "most." In the MAIL section of the Perl program, wherever $FORM{'most'} appears, the user's actual choice will be output. If the user did not make a choice, the default selection will appear, which is: I have no opinion.

In the second menu of the HTML-coded form, the user is asked to select a topic from the Main Menu that he or she found the least interesting. That menu was given the label "least." In the MAIL section of the Perl program, wherever $FORM{'least'} appears, the user's actual choice will be output. If the user did not make a choice, the default selection will appear, which is: I have no opinion.

In the next menu of the HTML-coded form, the user is asked to assign a rating to the content of the Web pages. Each choice in this category is labelled "rate1." Wherever $FORM{'rate1'} appears in the MAIL section of the Perl program, the user's actual choice will be output.

In the next menu of the HTML-coded form, the user is asked to assign a rating to the organization of the Web pages. Each choice in this category is labelled "rate2." Wherever $FORM{'rate2'} appears in the MAIL section of the Perl program, the user's actual choice will be output.

In the TEXTAREA of the HTML-coded form, the user is invited to comment further. This multiline text field is labelled "comments." Wherever $FORM{'comments'} appears in the MAIL portion of the Perl program, the user's actual comments will be output.

The environmental variable near the end of the Perl script returns the user's browser type. It is written as:

```
$ENV{'HTTP_USER_AGENT'}
```

This might be useful information to collect as when the evaluation form is processed. Depending on the type of browser used by a majority of visitors, this information may influence how you design your Web pages.

All of the lines in the MAIL section of the Perl program must end with `\n";`, which is used to indicate a new line. You can specify a skipped line between output text items to make the output easier to read by using the following command sequence: `print MAIL "\n";` you also can indicate the start and end of the user comments with dotted lines to make that text stand out when the form results are output. The MAIL section of the Perl script is closed using the `close (MAIL);` command sequence.

The output of the processed evaluation form, as received via e-mail, is shown in Figure 7.2.

The last three lines in the Perl script are part of the acknowledgment message sent to the user after the form is submitted. An acknowledgment message is not only a courtesy, but it provides some indication to the user that the form was indeed submitted. Notice the structure of the hypertext link back to the Main Menu; the entire URL is encapsulated with forward slashes.

Figure 7.3 shows how the acknowledgment message is rendered by Netscape Navigator.

You can change the text in the HTML form to suite your own needs. You can even add more menus, radio buttons, and multiline text fields. To make the revised form work, however, you must reference the changes in the Perl script so the users' inputs will show up on the processed form sent to you via e-mail. Before you make any changes, you should get the original form working.

Date: Mon, 17 Jul 1995 11:56:50 -0500
To: nmuller@ddx.com

This is a Web page evaluation from Charlie Tyke who is reachable at: tyke@system2000.com

I would say the most useful item on the Main Menu is: The_Role_of_CGI

I would say the least useful item on the Main Menu is: Internet_Sources

I give the content of these pages a rating of: Outstanding

I give the organization of these pages a rating of: Outstanding

----
Here is what else Charlie Tyke had to say:

Please add more content instead of graphics.
It slows down loading.

The browser used to access my Web page: Mozilla/1.1N (Windows; I; 16bit)

Figure 7.2

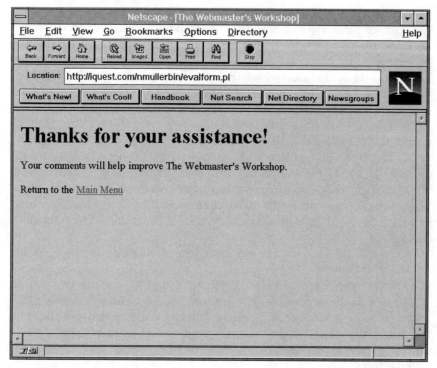

Figure 7.3

Creating a Guest Book Form

Many Web pages include a hypertext link to a guest book. The purpose of a guest book is to obtain useful information about the people who visit your Web page and their interests. From that information, you can get a sense of who your audience is, what their interests are, and how they learned about your Web page. As you accumulate this kind of information, an audience profile will begin to emerge, which may influence what you publish in your Web pages.

HTML coding for a guest book form

What follows is the HTML coding for a simple guest book:

```
<HTML>
<HEAD>
<TITLE>The Webmaster's Workshop</TITLE>
</HEAD>
<BODY>
<H2>Please sign in here . . . </H2>
<P>
<HR>
<P>
We would like to find out who is accessing
```

```
<B>The Webmaster's Workshop</B> and would appreciate it if you would
take a few moments to complete the form below. Signing the guest book
will help us to better fulfill your information needs in a timely
way.
<P>
<HR>
<form method="POST" action="/nmullerbin/guestfrm.pl">
<P>
<PRE>
<B>Your Name:</B> <INPUT VALUE="" SIZE=49 NAME="name">
<P>
<B>Organization:</B> <INPUT VALUE="" SIZE=49 NAME="organization">
<P>
<B>E-mail Address:</B> <INPUT VALUE="" SIZE=49 NAME="e-mail">
</PRE>
<P>
<HR>
<P>
<B>What topics would you like to know more about?</B>
<TEXTAREA ROWS=8 COLS=65 INPUT VALUE="" NAME="topics"></TEXTAREA><BR>
<P>
<HR>
<P>
<B>How did you learn about The Webmaster's Workshop?</B>
<TEXTAREA ROWS=8 COLS=65 INPUT VALUE=""
NAME="sources"></TEXTAREA><BR>
<P>
<INPUT TYPE="submit" VALUE="Submit">
<INPUT TYPE="reset" VALUE="Clear"><BR>
</FORM>
<P>
<HR SIZE=5>
<P>
<A HREF="index.html"><IMG SRC="al03.gif" ALIGN=MIDDLE></A>
<EM> Go back to Main Menu</EM>
</BODY>
</HTML>
```

Figure 7.4 shows how the guest book form is rendered by Netscape Navigator. Notice the way this form is presented using horizontal rules and the <PRE> and </PRE> tags to align the input fields. There is also a return icon at the end of the form to allow users to go back to the Main Menu if they do not wish to fill out the form.

Perl script for processing a guest book form

The Perl script for the guest book form contains the same basic elements as the evaluation form discussed earlier.

```
#!/usr/local/bin/perl

$mailprog = '/usr/bin/mail';
$recipient = 'nmuller@ddx.com';
print "Content-type: text/html\n\n";
print "<Head><Title>The Webmaster's Workshop</Title></Head>";
print "<Body><H1>Thank you for signing the Guest Book . . . </H1>
      </Body>";
read(STDIN, $buffer, $ENV{'CONTENT_LENGTH'});
@pairs = split (/&/,$buffer);
foreach $pair (@pairs)
```

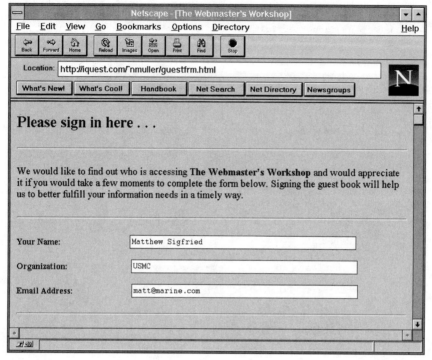

Figure 7.4

```
{
 ($name, $value) = split(/=/, $pair);
 $value =~ tr/+/ /;
 $value =~ s/%([a-fA-F0-9][a-fA-F0-9])/pack("C", hex($1))/eg;
 $FORM{$name} = $value;
}

open (MAIL, "|$mailprog $recipient $FORM{'e-mail'} $FORM{'NAME'}") ||
die "Can't open $mailprog!\n";
print MAIL "This is a Guest Book entry from $FORM{'name'} who is
reachable at: $FORM{'e-mail'}\n";
print MAIL "\n";
print MAIL "$FORM{'name'}'s organization is:
$FORM{'organization'}\n";
print MAIL "\n";
print MAIL "-----------------------------------------------------\n";
print MAIL "\n";
print MAIL "Here are the topics $FORM{'name'} would like to know more
about:\n";
print MAIL "\n";
print MAIL "$FORM{'topics'}\n";
print MAIL "\n";
print MAIL "-----------------------------------------------------\n";
print MAIL "\n";
print MAIL "Here is how $FORM{'name'} learned about The Webmaster's
Workshop:\n";
print MAIL "\n";
print MAIL "$FORM{'sources'}\n";
```

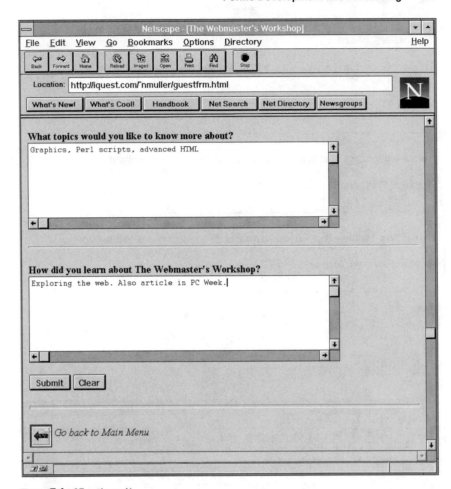

Figure 7.4 *(Continued)*

```
print MAIL "\n";
print MAIL "-------------------------------------------------------\n";
close (MAIL);

print "Your input will assist us in our continuing efforts to develop
and improve <STRONG>The Webmaster's Workshop</STRONG>.\n";
print MAIL "\n";
print "Return to the <A HREF=\"http://iquest.com/~nmuller/index.shtml\">
   Main Menu</a>
<P>
\n";
```

The output of the processed Guest Book form, as received via e-mail, is shown in Figure 7.5.

Figure 7.6 shows how the acknowledgment message is rendered by Netscape Navigator.

Date: Mon, 17 Jul 1995 12:08:29 -0500
To: nmuller@ddx.com

This is a Guest Book entry from Matthew Sigfried who is reachable at:
matt@marine.com

Matthew Sigfried's organization is: USMC

Here are the topics Matthew Sigfried would like to know more about:

Graphics, Perl scripts, advanced HTML

Here is how Matthew Sigfried learned about The Webmaster's Workshop:

Exploring the web. Also article in PC Week.

Figure 7.5

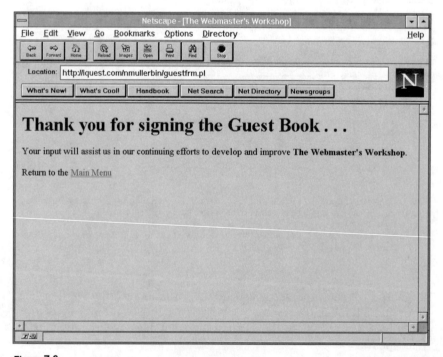

Figure 7.6

Creating a Catalog Request Form

Many companies advertise the availability of their product catalogs on the World Wide Web. In addition to meeting the immediate information needs of potential new customers, the Web can be a good vehicle for building mailing lists for future catalog mailings.

HTML coding for a catalog request form

What follows is the HTML coding for a simple catalog request form, with discussion items highlighted in bold:

```
<HTML>
<HEAD>
<TITLE>NJM Systems Inc.</TITLE></HEAD>
<BODY>
<CENTER><H1>Catalog Request Form</H1></CENTER>
<P>
<form method="POST" action="/nmullerbin/catreq.pl"><HR>
<CENTER><H3>Use this form to request an NJM Systems catalog and get
10% off on your next purchase!</H3></CENTER>
<P>
<HR>
<P>
<H4>Contact Information</H4>
<P>
Name:<BR>
<input TYPE="text" NAME="name" size=56>
<P>
Company:<BR>
<input type="text" NAME="company" size=56>
<P>
Phone:<BR>
<input type="text" NAME="phone" size=56>
<P>
Street Address: <BR>
<input type="text" NAME="address" size=56>
<P>
City: <input type="text" NAME="city" size=20> State: <input
type="text" NAME="state" size=3> Zip Code: <input type="text"
NAME="zip" size=10>
<P>
E-mail Address: <input type="text" NAME="e-mail" size=42>
<P>
<HR>
<P>
<H4>Please select the catalog you are interested in:</H4>
<I>(Check all that apply)</I>
<P>
<input type="radio" NAME="info_type1" VALUE="Car Stereo Systems"> Car
Stereo Systems
<P>
<input type="radio" NAME="info_type2" VALUE="Home Audio Systems">
Home Audio Systems
<P>
<input type="radio" NAME="info_type3" VALUE="Home Theater Systems">
Home Theater Systems
<P>
<input type="radio" NAME="info_type4" VALUE="Public Address Systems">
Public Address Systems
```

```
<P>
I intend to use the <STRONG>NJM Systems</STRONG> catalog(s) for the
following purpose:
<SELECT NAME="purchase" SIZE="3">
<OPTION>Corporate Purchase
<OPTION>Value-Added Reseller Purchase
<OPTION>Personal Purchase
<OPTION>Governmental Purchase
<OPTION>Educational Institution Purchase
<OPTION>Non-profit Organization Purchase
</SELECT>
<P>
<HR>
<P>
<H4>Can we be of further assistance?</H4>
<P>
<TEXTAREA NAME="assistance" ROWS=8 COLS=50></TEXTAREA>
<P>
<input type=Submit value="Send"> <input type=Reset value="Clear">
<P>
</FORM>
<P>
Return to the <A HREF="http://iquest.com/~nmuller/index.html">Main
Menu</A>
<BODY>
</HTML>
```

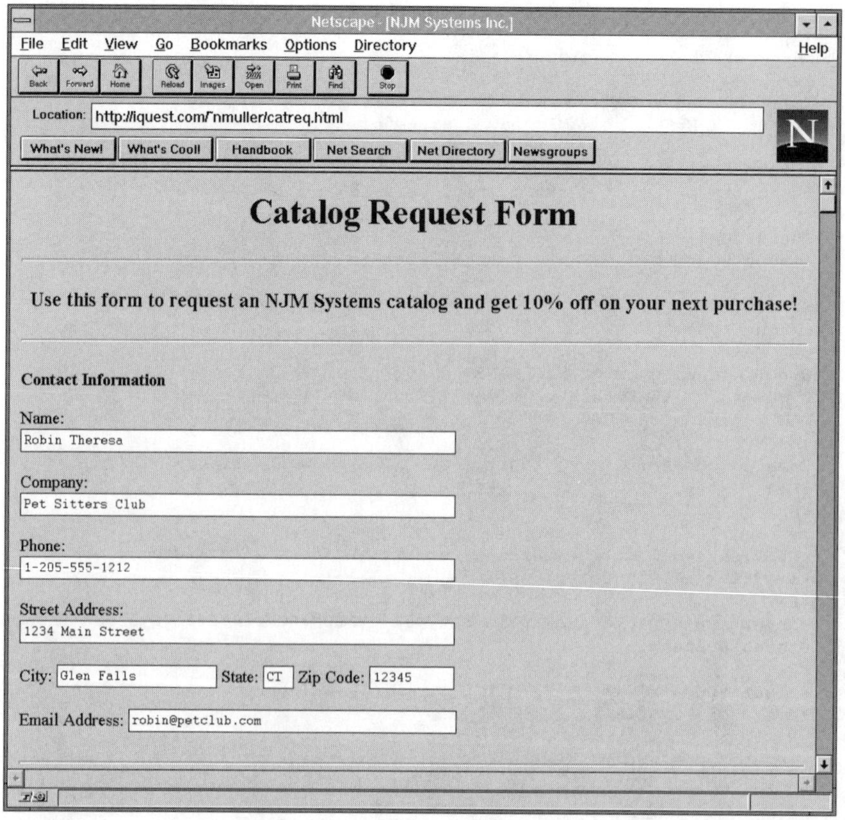

Figure 7.7

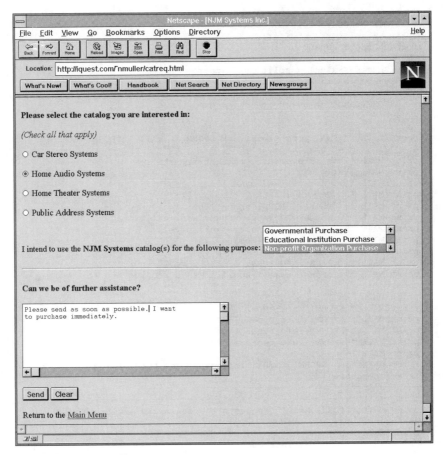

Figure 7.7 *(Continued)*

There are two noteworthy features of this form. One is that the user may select multiple items from the list of catalogs. The second feature is the scrollable multiline text field that lists the possible ways the user intends to use the catalog(s).

Figure 7.7 shows how the catalog request form is rendered by Netscape Navigator.

Perl script for processing a catalog request form

The Perl script for the catalog request form is as follows:

```
#!/usr/local/bin/perl

$mailprog = '/usr/bin/mail';
$recipient = 'nmuller@ddx.com';
print "Content-type: text/html\n\n";
print "<Head><Title>NJM Systems</Title></Head>";
print "<Body><H1>Thank you for checking out NJM Systems' products.
```

```
</H1></Body>";
read(STDIN, $buffer, $ENV{'CONTENT_LENGTH'});
@pairs = split(/&/,$buffer);
foreach $pair (@pairs)
{
    ($name, $value) = split(/=/, $pair);
    $value =~ tr/+/ /;
    $value =~ s/%([a- fA-F0-9][a-fA-F0-9])/pack("C", hex($1))/eg;
    $FORM{$name} = $value;
}


open (MAIL, "|$mailprog $recipient $FORM{'e-mail'} $FORM{'NAME'}") ||
die "Can't open $mailprog!\n";
print MAIL "This is a catalog request from:\n";
print MAIL "\n";
print MAIL "1. Name: $FORM{'name'}\n";
print MAIL "2. Company: $FORM{'company'}\n";
print MAIL "3. Phone: $FORM{'phone'}\n";
print MAIL "4. Street Address: $FORM{'address'}\n";
print MAIL "5. City: $FORM{'city'}\n";
print MAIL "6. State: $FORM{'state'}\n";
print MAIL "7. Zip Code: $FORM{'zip'}\n";
print MAIL "8. E-mail Address: $FORM{'e-mail'}\n";
print MAIL "9. $FORM{'name'} would like to receive the following
catalogs:\n";
print MAIL "\n";
print MAIL " $FORM{'info_type1'}\n";
print MAIL " $FORM{'info_type2'}\n";
print MAIL " $FORM{'info_type3'}\n";
print MAIL " $FORM{'info_type4'}\n";
print MAIL "\n";
print MAIL "10. $FORM{'name'} intends to use the catalog(s) for a:
$FORM{'purchase'}\n";
print MAIL "\n";
print MAIL "----------------------------------------------------\n";
print MAIL "$FORM{'name'} requests the following additional
assistance:\n";
print MAIL "\n";
print MAIL "$FORM{'assistance'}\n";
print MAIL "\n";
print MAIL "----------------------------------------------------\n";
close (MAIL);

print "The information you requested is on the way!
<P>
\n";
print "Return to the<A HREF=\"http://iquest.com/~nmuller/index.shtml\">
Main Menu</a>\n";
```

The output of the processed catalog request form, as received via e-mail, is shown in Figure 7.8.

Figure 7.9 shows how the acknowledgment message is rendered by Netscape Navigator.

Creating a Single-Product Order Form

An increasing number of companies are providing Internet users with the convenience of ordering products via e-mail. E-mail is suitable for transmit-

Date: Mon, 17 Jul 1995 12:12:45 -0500
To: nmuller@ddx.com

This is a catalog request from:

1. Name: Robin Theresa
2. Company: Pet Sitters Club
3. Phone: 1-205-555-1212
4. Street Address: 1234 Main Street
5. City: Glen Falls
6. State: CT
7. Zip Code: 12345
8. Email Address: robin@petclub.com
9. Robin Theresa would like to receive the following catalogs:

Home Audio Systems

10. Robin Theresa intends to use the catalog(s) for a: Non-profit Organization
Purchase

Robin Theresa requests the following additional assistance:

Please send as soon as possible. I want
to purchase immediately.

Figure 7.8

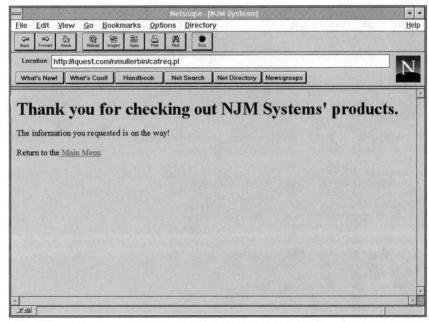

Figure 7.9

ting order forms, along with purchase order numbers and credit card numbers. To safeguard financial information as it traverses the Internet, you should have a secure server. If you do not have a secure server, you can still take credit card orders via e-mail, but you should state in your form that the transmission will not be secure. As an alternative, you should provide an 800 number to take credit card orders over the phone from those who are reluctant to e-mail them.

One more thing—to actually turn credit card orders into money, you must be a credit card merchant registered with a bank or third-party credit card processing service.

HTML coding for a single-product order form

What follows is the HTML coding for a simple mail order form, with discussion items highlighted in bold:

```
<HTML>
<HEAD>
<TITLE>Tapes By Mail, Inc.</TITLE>
</HEAD>
<BODY>
<CENTER><H1>Tapes By Mail, Inc.</H1></CENTER>
<P>
<CENTER><H3>Use this form to order audio cassette tapes from Tapes By
Mail</H3></CENTER>
<P>
<HR>
<P>
<I>This week's featured selection:</I>
<P>
<H3>Competing Effectively in the Global Marketplace</H3>
<P>
Join Fortune 500 managers, industry consultants and government policy
makers for this informative audio cassette course on international
trade and development issues. The complete 10 session program sells
for only $99. Order online now by filling out the form below or call
our toll-free number.
<P>
<center><H3>Guarantee</H3></center>
We offer a complete 100% money back guarantee. If you are not fully
satisfied with your purchase, we will gladly refund the entire
purchase price.
<P>
<form method="POST" action="/nmullerbin/mailord.pl">
<HR>
<P>
Name:<BR>
<input TYPE="text" NAME="name" size=56>
<P>
Title:<BR>
<input type="text" NAME="title" size=56>
<P>
Company:<BR>
<input type="text" NAME="company" size=56>
<P>
Phone:<BR>
<input type="text" NAME="phone" size=56>
<P>
Street Address: <BR>
```

```
<input type="text" NAME="address" size=56>
<P>
City: <input type="text" NAME="city" size=20> State: <input
type="text" NAME="state" size=3> Zip Code: <input type="text"
NAME="zip" size=10>
<P>
E-mail Address: <input type="text" NAME="e-mail" size=42>
<P>
<HR>
<P>
<H3>Choose Your Method of Payment:</H3>
<P>
Purchase Order No.: <input type="text" Name="order" size=20>
<P>
<HR>
<P>
Credit Card:
<select name="card">
<option selected> Not Applicable
<option value="Amex"> American Express
<option value="MasterCard"> Master Card
<option value="VISA"> VISA
</select>
<P>
Account Number: <input type="text"<P> <B>Name="account" size=31><BR>
Expiration Date: <input type="text" Name="expires" size=32>
<P>
<I>Warning: Credit card transactions are not secure.</I>
<P>
<HR>
<P>
<input type=submit value="Click Here To Order Now!"> or <input
type=Reset value="Clear">
<P>
<P>
</FORM>
<H3><I>You can place your order by phone: 1-800-000-0000. Please have
your credit card handy.</I></H3>
</BODY>
</HTML>
```

The multiline text field is coded in a similar manner as those in previous examples, except that the names of credit cards are the selections. Whenever credit cards are the selections, you also must ask for the credit card number and expiration date. Both items are required for processing the charge order.

Figure 7.10 shows how the single-product order form is rendered by Netscape Navigator.

Perl script for processing a single-product order form

The Perl script for the single-product order form is as follows:

```
#!/usr/local/bin/perl

$mailprog = '/usr/bin/mail';
$recipient = 'nmuller@ddx.com';
print "Content-type: text/html\n\n";
print "<Head><Title>Tapes By Mail, Inc.</Title></Head>";
print "<Body><H1>Thank you for your order.</H1></Body>";
```

Figure 7.10

```
read(STDIN, $buffer, $ENV{'CONTENT_LENGTH'});
@pairs = split(/&/,$buffer);
foreach $pair (@pairs)
{
    ($name, $value) = split(/=/, $pair);
    $value =~ tr/+/ /;
    $value =~ s/%([a-fA-F0-9][a-fA-F0- 9])/pack("C", hex($1))/eg;
    $FORM{$name} = $value;
}

open (MAIL, "|$mailprog $recipient $FORM{'e-mail'} $FORM{'NAME'}") ||
die "Can't open $mailprog!\n";
print MAIL "Please send $FORM{'name'} the 10-session audio cassette
program on, Competing Effectively in the Global Marketplace.\n";
print MAIL "\n";
print MAIL "1. Name: $FORM{'name'}\n";
print MAIL "2. Title: $FORM{'title'}\n";
print MAIL "3. Company: $FORM{'company'}\n";
print MAIL "4. Phone: $FORM{'phone'}\n";
```

```
┌─────────────────────────────────────────────────────────────────────┐
│ —                    Netscape - [Tapes By Mail, Inc..]        ▼  ▲   │
├─────────────────────────────────────────────────────────────────────┤
│ File   Edit   View   Go   Bookmarks   Options   Directory      Help  │
├─────────────────────────────────────────────────────────────────────┤
│  ⇦      ⇨      🏠      ®      🔟      🔁      🖨      🔍      ●       │
│ Back  Forward  Home   Reload  Images  Open    Print   Find    Stop    │
├─────────────────────────────────────────────────────────────────┬────┤
│ Location: http://iquest.com/~nmuller/mailord.html               │ N  │
├─────────────────────────────────────────────────────────────────┴────┤
│ [What's New!] [What's Cool!] [Handbook] [Net Search] [Net Directory] [Newsgroups] │
├─────────────────────────────────────────────────────────────────────┤
│ Phone:                                                             ↑  │
│ ┌─────────────────────────────────────────────────────────┐         │
│ │ 1-123-555-1212                                          │         │
│ └─────────────────────────────────────────────────────────┘         │
│                                                                      │
│ Street Address:                                                      │
│ ┌─────────────────────────────────────────────────────────┐         │
│ │ 6789 San Diego Ave.                                     │         │
│ └─────────────────────────────────────────────────────────┘         │
│                                                                      │
│ City: ┌───────────────┐  State: ┌──┐  Zip Code: ┌──────────┐        │
│       │ Grand Rapids  │         │MI│            │ 65432    │        │
│       └───────────────┘         └──┘            └──────────┘        │
│                                                                      │
│ Email Address: ┌──────────────────────────────┐                     │
│                │ shirley@system2000.com       │                     │
│                └──────────────────────────────┘                     │
│ ─────────────────────────────────────────────────────────────────── │
│                                                                      │
│ **Choose Your Method of Payment:**                                  │
│                                                                      │
│ Purchase Order No.: ┌──────────────────────┐                        │
│                     │                      │                        │
│                     └──────────────────────┘                        │
│ ─────────────────────────────────────────────────────────────────── │
│                                                                      │
│ Credit Card: ┌──────────────────┐                                   │
│              │ Master Card    ▼ │                                   │
│              └──────────────────┘                                   │
│                                                                      │
│ Account Number: ┌──────────────────────────────┐                    │
│                 │ xxxx xxxx xxxx xxxx          │                    │
│ Expiration Date: ┌──────────────────────────────┐                   │
│                  │ 03/98                        │                   │
│                  └──────────────────────────────┘                   │
│ ─────────────────────────────────────────────────────────────────── │
│                                                                      │
│ ┌──────────────────────────────┐      ┌───────┐                     │
│ │ Click Here To Order Now!     │  or  │ Clear │                     │
│ └──────────────────────────────┘      └───────┘                     │
│                                                                      │
│ *You can place your order by phone: 1-800-000-0000. Please have your credit card* │
│ *handy.*                                                          ↓  │
├─────────────────────────────────────────────────────────────────────┤
│ ⚁                                                                    │
└─────────────────────────────────────────────────────────────────────┘
```

Figure 7.10   *(Continued)*

```perl
print MAIL "5. Street Address: $FORM{'address'}\n";
print MAIL "6. City: $FORM{'city'}\n";
print MAIL "7. State: $FORM{'state'}\n";
print MAIL "8. Zip Code: $FORM{'zip'}\n";
print MAIL "9. E-mail Address: $FORM{'e-mail'}\n";
print MAIL "\n";
print MAIL "Method of Payment:\n";
print MAIL "\n";
print MAIL "10. Purchase Order No.: $FORM{'order'}\n";
print MAIL "11. Credit Card: $FORM{'card'}\n";
print MAIL "12. Account No.: $FORM{'account'}\n";
print MAIL "13. Expiration Date: $FORM{'expires'}\n";
close (MAIL);

print "Please allow 10 days for delivery.
<P>
\n";
print "Return to the<A HREF=\"http://iquest.com/~nmuller/index.shtml\">
Main Menu</a>\n";
```

Typically, when Internet credit card orders are received they are imported into a software program provided by the bank or third-party processing firm. This program batch processes credit card numbers, verifying that the customer's address and zip code match the address and zip code to which the card was issued. This type of verification can eliminate some attempts at fraud. When batch processing is complete, the software automatically calls a central processor through a non-Internet direct line. The transaction information is uploaded to the processor, and within 48 hours the money is deposited into your bank account. There are more automated software solutions available that tie into either the Internet or your existing software. For example, you can get the credit card processing protocols that run on the central processor and use that information to develop and further automate your own system.

The output of the processed single-product order form, as received via e-mail, is shown in Figure 7.11.

Figure 7.12 shows how the acknowledgment message is rendered by Netscape Navigator.

Creating a Multiproduct Order Form

The Web is ideally suited for small catalog companies because it enables them to extend their reach beyond what their printing and mailing budgets would normally allow. Such a company can post its catalog on the Web and take credit card orders via a multiproduct order form that is submitted as

Date: Mon, 17 Jul 1995 12:46:57 -0500
To: nmuller@ddx.com

Please send Shirley Mae the 10-session audio cassette program on, Competing Effectively in the Global Marketplace.

1. Name: Shirley Mae
2. Title: Manager Public Relations
3. Company: System2000, Inc
4. Phone: 1-123-555-1212
5. Street Address: 6789 San Diego Ave.
6. City: Grand Rapids
7. State: MI
8. Zip Code: 65432
9. Email Address: shirley@system2000.com

Method of Payment:

10. Purchase Order No.:
11. Credit Card: MasterCard
12. Account No.: xxxx xxxx xxxx xxxx
13. Expiration Date: 03/98

Figure 7.11

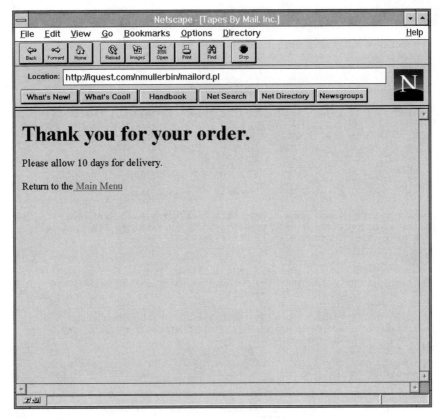

Figure 7.12

e-mail. Even print catalogs can contain the URL of the Web version of the catalog to stimulate e-mail orders.

HTML coding for a multiproduct order form

The HTML coding for a simple multiproduct order form is shown below. Items for discussion are highlighted in bold.

```
<HTML>
<HEAD>
<TITLE>Order Form</TITLE>
</HEAD>
<BODY>
<CENTER><H2>Big Sky Catalog Company</H2>
<P>
<H3><I>Adventure Wear for the City Slicker!</I></H3>
</CENTER>
<form method="POST" action="/nmullerbin/ordersht.pl"><HR>
<P>
<H4>When ordering electronically from the Big Sky catalog, please
provide the following information:</H4>
<HR>
<B>Your Full Name:</B> <INPUT TYPE="text" NAME="name" SIZE=45>
```

```
<P>
<B>Billing Address:</B> <INPUT TYPE="text" NAME="address" SIZE=46>
<P>
<B>City:</B> <INPUT TYPE="text" NAME="city" SIZE=40>
<B>State:</B> <INPUT TYPE="text" NAME="state" SIZE=8>
<P>
<B>Zip Code:</B> <INPUT TYPE="text" NAME="zip" SIZE=15>
<B>Country:</B> <INPUT TYPE="text" NAME="country" SIZE=26>
<P>
<B>E-mail Address:</B> <INPUT TYPE="text" NAME="e-mail" SIZE=46>
<P>
<B>Telephone:</B> <INPUT TYPE="text" NAME="phone" SIZE=20>
<B>Fax Number:</B> <INPUT TYPE="text" NAME="fax" SIZE=16>
<P>
<HR>
<P>
<PRE> Qty     Catalog No.     Product     Price</PRE>
<P>
<INPUT TYPE="text" NAME="qty1" SIZE=7><INPUT TYPE="text" NAME=
"catalog1" SIZE=24><INPUT TYPE="text"<P> <B>NAME="prod1" SIZE=38>
<INPUT TYPE="text" NAME="price1" SIZE=20>
<P>
<P>
<INPUT TYPE="text" NAME="qty2" SIZE=7><INPUT TYPE="text" NAME=
"catalog2" SIZE=24><INPUT TYPE="text" NAME="prod2" SIZE=38><INPUT
TYPE="text" NAME="price2" SIZE=20>
<P>
<INPUT TYPE="text" NAME="qty3" SIZE=7><INPUT TYPE="text" NAME=
"catalog3" SIZE=24><INPUT TYPE="text" NAME="prod3" SIZE=38><INPUT
TYPE="text" NAME="price3" SIZE=20>
<P>
<INPUT TYPE="text" NAME="qty4" SIZE=7><INPUT TYPE="text" NAME=
"catalog4" SIZE=24><INPUT TYPE="text" NAME="prod4" SIZE=38><INPUT
TYPE="text" NAME="price4" SIZE=20>
<P>
<INPUT TYPE="text" NAME="qty5" SIZE=7><INPUT TYPE="text" NAME=
"catalog5" SIZE=24><INPUT TYPE="text" NAME="prod5" SIZE=38><INPUT
TYPE="text" NAME="price5" SIZE=20>
<P>
<HR>
<P>
Shipping Method:<BR>
<SELECT NAME="ship"><OPTION>UPS GroundTRAC <OPTION>UPS 2nd Day Air
<OPTION>UPS Next Day Air <OPTION>FedEx Priority <OPTION> FedEx
International </SELECT>
<P>
<HR>
<P>
Credit Card:<BR>
<select name="card"><option selected> American Express

<option value="MasterCard"> Master Card
<option value="VISA"> VISA
<option value="Discover"> Discover
</select>
<P>
Account Number: <BR>
<input type="text" Name="account" size=32>
<P>
Expiration Date: <BR>
<input type="text" Name="expires" size=32>
<P>
<I>Warning: Credit card transactions are not secure.</I>
<P>
<HR>
```

```
<P>
<input type=submit value="Click Here To Order Now!"> or <input
type=Reset value="Clear">
<P>
<P>
</FORM>
<H3><I>You can place your order by phone: 1-800-000-0000. Please have
your credit card handy.</I></H3>
</FORM>
</BODY>
</HTML>
```

In this HTML-coded form, the entry fields are arranged in four columns and five rows. Up to five products can be ordered from this form. For each product, the user is asked to enter the quantity, catalog order number, product, and price of the item. You can enlarge the order form by adding more columns and rows. Just be sure that the input text variables are named differently for each item of information. For example, the HTML coding for a sixth row would look like this:

```
<INPUT TYPE="text" NAME="qty6" SIZE=7><INPUT TYPE="text"
NAME="catalog6" SIZE=24><INPUT TYPE="text" NAME="prod6" SIZE=38>
<INPUT TYPE="text" NAME="price6" SIZE=20>
```

Figure 7.13 shows how the multiproduct order form is rendered by Netscape Navigator.

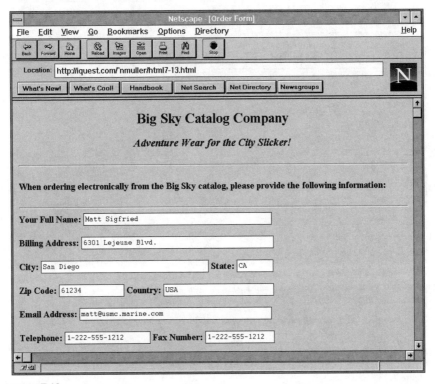

Figure 7.13

Qty	Catalog No.	Product	Price
1	654-9233	Sheepskin vest	99.50
1	888-3712	Cowboy hat	29.50
4	932-0021	Ammo box	19.50
2	511-9907	Thermal underwear	9.50
1	712-4522	Campfire grill kit	29.50

Shipping Method:
UPS 2nd Day Air

Credit Card:
American Express

Account Number:
xxxx xxxx xxxx xxxx

Expiration Date:
6/98

Warning: Credit card transactions are not secure.

Click Here To Order Now!   or Clear

You can place your order by phone: 1-800-000-0000. Please have your credit card handy.

Figure 7.13 *(Continued)*

Perl script for processing a multiproduct order form

The Perl script for the multiproduct order form is as follows, with discussion points highlighted in bold:

```perl
#!/usr/local/bin/perl

$mailprog = '/usr/bin/mail';
$recipient = 'nmuller@ddx.com';
print "Content-type: text/html\n\n";
print "<Head><Title>Big Sky Catalog Company</Title></Head>";
print "<Body><H1>Thanks for your order city slicker.</H1></Body>";
read(STDIN, $buffer, $ENV{'CONTENT_LENGTH'});
@pairs = split(/&/, $buffer);
foreach $pair (@pairs)
{
     ($name, $value) = split(/=/, $pair);
     $value =~ tr/+/ /;
     $value =~ s/%([a-fA- F0-9][a-fA-F0-9])/pack("C", hex($1))/eg;
     $FORM{$name} = $value;
}

open (MAIL, "|$mailprog $recipient $FORM{'e-mail'} $FORM{'NAME'}") ||
die "Can't open $mailprog!\n";
print MAIL "This is an electronic order from $FORM{'name'} for items
listed in the 1995 issue of the Big Sky catalog.\n";
print MAIL "\n";
print MAIL "1. Contact Information:\n";
print MAIL " Name: $FORM{'name'}\n";
print MAIL " Billing Address: $FORM{'address'}\n";
print MAIL " City: $FORM{'city'}\n";
print MAIL " State: $FORM{'state'}\n";
print MAIL " Zip Code: $FORM{'zip'}\n";
print MAIL " Country: $FORM{'country'}\n";
print MAIL " E-mail Address: $FORM{'e-mail'}\n";
print MAIL " Telephone: $FORM{'phone'}\n";
print MAIL " Fax number: $FORM{'fax'}\n";
print MAIL "\n";
print MAIL "2. Send the following items:\n";
print MAIL "\n";
print MAIL " Qty: $FORM{'qty1'} #$FORM{'catalog1'} $FORM{'prod1'}
$FORM{'price1'}\n";
print MAIL " ------------------------------------------------- \n";
print MAIL "\n";
print MAIL " Qty: $FORM{'qty2'} #$FORM{'catalog2'} $FORM{'prod2'}
$FORM{'price2'}\n";
print MAIL " -------------------------------------------------\n";
print MAIL "\n";
print MAIL " Qty: $FORM{'qty3'} #$FORM{'catalog3'} $FORM{'prod3'}
$FORM{'price3'}\n";
print MAIL " -------------------------------------------------\n";
print MAIL "\n";
print MAIL " Qty: $FORM{'qty4'} #$FORM{'catalog4'} $FORM{'prod4'}
$FORM{'price4'}\n";
print MAIL " -------------------------------------------------\n";
print MAIL "\n";
print MAIL " Qty: $FORM{'qty5'} #$FORM{'catalog5'} $FORM{'prod5'}
$FORM{'price5'}\n";
print MAIL " -------------------------------------------------\n";
print MAIL "\n";
$TOTAL = $FORM{'price1'} *<P> <B>$FORM{'qty1'} + $FORM{'price2'} *
$FORM{'qty2'} + $FORM{'price3'} * $FORM{'qty3'} + $FORM{'price4'} *
$FORM{'qty4'} + $FORM{'price5'} * $FORM{'qty5'};
print MAIL " The total charge for this order is: \$ ";
```

```
printf MAIL "%.2f", $TOTAL;
print MAIL "\n";
print MAIL "\n";
print MAIL "3. Shipping Method:\n";
print MAIL " $FORM{'ship'}\n";
print MAIL "\n";
print MAIL "4. Method of Payment:\n";
print MAIL " Credit Card: $FORM{'card'}\n";
print MAIL " Account No.: $FORM{'account'}\n";
print MAIL " Exp. Date: $FORM{'expires'}\n";
close (MAIL);

print "The total amount of your order is: \$\n";
printf "%.2f", $TOTAL;
print "
<P>
\n";
print "Please allow 10 days<P> <B>for delivery.
<P>
\n";
print "
<P>
\n";
print "Return to the <A HREF=\"http://iquest.com/~nmuller/ordersht.
html\">
Order Form</A>\n";
print "
<P>
\n";
print "Return to the <A HREF=\"http://iquest.com/~nmuller/index.shtml
\"> Main Menu</A>\n";
```

There are two noteworthy features in this script. One is the automatic calculation of the total price of the order (see section in bold). In essence, we have defined $TOTAL as price × quantity for each item ordered. The other feature is the return of the total price in the acknowledgment message (also highlighted in bold). This assures the user that the correct amount will be charged to his or her credit card.

The output of the processed multiproduct order form, as received via e-mail, is shown in Figure 7.14.

Figure 7.15 shows how the acknowledgment message is rendered by Netscape Navigator. Notice that the total amount of the order is included as part of the message. A link back to the order form also has been added.

Creating a Subscription Form

With today's sophisticated desktop publishing software, virtually anyone can start a newsletter, write a book, or create an update service on a specialized topic. The World Wide Web offers the means to publicize homegrown publications. With a Web page, sample newsletters can be posted along with subcription forms that are sent via electronic mail. Not all publications involve subscription charges. Many publishers offer controlled circulation magazines and newsletters, which require subscribers to fill out detailed questionnaires that qualify them for a free subscription. The forms are verified by auditors and the circulation numbers are used to set advertising rates. The demographic in-

Date: Tue, 18 Jul 1995 10:58:56 -0500
To: nmuller@ddx.com

This is an electronic order from Matt Sigfried for items listed in the 1995 issue of the Big Sky catalog.

1. Contact Information:
    Name: Matt Sigfried
    Billing Address: 6301 Lejeune Blvd.
    City: San Diego
    State: CA
    Zip Code: 61234
    Country: USA
    Email Address: matt@usmc.marine.com
    Telephone: 1-222-555-1212
    Fax number: 1-222-555-1212

2. Send the following items:

Qty: 1	#654-9233	Sheepskin vest	99.50
Qty: 1	#888-3712	Cowboy hat	29.50
Qty: 4	#932-0021	Ammo box	19.50
Qty: 2	#511-9907	Thermal underwear	9.50
Qty: 1	#712-4522	Campfire grill kit	29.50

The total charge for this order is: $ 255.50

3. Shipping Method:
    UPS 2nd Day Air

4. Method of Payment:
    Credit Card: American Express
    Account No.:   xxxx xxxx xxxx xxxx
    Exp. Date: 6/98

Figure 7.14

formation is used to sell mailing lists. In addition, many companies offer free newsletters to customers, which essentially are vehicles for self-promotion.

HTML coding for a subscription form

The following HTML coding example is for a free newsletter subscription. You can use this form as the starting point for developing your own sub-

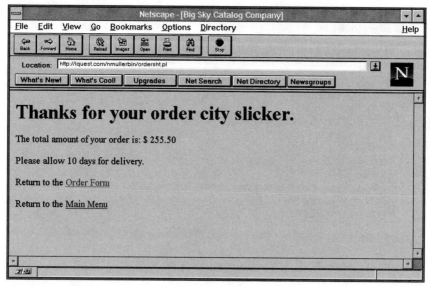

Figure 7.15

scription form—for paid or free publications. If your publication involves subscription charges, you can add into this form (and the associated Perl script) the credit card and purchase order elements from the previous forms and scripts.

```
<HTML>
<HEAD>
<TITLE>The Webmaster's Newsletter</TITLE>
</HEAD>
<BODY>
<FONT SIZE=5><I>Free Subscription For Qualified Webmasters</I></FONT>
<P>
<H4>To receive your free subscription to <I>The Webmaster's Newsletter,
</I> please fill out this form as completely as possible.</H4>
To qualify, please answer ALL questions. Incomplete forms will not be
processed or acknowledged.
<HR>
<form method="POST" action="/nmullerbin/newsub.pl">
Do you wish to receive/continue to receive <I>The Webmaster's
Newsletter? <BR>
<PRE>
<INPUT NAME="receive" TYPE="radio" VALUE="yes">
<B>Yes</B> <INPUT NAME="receive" TYPE="radio" VALUE="no">
<B>No</B><BR>
</PRE>
<P>
<PRE>
<B>Name:</B>      <INPUT SIZE=40 NAME="name"><BR>
<B>Title:</B>     <INPUT SIZE=40 NAME="title"><BR>
<B>Company:</B>   <INPUT SIZE=40 NAME="company"><BR>
<B>Address:</B>   <INPUT SIZE=40 NAME="address"><BR>
<B>City, State, Zip:</B> <INPUT SIZE=24 NAME="city"><INPUT SIZE=2
NAME="state"><INPUT SIZE=12 NAME="zip"><BR>
<B>Telephone No:</B>      <INPUT SIZE=40 NAME="phone"><BR>
```

```
<B>Fax Number:</B> <INPUT SIZE=40 NAME="fax"><BR>
<B>E-Mail:</B>      <INPUT SIZE=40 NAME="e-mail"><BR>
<P>
<HR>
<P>
Do you wish to receive EMAIL notices of our books and special reports
about the Internet? <BR>
<INPUT NAME="notice" TYPE="radio" VALUE="yes" CHECKED>
<B>Yes</B> <INPUT NAME="notice" TYPE="radio" VALUE="no">
<B>No</B>
</PRE>
<HR>
<P>
<B>The primary application of your Web site. </B> <I>(Check the one
that best describes your Web site.) </I>
<OL>
<LI><INPUT type="radio" NAME="app" VALUE="internal information
distribution"> Internal information distribution
<LI><INPUT type="radio" NAME="app" VALUE="provides services to
corporations"> Provide services to corporations
<LI><INPUT type="radio" NAME="app" VALUE="provides services to
government agencies"> Provide services to government agencies
<LI><INPUT type="radio" NAME="app" VALUE="provides services to
individuals"> Provide services to individuals
<LI><INPUT type="radio" NAME="app" VALUE="Other"> Other
</OL>
<HR>
<P>
<B>Number of users/subscribers of your Web site.</B>
<OL>
<LI><INPUT type="radio" NAME="users" VALUE="Under 100"> Under 100
<LI><INPUT type="radio" NAME="users" VALUE="101-500"> 101-500
<LI><INPUT type="radio" NAME="users" VALUE="501-1000"> 501- 1000
<LI><INPUT type="radio" NAME="users" VALUE="Over 1000"> Over 1000
</OL>
<HR>
<P>
<B>Do you help to evaluate, recommend, specify or approve purchase of
products or services described below?</B><BR>
<I>(Check <B>all</B> that apply.)</I>
<OL>
<LI><INPUT type="checkbox" NAME="help1" VALUE="Computers/workstations">
Computer/Workstation Systems (including micros, minis, mainframes,
etc.)
<LI><INPUT type="checkbox" NAME="help2" VALUE="Peripherals">
Peripherals (including printers, disk/tape drives, modems, boards, etc.)
<LI><INPUT type="checkbox" NAME="help3" VALUE="Software"> Software
(including applications, utilities, RDBMS, communication software,
etc.)
<LI><INPUT type="checkbox" NAME="help4" VALUE="Networks"> Networks
(including LANs, WANs, communications servers, etc.)
<LI><INPUT type="checkbox" NAME="help5" VALUE="Services"> Services
(including maintenance, education, training, etc.)
<LI><INPUT type="checkbox" NAME="help6" VALUE="None"> None of the
above
</OL>
<HR>
<P>
<B>Do you plan to purchase any of the following in the next 12
months?</B> <I>(Check <B>all</B> that apply.)</I>
<OL>
<LI><INPUT type="checkbox" NAME="buy1" VALUE="Computers/workstations">
Computer/Workstation Systems
<LI><INPUT type="checkbox" NAME="buy2" VALUE="Peripherals"> Peripherals
```

```
<LI><INPUT type="checkbox" NAME="buy3" VALUE="Software"> Software
<LI><INPUT type="checkbox" NAME="buy4" VALUE="Networks"> Networks
<LI><INPUT type="checkbox" NAME="buy5" VALUE="None"> None
</OL>
<HR>
<P>
<B>Which operating system are you using for your Web server? </B>
<OL>
<LI><INPUT type="radio" NAME="os" VALUE="Windows"> Windows 3.1
<LI><INPUT type="radio" NAME="os" VALUE="Windows 3.11"> Windows 3.11
<LI><INPUT type="radio" NAME="os" VALUE="Windows NT"> Windows NT
<LI><INPUT type="radio" NAME="os" VALUE="Windows 95"> Windows 95
<LI><INPUT type="radio" NAME="os" VALUE="OS/2"> OS/2
<LI><INPUT type="radio" NAME="os" VALUE="UNIX"> UNIX
</OL>
<HR>
<P>
<B>What is your estimated annual budget for Web site products/
services? </B>
<OL>
```

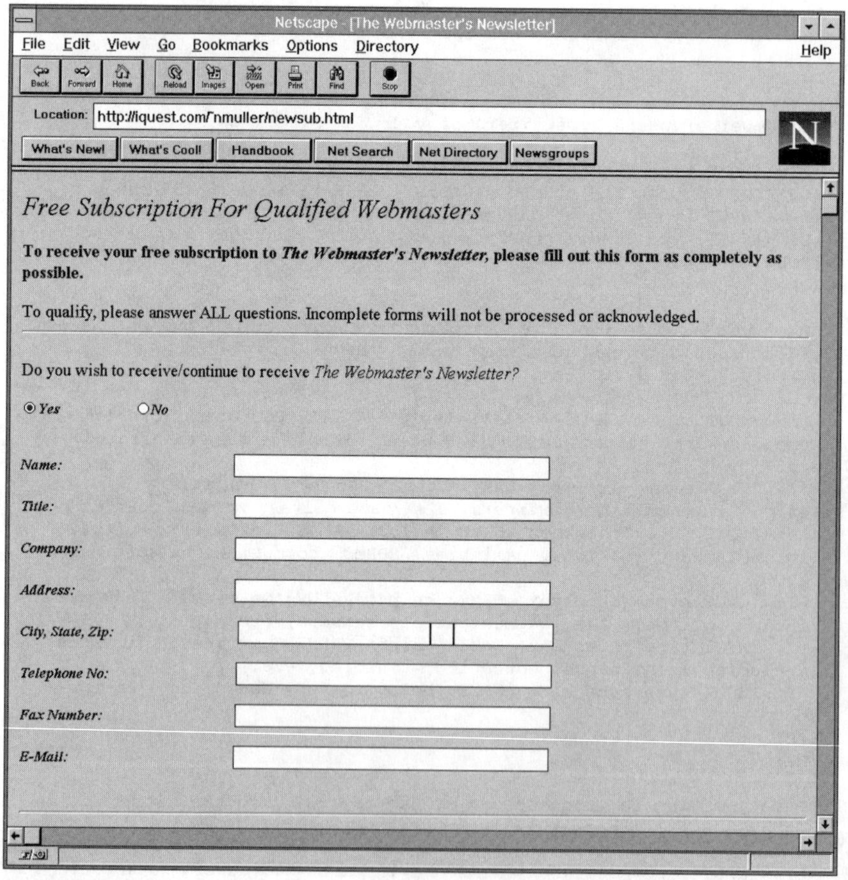

Figure 7.16

```
                    Netscape - [The Webmaster's Newsletter]
File   Edit   View   Go   Bookmarks   Options   Directory                    Help

 Back   Forward   Home   Reload   Images   Open   Print   Find   Stop

 Location: http://iquest.com/nmuller/newsub.html                          N

  What's New!   What's Cool!   Handbook   Net Search   Net Directory   Newsgroups

Free Subscription For Qualified Webmasters

To receive your free subscription to The Webmaster's Newsletter, please fill out this form as completely as possible.

To qualify, please answer ALL questions. Incomplete forms will not be processed or acknowledged.


Do you wish to receive/continue to receive The Webmaster's Newsletter?

 ⦿ Yes        ◯ No


Name:              Linda Lee

Title:             Mgr. Internet Services

Company:           LTM Inc.

Address:           9 Huckleberry Lane

City, State, Zip:  Albany          NY  92183

Telephone No:      1-123-555-1212

Fax Number:

E-Mail:            linda@ltm.com
```

Figure 7.16   *(Continued)*

```
<LI><INPUT type="radio" NAME="budget" VALUE="$5 million or more"> $5
million or more
<LI><INPUT type="radio" NAME="budget" VALUE="$1 million - $4.9
million"> $1 million - $4.9 million
<LI><INPUT type="radio" NAME="budget" VALUE="$500,000 - $1 million">
$500,000 - $1 million
<LI><INPUT type="radio" NAME="budget" VALUE="$99,999 - $499,999">
$99,999 - $499,999
<LI><INPUT type="radio" NAME="budget" VALUE="Under $99,999"> Under
$99,999
</OL>
<HR>
<P>
<INPUT type=submit VALUE="Submit"> or <INPUT type=Reset
VALUE="Clear">
<P>
</FORM>
</BODY>
</HTML>
```

Figure 7.16 (pages 158 through 161) shows how the subscription form is rendered by Netscape Navigator.

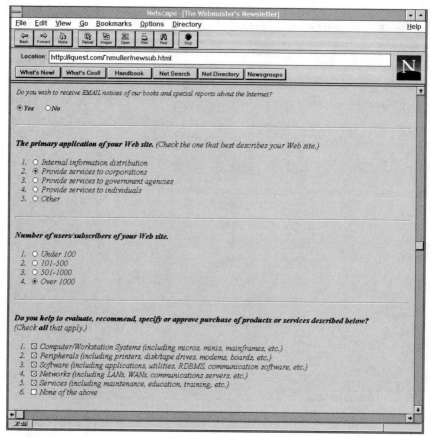

Figure 7.16 *(Continued)*

Perl script for processing a subscription form

The Perl script for the subscription form is as follows:

```
#!/usr/local/bin/perl

$mailprog = '/usr/bin/mail';
$recipient = 'nmuller@ddx.com';
print "Content-type: text/html\n\n";
print "<Head><Title>The Webmaster's Newsletter</Title></Head>";
print "<Body><H2>Thank you for subscribing to <EM>The Webmaster's
Newsletter</EM>.</H2></Body>";
read(STDIN, $buffer, $ENV{'CONTENT_LENGTH'});
@pairs = split /&/,$buffer);
foreach $pair (@pairs)
{
    ($name, $value) = split(/=/, $pair);
    $value =~ tr/+/ /;
    $value =~ s/%([a-fA-F0-9][a-fA-F0-9])/pack("C", hex($1))/eg;
    $FORM{$name} = $value;
}

open (MAIL, "|$mailprog $recipient $FORM{'e-mail'} $FORM{'NAME'}") ||
```

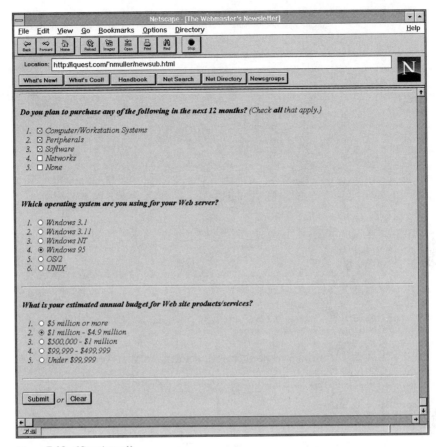

Figure 7.16 *(Continued)*

```perl
die "Can't open $mailprog!\n";
print MAIL "This is a subscription request for The Webmaster's
Newsletter.\n";
print MAIL "\n";
print MAIL "1 Contact Information\n";
print MAIL " Name: $FORM{'name'}\n";
print MAIL " Title: $FORM{'title'}\n";
print MAIL " Company: $FORM{'company'}\n";
print MAIL " Street Address: $FORM{'address'}\n";
print MAIL " City: $FORM{'city'}\n";
print MAIL " State: $FORM{'state'}\n";
print MAIL " Zip Code: $FORM{'zip'}\n";
print MAIL " Phone: $FORM{'phone'}\n";
print MAIL " E-mail Address: $FORM{'e-mail'}\n";
print MAIL "\n";
print MAIL "2. Does $FORM{'name'} wish to be notified of new books
and reports: $FORM{'notice'}\n";
print MAIL "\n";
print MAIL "3. The primary activity of this Web site is:
$FORM{'app'}\n";
print MAIL "\n";
print MAIL "4. The number of users/subscribers at this Web site is:
$FORM{'users'}\n";
```

```
print MAIL "\n";
print MAIL "5. $FORM{'name'} participates in purchasing decisions for
the following types of products: $FORM{'help6'}
 $FORM{'help1'}
 $FORM{'help2'}
 $FORM{'help3'}
 $FORM{'help4'}
 $FORM{'help5'}\n";
print MAIL "\n";
print MAIL "6. $FORM{'name'} plans to purchase the following types of
products in the next 12 months: $FORM{'buy5'}
 $FORM{'buy1'}
 $FORM{'buy2'}
 $FORM{'buy3'}
 $FORM{'buy4'}\n";
print MAIL "\n";
print MAIL "7. The operating system at this Web site is: $FORM{'os'}
\n";
print MAIL "\n";
print MAIL "8. The estimated annual budget for Web site products/
services is: $FORM{'budget'}\n";
print MAIL "\n";
close (MAIL);
print "Your subscription request will be processed immediately. You
can expect your first issue within 30 days.
<P>
\n";
print "Return to the<A HREF=\"http://iquest.com/~nmuller/index.shtml
\"> Main Menu</a>\n";
```

The output of the processed subscription form, as received via e-mail, is shown in Figure 7.17.

Figure 7.18 shows how the acknowledgment message is rendered by Netscape Navigator.

Creating a Seminar Registration Form

The Web offers a good way for seminar providers to augment their visibility before a vast potential audience. Of course, the URL of the seminar provider's Web page would have to be advertised to appropriate newsgroups and registered with the major search engines on the Internet to ensure maximum exposure. Corporations often provide free seminars on industry trends, products and applications, and technology management—all with the goal of obtaining sales leads and, eventually, new customers. So whether you are an individual, a seminar company, or a corporation, you can probably make use of a seminar registration form.

HTML coding for a seminar registration form

The HTML coding for a simple seminar registration form is shown below. Credit card information is embedded in the form, but if it does not apply to you, it can just as easily be left out. Items for discussion are highlighted in bold.

```
<HTML>
<HEAD>
```

Date: Mon, 17 Jul 1995 13:30:54 -0500
To: nmuller@ddx.com

This is a subscription request for The Webmaster's Newsletter.

1 Contact Information
      Name: Linda Lee
      Title: Mgr. Internet Services
      Company: LTM Inc.
      Street Address: 9 Huckleberry Lane
      City: Albany
      State: NY
      Zip Code: 92183
      Phone: 1-123-555-1212
      Email Address: linda@ltm.com

2. Does Linda Lee wish to be notified of new books and reports: yes

3. The primary activity of this Web site is: provides services to corporations

4. The number of users/subscribers at this Web site is: Over 1000

5. Linda Lee participates in purchasing decisions for the following types of products:
          Computers/workstations
          Peripherals
          Software
          Networks
          Services

6. Linda Lee plans to purchase the following types of products in the next 12 months:
          Computers/workstations
          Peripherals
          Software

7. The operating system at this Web site is: Windows 95

8. The estimated annual budget for Web site products/services is: $1 million - $4.9 million

Figure 7.17

```
<TITLE>Seminar Registration Form</TITLE>
</HEAD>
<BODY>
<CENTER><H2>The Webmaster's Workshop</H2></CENTER>
<form method="POST" action="/nmullerbin/regform.pl">
<P>
<HR>
Join our panel of experts for a three-day, information-packed seminar
that will help you understand key client/server and Internet concepts,
get updated on Web developments and standards, administer a growing
subscriber base, implement security, and prepare for the next
generation of Internet services. Hands-on workshops will offer tips
on site administration, HTML coding, programming and more. You'll
also see the latest Web products and demonstrations by vendors. The
```

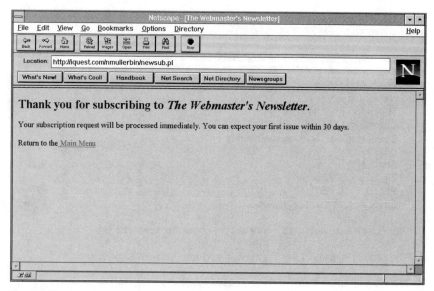

Figure 7.18

```
registration fee includes a free 6-issue subscription to <I>The
Webmaster's Newsletter.</I>
<HR>
Upon sending a completed form, the amount that will be charged to
your credit card and the selected location and date of <B> The
Webmaster's Workshop </B> will be confirmed. You<P><B>may call the
toll-free number below for assistance with hotel reservations.
<P>
You will need a Visa, Mastercard or American Express to use this
electronic registration form. Submit only one form per attendee.
<P>
Name<BR>
<input size=40 name="name"><BR>
Name for Meeting Badge<BR>
<input size=40 name="badge"><BR>
Organization<BR>
<input size=40 name="organ"><BR>
Mailing Address<BR>
<input size=40 name="address"><BR>
City<BR>
<input size=40 name="city"><BR>
State<BR>
<input size=40 name="state"><BR>
Zip Code<BR>
<input size=40 name="zip"><BR>
E-Mail<BR>
<input size=40 name="e-mail"><BR>
Telephone<BR>
<input size=40 name="phone"><BR>
Fax<BR>
<input size=40 name="fax"><BR>
<P>
<HR>
<P>
<B>Workshop Locations/Dates</B><BR>
<MENU><INPUT name="location" value="New York City on January 15-18th
```

```
at the Twin Towers Hotel" TYPE="radio"> New York City/January 15-18th
at the Twin Towers Hotel<BR>
<INPUT name="location" value="Dallas on February 12-14th at the
Hightower Hotel" TYPE="radio"> Dallas/February 12-14th at the
Hightower Hotel<BR>
<INPUT name="location" value="Chicago on March 11-13th at the Park
Hotel" TYPE="radio"> Chicago/March 11-13th at the Park Hotel<BR>
<INPUT name="location" value="Seattle on April 15-17th at the Central
West Hotel" TYPE="radio"> Seattle/April 15-17th at the Central West
Hotel<BR>
<INPUT name="location" value="Atlanta on May 13-15th at the Piedmont
Hotel" TYPE="radio"> Atlanta/May 13-15th at the Piedmont Hotel<BR>
</MENU>
<HR>
<P>
<B>Registration Fees</B> (Registration form and credit card information
must be received at The Webmaster's Workshop three days before the
event. Fees will be charged on the receipt date).
<P>
<MENU><input type="radio" name="fee" value="$495"> $495: All sessions,
hands-on workshops, and exhibits<BR>
<input type="radio" name="fee" value="$295"> $295: Sessions and
exhibits only<BR>
<input type="radio" name="fee" value="$95"> $95: Exhibits only<BR>
</MENU>
<HR>
<P>
<B>Method of Payment</B>
<P>
<MENU>
<select name="card"><option selected> American Express
<option value="MasterCard"> Master Card
<option value="VISA"> VISA
<option value="Discover"> Discover
</select>
<P>
Account Number: <BR>
<input type="text" Name="account" size=32>
<P>
Expiration Date: <BR>
<input type="text" Name="expires" size=32>
<P>
<I>Warning: Credit card transactions are not secure.</I>
</MENU>
<P>
<HR>
<P>
<input type=submit value="Submit"> or <input type=Reset
value="Clear">
<P>
<P>
</FORM>
<H4><I>If you prefer to register by phone, or need assistance with
hotel reservations, call: 1-800-000-0000. Please have your credit
card handy.</I></H4>
</BODY>
</HTML>
```

Figure 7.19, appearing on pages 166 through 169, shows how the seminar registration form is rendered by Netscape Navigator.

Notice that the user is informed that the credit card charge, as well as the location and date of the seminar, will be confirmed upon submitting the form.

```
┌─────────────────────────────────────────────────────────────────┐
│ —              Netscape - [Electronic Registration Form]    ▼ ▲  │
├─────────────────────────────────────────────────────────────────┤
│ File   Edit   View   Go   Bookmarks   Options   Directory   Help │
│ ┌──┐ ┌──┐ ┌──┐ ┌──┐ ┌──┐ ┌──┐ ┌──┐ ┌──┐ ┌──┐                     │
│ Back Forward Home Reload Images Open Print Find Stop             │
│ Location: http://iquest.com/~nmuller/regform.html         ┌───┐  │
│                                                           │ N │  │
│ What's New!  What's Cool!  Handbook  Net Search  Net Directory  Newsgroups │
└─────────────────────────────────────────────────────────────────┘
```

The Webmaster's Workshop

Join our panel of experts for a three-day, information-packed siminar that will help you understand key client/server and Internet concepts, get updated on Web developments and standards, administer a growing subscriber base, implement security, and prepare for the next generation of Internet services. Hands-on workshops will offer tips on site administration, HTML coding, programming and more. You'll also see the latest Web products and demonstrations by vendors. The registration fee includes a free 6-issue subscription to *The Webmaster's Newsletter*.

Upon sending a completed form, the amount that will be charged to your credit card and the selected location and date of **The Webmaster's Workshop** will be confirmed. You may call the toll-free number below for assistance with hotel reservations.

You will need a Visa, Mastercard or American Express to use this electronic registration form. Submit only one form per attendee.

Name
```
Douglas Young
```
Name for Meeting Badge
```
Doug Young
```
Organization
```
JD Corp.
```
Mailing Address
```
822 Hollywood Ave
```
City
```
Bayonne
```
State
```
NJ
```

Figure 7.19

Perl script for processing a seminar registration form

The Perl script for the seminar registration form is as follows:

```perl
#!/usr/local/bin/perl

$mailprog = '/usr/bin/mail';
$recipient = 'nmuller@ddx.com';
print "Content-type: text/html\n\n";
print "<Head><Title>The Webmaster's Workshop</Title></Head>";
print "<Body><H2>Thanks for registering for <I>The Webmaster's
Workshop</I>.</H2></Body>";
read(STDIN, $buffer, $ENV{'CONTENT_LENGTH'});
@pairs = split(/&/, $buffer);
foreach $pair (@pairs)
{
  ($name, $value) = split(/=/, $pair);
  $value =~ tr/+/ /;
  $value =~ s/%([a-fA-F0-9][a-fA-F0-9])/pack("C", hex($1))/eg;
  $FORM{$name} = $value;
}
```

```
open (MAIL, "|$mailprog $recipient $FORM{'e-mail'} $FORM{'NAME'}") ||
die "Can't open $mailprog!\n";
print MAIL "This is an electronic registration form from
$FORM{'name'}, who will attend The Webmaster's Workshop.\n";
print MAIL "\n";
print MAIL "1. Registration Information:\n";
print MAIL " Name: $FORM{'name'}\n";
print MAIL " Badge: $FORM{'badge'}\n";
print MAIL " Organization: $FORM{'organ'}\n";
print MAIL " Address: $FORM{'address'}\n";
print MAIL " City: $FORM{'city'}\n";
print MAIL " State: $FORM{'state'}\n";
print MAIL " Zip Code: $FORM{'zip'}\n";
print MAIL " E-mail Address: $FORM{'e-mail'}\n";
print MAIL " Telephone: $FORM{'phone'}\n";
print MAIL " Fax number: $FORM{'fax'}\n";
print MAIL "\n";
print MAIL "2. Workshop location/date: $FORM{'location'}\n";
print MAIL "\n";
print MAIL "3. The registration fee is: $FORM{'fee'}\n";
print MAIL "\n";
```

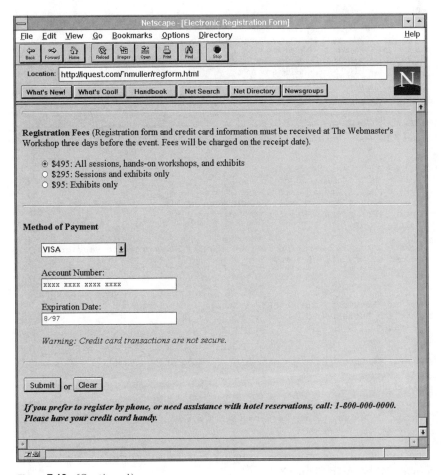

Figure 7.19 *(Continued)*

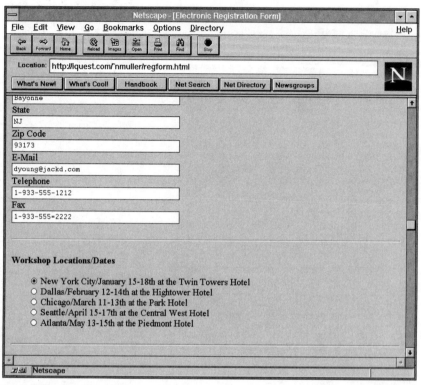

Figure 7.19 *(Continued)*

```
print MAIL "4. Method of Payment:\n";
print MAIL " Credit Card: $FORM{'card'}\n";
print MAIL " Account No.: $FORM{'account'}\n";
print MAIL " Exp. Date: $FORM{'expires'}\n";
close (MAIL);

print "Your registration fee, which will be charged to your credit
card, is: ", $FORM{'fee'};
print "
<P>
\n";
print "Return to the <A HREF=\"http://iquest.com/~nmuller/regform.
html\"> Registration Form</A>\n";
print "
<P>
\n";
print "Return to the <A HREF=\"http://iquest.com/~nmuller/index.shtml
\"> Main Menu</A>\n";
print "
<P>
\n";
print "<EM>See you at The Webmaster's Workshop in ", $FORM{'location'};
</EM>
```

The output of the processed seminar registration form, as received via
e-mail, is shown in Figure 7.20.

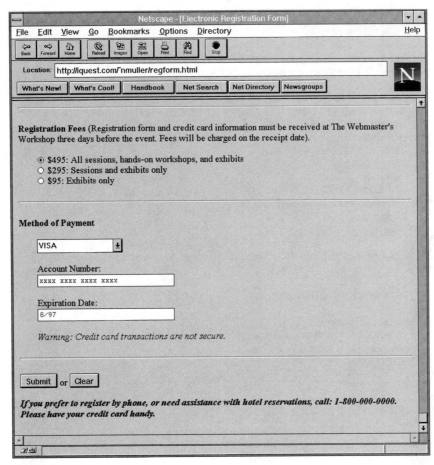

Figure 7.19 *(Continued)*

Figure 7.21 shows how the acknowledgment message is rendered by Netscape Navigator. Notice that the city, date, hotel and registration fee are returned in the message as well, providing added assurance to the user that the correct information has been processed.

Creating a Help Request Form

Using HTML tags, a simple help request form can be designed to be sent via the Web to a company's central help desk facility. Although many network management systems can detect specified events, raise alarms when predefined performance thresholds are reached, and implement automated procedures for problem resolution, they do so only for devices connected to the network. There may be many desktop systems and

Date: Mon, 17 Jul 1995 13:48:33 -0500
To: nmuller@ddx.com

This is an electronic registration form from Douglas Young, who will attend The Webmaster's Workshop.

1. Registration Information:
    Name: Douglas Young
    Badge: Doug Young
    Company: JD Corp.
    Address: 822 Hollywood Ave
    City: Bayonne
    State: NJ
    Zip Code: 93173
    Email Address: dyoung@jackd.com
    Telephone: 1-933-555-1212
    Fax number: 1-933-555=2222

2. Workshop location/date: New York City on January 15-18th at the Twin Towers Hotel

3. The registration fee is: $495

4. Method of Payment:
    Credit Card: VISA
    Account No.:   xxxx xxxx xxxx xxxx
    Exp. Date: 8/97

Figure 7.20

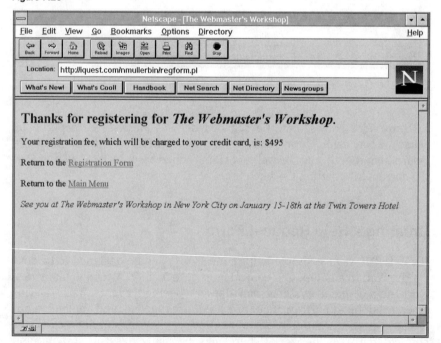

Figure 7.21

workgroup clusters that are not connected to the corporate backbone, but that may need a convenient facility for reporting problems and requesting troubleshooting assistance. A simple HTML-coded form that can be sent via e-mail over a cheap dialup Internet connection can fulfill this need.

HTML coding for a help request form

What follows is the HTML coding for a simple help request form:

```
<HTML>
<HEAD>
<TITLE>Help Request Form</TITLE>
</HEAD>
<BODY>
<P>
<form method="POST" action="/nmullerbin/helpreq.pl">
<P>
<CENTER><H2>Help Request Form</H2></CENTER>
<P>
<HR SIZE=5>
<P>
<PRE><STRONG>
  Your name: <INPUT SIZE=30 NAME="name">
  Your location: <INPUT SIZE=30 NAME="location">
  Your phone number: <INPUT SIZE=30 NAME="phone">
Your e-mail address: <INPUT SIZE=30 NAME="e-mail">
</PRE></STRONG>
<P>
<P>
<HR SIZE=5>
<P>
<H4>What type of technical assistance do you need?</H4>
<PRE> <SELECT NAME="assistance">
  <OPTION VALUE="application-specific"> Application-Specific
  <OPTION VALUE="operating-system"> Operating-System
  <OPTION VALUE="drivers"> Drivers
  <OPTION VALUE="hardware_installation"> Hardware Installation
  <OPTION VALUE="software_installation"> Software Installation
</SELECT>
</PRE>
<P>
<HR SIZE=5>
<P>
<H4>Please provide information about the type of system you are
using:</H4>
<PRE><STRONG>
  Vendor: <INPUT SIZE=15 NAME="vendor">
  Model: <INPUT SIZE=15 NAME="model">
  Operating System: <INPUT SIZE=15 NAME="os">
  OS Version: <INPUT SIZE=15 NAME="osver">
</PRE></STRONG>
<P>
<HR SIZE=5>
<P>
<H4>How would you categorize the severity of the problem?</H4>
<INPUT TYPE="radio" NAME="severity" VALUE="CRITICAL"> Critical — We
will contact you immediately.
<P>
<INPUT TYPE="radio" NAME="severity" VALUE="SERIOUS"> Serious — We
will contact you today.
```

```
<P>
<INPUT TYPE="radio" NAME="severity" VALUE="MEDIUM"> Medium — We will
contact you on or before the next working day.
<P>
<INPUT TYPE="radio" NAME="severity" VALUE="LOW"> Low — We will contact
you within 24-48 hours.
<P>
<HR SIZE=5>
<P>
<H4>When does the problem seem to occur?</H4>
<PRE>
  <SELECT NAME="when" SIZE=4>
  <OPTION VALUE="Start" SELECTED> At start-up
  <OPTION VALUE="within_application"> Within application
  <OPTION VALUE="during_file_transfers"> During file transfers
  <OPTION VALUE="during testing"> During testing
  <OPTION VALUE="intermittently"> Intermittently
  <OPTION VALUE="Other"> Other
  </SELECT>
</PRE>
<P>
<HR SIZE=5>
<P>
```

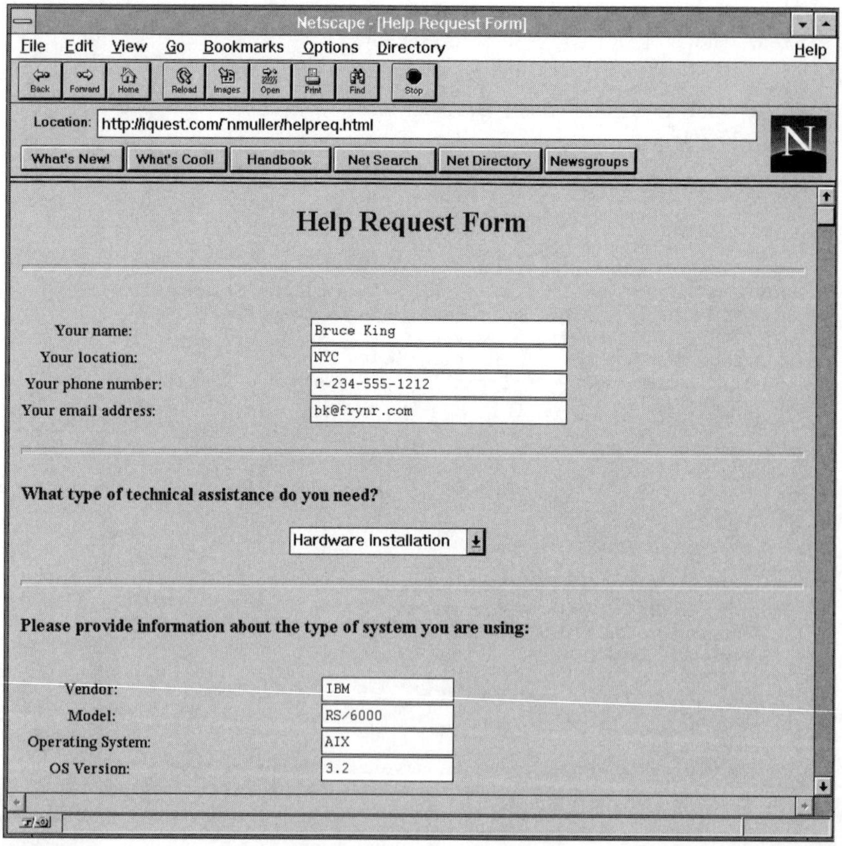

Figure 7.22

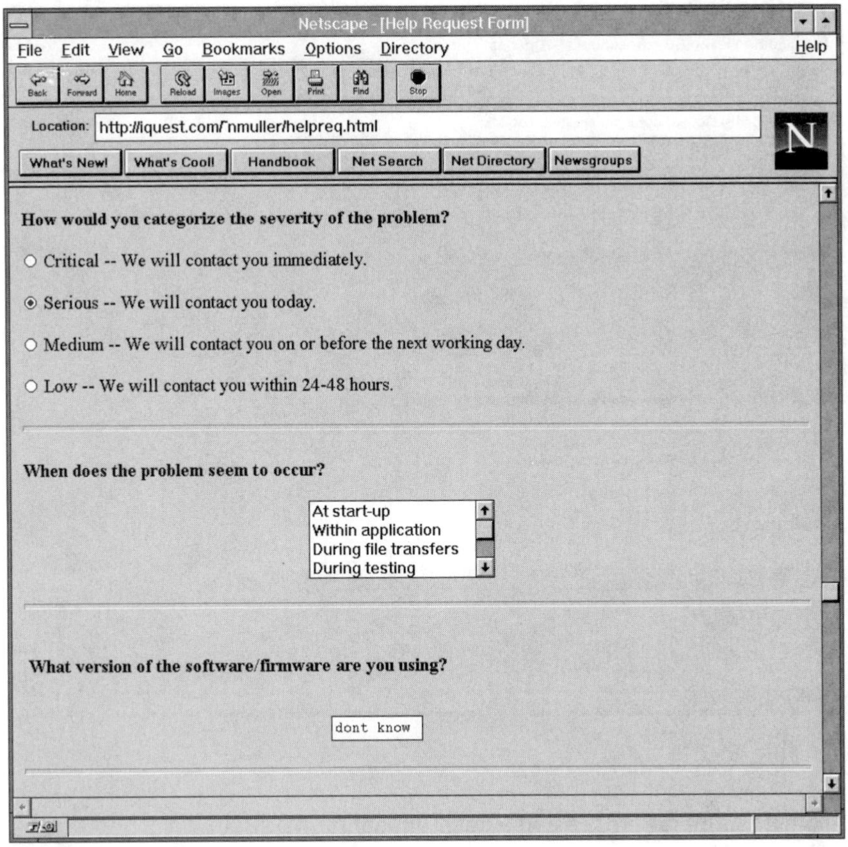

Figure 7.22 *(Continued)*

```
<PRE><STRONG>
<H4> What version of the software/firmware are you using?</H4>
<P>
<INPUT SIZE=10 NAME="version">
</PRE>
</STRONG>
<P>
<HR SIZE=5>
<P>
<H4>Please add any other information you think is relevant:</H4>
<P>
<TEXTAREA NAME="comments" ROWS=8 COLS=70></TEXTAREA>
<P>
<INPUT TYPE="submit" VALUE="Submit">
<INPUT TYPE="reset" VALUE="Clear">
</FORM>
</BODY>
</HTML>
```

Figure 7.22 on pages 172 through 174 shows how the help request form is rendered by Netscape Navigator.

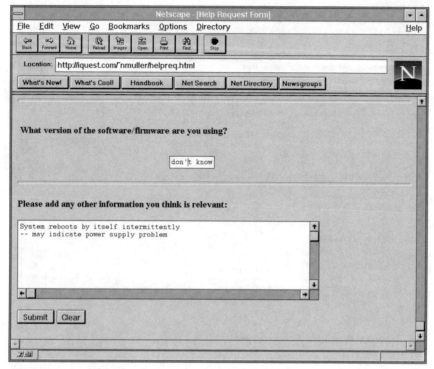

Figure 7.22 *(Continued)*

The Perl script for processing a help request form

The Perl script for a help request form is as follows, with discussion items highlighted in bold:

```perl
#!/usr/local/bin/perl

$mailprog = '/usr/bin/mail';
$recipient = 'nmuller@ddx.com';
print "Content-type: text/html\n\n";
print "<Head><Title>Strategic Information Resources</Title></Head>";
print "<Body><H1>Thank you for reporting this problem.</H1></Body>";
read(STDIN, $buffer, $ENV{'CONTENT_LENGTH'});
@pairs=split(/&/,$buffer);
foreach $pair (@pairs)
{
  ($name, $value) = split(/=/, $pair);
  $value =~ tr/+/ /;
  $value =~ s/%([a-fA-F0-9][a-fA-F0-9])/pack("C", hex($1))/eg;
  $FORM{$name} = $value;
}

open (MAIL, "|$mailprog $recipient $FORM{'e-mail'} $FORM{'NAME'}") ||
die "Can't open $mailprog!\n";
print MAIL "This is a request for help from $FORM{'name'}, who is
reachable at $FORM{'e-mail'}.\n";
print MAIL "\n";
```

```
print MAIL "$FORM{'name'} can also be reached as follows:\n";
print MAIL "\n";
print MAIL "Location: $FORM{'location'}\n";
print MAIL "Phone number: $FORM{'phone'}\n";
print MAIL "\n";
print MAIL "The kind of technical assistance $FORM{'name'} needs is
related to $FORM{'assistance'}.\n";
print MAIL "\n";
print MAIL "The type of system $FORM{'name'} has is:\n";
print MAIL "\n";
print MAIL "$FORM{'vendor'}\n";
print MAIL "$FORM{'model'}\n";
print MAIL "$FORM{'os'}\n";
print MAIL "$FORM{'osver'}\n";
print MAIL "\n";
print MAIL "$FORM{'name'} has categorized the severity of the problem
as: $FORM{'severity'}\n";
print MAIL "\n";
print MAIL "The problem seems to occur $FORM{'when'}\n";
print MAIL "\n";
print MAIL "The version of the software/firmware $FORM{'name'} uses
is: $FORM{'version'}\n";
print MAIL "\n";
print MAIL "-----------------------------------------------\n";
print MAIL "$FORM{'name'} believes the following additional information
is relevant:\n";
print MAIL "\n";
print MAIL "$FORM{'comments'}\n";
print MAIL "\n";
print MAIL "-----------------------------------------------\n";
print MAIL "Here is some information about $FORM{'name'}'s machine
and connections:\n";
print MAIL "\n";
print MAIL "Server protocol: $ENV{'SERVER_PROTOCOL'}\n";
print MAIL "Server port: $ENV{'SERVER_PORT'}\n";
print MAIL "Remote host: $ENV{'REMOTE_HOST'}\n";
print MAIL "Remote IP address: $ENV{'REMOTE_ADDR'}\n";
close (MAIL);

print "Your request has been logged. We will contact you based on the
severity of the problem, which you indicated is: ", $FORM{'severity'};
print "
<P>
\n";
print "Return to the <A HREF=\"http://iquest.com/~nmuller/index.shtml
\">Main Menu</a>\n";
```

In this Perl script, additional information will be included with the form's output. These items describe the user's environment: server protocol, server port, remote host, and remote IP address.

The output of the processed help request form, as received via e-mail, is shown in Figure 7.23.

Figure 7.24 shows how the acknowledgment message is rendered by Netscape Navigator. Notice that the message includes the problem's severity, as indicated by the user. This serves as assurance that the severity of the problem is understood by the help desk operator and that an appropriate action will be taken within the response time associated with that level of problem severity.

Date: Mon, 17 Jul 1995 13:55:00 -0500
To: nmuller@ddx.com

This is a trouble report and request for technical assistance from Bruce King, who is reachable at bk@frynr.com.

Bruce King can also be reached as follows:

Location: NYC
Phone number: 1-234-555-1212

The kind of technical assistance Bruce King needs is related to hardware_installation.

The type of system Bruce King has is:

IBM
RS/6000
AIX
3.2

Bruce King has categorized the severity of the problem as: SERIOUS

The problem seems to occur intermittently

The version of the software/firmware Bruce King uses is: dont know

----
Bruce King believes the following additional information is relevant:

System reboots by itself intermittently
-- may indicate power supply problem

Here is some information about Bruce King's machine and connections:

Server protocol: HTTP/1.0
Server port: 80
Remote host: bk.frynr.com
Remote IP address: 204.177.198.96

Figure 7.23

Debugging Checklist

Although these HTML forms and Perl programs have been tested extensively on the Web, if you have not worked very much with the Perl language, you may occasionally forget to do certain things with these programs that will prevent them from running properly. If you experience any problems with the Perl programs on HTMLdisk, here is a checklist of critical items that merit your attention:

- Your server must support Perl.

- The server must support the POST method of processing forms.

- You must put your e-mail address at $recipient in each Perl program (the third line).

- For the $mailprog line, you should find out from your system administrator the preferred reference to the server's e-mail program (mail alias).

- You must reference your own bin alias in the "form method" line of the HTML form.

- You must save the Perl programs as ASCII (not binary) and put them in your cgi-bin directory.

- Via a telnet session, you must make each Perl program executable with the following command: `chmod a+rx filename.pl` (or something similar). Alternatively, ask your system administrator to do this for you.

- You must change the hypertext links at the end of each Perl program (if any) to something that is appropriate for your Web page.

- If you want to change the Perl programs in any way, you must be careful not to deviate from the Perl syntax. For example, leaving out a colon, single-quote mark, or slash that is part of a command will cause the program not to work.

- If you have trouble isolating such errors, your system administrator probably has a debugging utility that can spot the problem immediately.

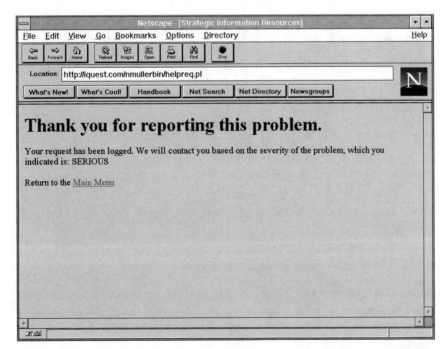

Figure 7.24

If you want to change the Perl programs, please feel free to do so and use them as you please. However, if you are not an experienced programmer, make only incremental changes and test them online to see what impact they have on the program's operation before proceeding further. If you make too many changes all at once, it will be tougher to isolate the true cause of any problem.

Enhancing the Scripts

The Perl scripts discussed in this chapter provide only very basic functionality. Admittedly, there is plenty of room for enhancement. For example, you could add a date-time stamp to the acknowledgment messages and add error detection to the various form fields. You could add both to the same Perl script. And you can expand error detection to make one field dependent on another field. The Perl programs used in this chapter allow for these and other types of enhancements.

Date-time stamp

Adding a date-time stamp to the acknowledgment messages is achieved by including the following lines to any of the previously discussed Perl scripts:

```
($sec, $min, $hour, $mday, $mon, $year, $wday, $yday, $isdst) =
localtime(time);%weekday = ("0", "Sunday","1", "Monday","2",
"Tuesday","3", "Wednesday","4", "Thursday","5", "Friday", "6",
"Saturday",);

%month = ("0", "January","1", "February","2", "March","3",
"April","4", "May","5", "June","6", "July","7", "August","8",
"September","9", "October","10", "November","11", "December",);
```

These lines must be placed before the following statement in each of the Perl scripts:

```
print "Content-type: text/html\n\n";
```

In addition, the following print statements must be added to the Perl script:

```
print "$weekday{$wday}<BR>";
print "$month{$mon} $mday, 19$year<BR>";print "$hour:$min:$sec CDT";
print "<HR>";
```

These lines are placed before the following statement in each of the Perl scripts:

```
open (MAIL, "¦$mailprog $recipient $FORM{'e-mail'} $FORM{'NAME'}")
¦¦ die "Can't open $mailprog!\n";
```

A date-time stamp is especially useful for credit card transactions, since it provides the user with an accurate record of when an order was placed. Figure 7.25 shows such an application of the date-time stamp in an acknowledgment message, as rendered by Netscape Navigator.

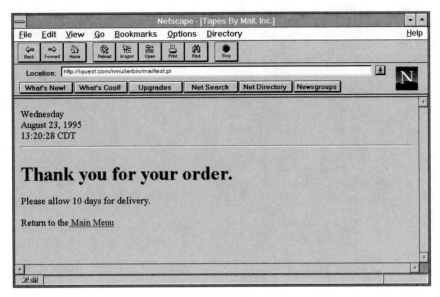

Figure 7.25

Error detection

Any field in an HTML form can be error checked, even for e-mail addresses, at least to the extent that the fields are filled in before the form is sent. If particular fields are not filled in by the user, an appropriate error message will be sent back until the entire form is completed.

For example, the following statements added to the Perl script will issue an error message if the use fails to fill in the "Name" field of an HTML form:

```
if (! $FORM{'name'}) {
print "<H2>Sorry, you failed to enter your name.</H2><P>\n",
"Please go back and do so.<P><HR><P>\n";
print "Or cancel this message by returning to the <A HREF=\"http://
iquest.com/~nmuller/index.shtml\">Main Menu</A><P>\n";
exit;
}
```

Of course, you must change the hypertext link to your own Main Menu. If the user fails to enter his or her name, these statements produce the error message shown in Figure 7.26, as rendered by Netscape Navigator.

If the user forgets to enter an e-mail address in the HTML form, the following statements added to the Perl script will issue an appropriate error message:

```
if ($FORM{'e-mail'} !~ /.+\@[\w.]+/) {
print "<H2>Sorry, you failed to enter a valid email address.</H2>
<P>\n",
"Please go back and do so.<P><HR><P>\n";
print "Or cancel this order by returning to the <A HREF=\"http://
iquest.com/~nmuller/index.shtml\">Main Menu</A><P>\n";
exit;
}
```

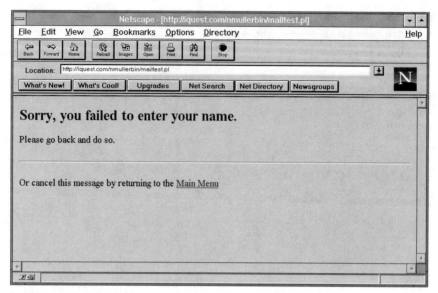

Figure 7.26

If the user fails to enter an e-mail address or fails to use a valid e-mail syntax, these statements produce the error message shown in Figure 7.27, as rendered by Netscape Navigator.

In this instance, the Perl script is looking for the @ sign as well as a period. Both characters are necessary components of any e-mail address. In both examples of error detection, the lines are placed before the following statement in each of the Perl scripts:

```
open (MAIL, "¦$mailprog $recipient $FORM{'e-mail'} $FORM{'NAME'}")
¦¦ die "Can't open $mailprog!\n";
```

However, if you are using the date-time stamp as well as error detection in the same script, the error detection statements must precede the statements for the date-time stamp.

This type of error detection can be used for any HTML form field. You just have to make sure the names of the form fields used in the Perl script correspond to those used in the HTML form. However, this error detection method does not ensure that valid information is filled in by the user; it only ensures that some type of information is entered in each field. Nevertheless, forcing the user to fill in each field can minimize the number of blank forms that are sent by curiosity seekers and pranksters.

Expanded error detection

Let's expand the use of error detection to include a comparison of two fields. If you go back to the Tapes By Mail order form in Figure 7.10, you will see that the user must select a method of payment, by entering either a purchase order number or selecting a credit card. To do error detection in this case, the Perl script must first examine the purchase order field of the HTML form. If this field is filled in, no check is done on the credit card field, and the form will be processed. However, if the purchase order field is not filled in, the error detection is done on the credit card field. If the user fails to choose either the purchase order or credit card method of payment, an appropriate error message will be sent.

If the user forgets to choose a method of payment, the following statements added to the Perl script will issue an appropriate error message:

```
if (! $FORM{'order'} == ! $FORM{'card'}) {
print "<H2>Sorry, you failed to select a method of
payment.</H2><P>\n",
"Please go back and do so.<P><HR><P>\n";
print "Or cancel this order by returning to the <A HREF=\"http://
iquest.com/~nmuller/index.shtml\">Main Menu</A><P>\n";
exit;
}
```

To use this statement in the Perl script, you must first change the HTML form so that the first choice in the credit card list is blank, instead of "Not Applicable." To the Perl script, "Not Applicable" is a valid choice. All you have to do is delete the words "Not Applicable" in the HTML form. This leaves "option" blank. If the user fails to select a method of payment, these statements produce the error message shown in Figure 7.28, as rendered by Netscape Navigator.

Let's say that the user selects a credit card as the method of payment. The next items that need error detection are the credit card number and the expiration date, which are essential for processing any credit card order. Error

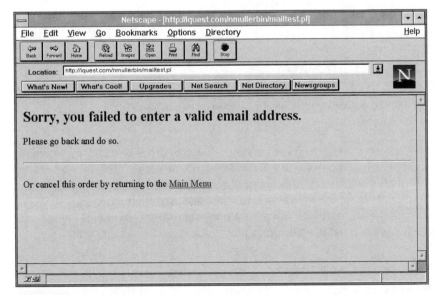

Figure 7.27

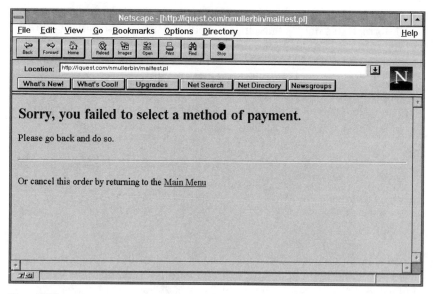

Figure 7.28

detection on these fields is accomplished by adding the following sets of statements to the Perl script:

```
if ($FORM{'card'} && ! $FORM{'account'}) {
print "<H2>Sorry, you failed to enter a credit card
number.</H2><P>\n",
"Please go back and do so.<P><HR><P>\n";
print "Or cancel this order by returning to the <A HREF=\"http://
iquest.com/~nmuller/index.shtml\">Main Menu</A><P>\n";
exit;
}

if ($FORM{'account'} && ! $FORM{'expires'}) {
print "<H2>Sorry, you failed to enter the expiration date of your
credit card.</H2><P>\n",
"Please go back and do so.<P><HR><P>\n";
print "Or cancel this order by returning to the <A HREF=\"http://
iquest.com/~nmuller/index.shtml\">Main Menu</A><P>\n";
exit;
}
```

The first set of statements are saying, "if credit card is selected and account number is missing, issue the following error message." The second set of statements are saying, "if account number is furnished and expiration date is missing," issue the following error message. Error detection in both cases will not ensure that valid information is entered into the fields—only that the fields are filled in with something which is assumed to be valid.

Enhancing the e-mail header

If you have tried using any of the previously discussed HTML forms and Perl scripts, you were probably not impressed with the e-mail headers; specifically, when viewing the e-mail messages in your favorite e-mail program, there is no "From" line indicating who sent the forms, and no "Subject" line indicating what the message is about. This is because we used a generic e-mail program—mailprog. To obtain additional detail in the e-mail header, you must use the Sendmail format in your Perl scripts. The Sendmail program is supported by most UNIX servers on the Internet.

The following Perl script is a revision of the one previously discussed, which processed the evaluation form coded in HTML. This time, however, the Perl script uses the Sendmail format to provide more information in the e-mail header. The changes are highlighted in bold.

```perl
#!/usr/local/bin/perl

$Sendmail = "/usr/lib/sendmail";
$to = "nmuller@ddx.com";

print "Content-type: text/html\n\n";
print "<Head><Title>The Webmaster's Workshop</Title></Head>";
print "<Body><H1>Thanks for your assistance!</H1></Body>";

read(STDIN, $buffer, $ENV{'CONTENT_LENGTH'});
@pairs = split(/&/, $buffer);

foreach $pair (@pairs)
{
    ($name, $value) = split(/=/, $pair);
    $value =~ tr/+/ /;
    $value =~ s/%([a-fA-F0-9][a-fA-F0-9])/pack("C", hex($1))/eg;

    $FORM{$name} = $value;
}
open (SMAIL, "|$Sendmail $to") || die "Can't open $Sendmail!\n";
print SMAIL "To: nmuller@ddx.com (Nathan Muller)\n";
print SMAIL "From: $FORM{'e-mail'} ($FORM{'name'})\n";
print SMAIL "Subject: Evaluation\n\n";
print SMAIL "This is a Web page evaluation from $FORM{'name'} who is
reachable at $FORM{'e-mail'}:\n";
print SMAIL "\n";
print SMAIL "I would say the most useful item on the Main Menu is:
$FORM{'most'}\n";
print SMAIL "\n";
print SMAIL "I would say the least useful item on the Main Menu is:
$FORM{'least'}\n";
print SMAIL ";\n";
print SMAIL "I give the content of these pages a rating of:
$FORM{'rate1'}\n";
print SMAIL "\n";
print SMAIL "I give the organization of these pages a rating of:
$FORM{'rate2'}\n";
print SMAIL "\n";
print SMAIL "-----------------------------------------------------\n";
print SMAIL "Here is what else $FORM{'name'} had to say:\n";
print SMAIL "\n";
print SMAIL "$FORM{'comments'}\n";
print SMAIL "\n";
print SMAIL "-----------------------------------------------------\n";
print SMAIL "\n";
print  SMAIL "The browser used to access my Web page: ENV{'HTTP_USER_AGENT'}\n";
```

```
close (SMAIL);
```

```
print "Your comments will help improve The Webmaster's Workshop.<P>\n";
print "\n";
print "Return to the <A HREF=\"http://iquest.com/~nmuller/
index.shtml\">Main Menu</a>\n";
```

The output of the processed evaluation form is shown in Figure 7.29. Note the additional detail provided in the header.

```
Date: Sun, 15 Oct 1995 16:03:21 -0500
To: nmuller@ddx.com (Nathan Muller)
From: nmuller@iquest.com (Nathan Muller)
Subject: Evaluation

This is a Web page evaluation from Nathan Muller who is reachable at
nmuller@iquest.com:

I would say the most useful item on the Main Menu is:
Programming_in_Perl

I would say the least useful item on the Main Menu is: Internet_Sources

I give the content of these pages a rating of: Outstanding

I give the organization of these pages a rating of: Outstanding

-------------------------------------------------------------------
Here is what else Nathan Muller had to say:




-------------------------------------------------------------------

The browser used to access my Web page: Mozilla/1.1N (Windows; I; 16bit)
```

Figure 7.29

WWW and Database Integration

The HTML forms and Perl scripts presented in this chapter are relatively simple and, with minor tweaking, would suit the needs of most casual users. However, in high transaction environments that involve such things as database queries or order processing, you may need to integrate your existing database with the Web. The methods for accomplishing this are becoming available.

One method is Sybperl, develped by Michael Pepper. Sybperl is the Sybase extensions for Perl 5, which consists of three modules: Dblib, Sybperl. and CTlib.

The Sybase Dblib module implements the Perl 5 version of the DB-library application programming interface (API). The Sybase Sybperl module implements the Sybperl 1.0xx API, and is built on top of Sybase Dblib. Sybase

CTlib implements an experimental implementation of the Client Library API.

The beta version of Sybperl is downloadable from the following URL:

```
http://www.sybase.com/WWW/Sybperl/index.html
```

If you are not inclined to writing a lot of code to integrate your Sybase with the Web, you might want to try a toolset called Web/Genera, developed by Stan Letovsky. Web/Genera simplifies the integration of Sybase databases into the World Wide Web, letting you provide Web access to the contents of Sybase databases without writing code. All you do is describe how you want your data objects to appear using the Genera schema notation, and Genera will automatically extract objects from your database and format them into HTML for distribution over the Web. Genera supports URLs to database objects, as well as query forms that provide the power of relational queries with the simplicity of fill-in-the-blanks—without the need for Structured Query Language (SQL). Genera is also useful for providing full-text search of Sybase databases via Web/WAIS and Gopher/WAIS hookups.

The beta version of Web/Genera is downloadable from the following URL:

```
http://gdbdoc.gdb.org/letovsky/genera/genera.html
```

Other popular databases can be integrated with the World Wide Web. In the case of Oracle, integration is achieved with Oraperl, the Oracle extensions to Perl. At the following URL, there is a tutorial on the subject, along with several demonstrations on querying and updating a database:

```
http://moulon.inra.fr/oracle/www_oracle_eng.html
```

Oraperl can be downloaded from the following URL:

```
ftp://moulon.inra.fr/pub/www-oracle/
```

Summary

This chapter has presented some of the most common types of forms that are likely to be required somewhere in your Web pages, as well as the Perl scripts that process the data entered into the forms. Hopefully, you will be able to apply this information to your own application needs. After seeing the power of Perl in action, you may be motivated to learn more about Perl. Toward that end, the following references may prove useful:

Learning Perl by Randal L. Schwartz, published by O'Reilly & Associates, Inc. [ISBN 1-56592-042-2]

Programming Perl by Larry Wall and Randal L. Schwartz, published by O'Reilly & Associates, Inc. [ISBN 0-937175-64-1]

Other useful resources on Perl and CGI programming and HTML include the following newsgroups which can be accessed via your Web browser or news reader:

comp.infosystems.www.authoring.cgi
comp.infosystems.www.authoring.html
comp.infosystems.www.authoring.misc
comp.lang.perl.announce
comp.lang.perl.misc

Perl documentation and sample scripts are available from dozens of sources on the World Wide Web, including:

www.wwu.edu
pubweb.nexor.co.uk/public/perl/perl.html
www.eecs.nwu.edu/perl/perl.html
www.cis.ufl.edu/perl/

Building Tables

The ability to code tables is the major new feature of HTML version 3.0. At this writing, not very many Web browsers support tables because the HTML 3.0 specification is still in draft form. Fortunately, the Netscape browser supports tables. If you do not have the Netscape browser, you can use your current Web browser to download a copy from the home page of Netscape Communications Corp. (http://www.netscape.com/).

Table layout

Tables comprise rows (horizontal) and columns (vertical) of data and often include titles, lines of text, and column heads. They can even include graphical objects and other, smaller tables. Headers or data can be flushed left or right and even centered within the cells. Cells can stretch across multiple rows and columns. The content of cells also can include hypertext links to other tables or files.

Essential tags

Table 8.1 describes the essential tags that are used to create tables, as proposed in the draft HTML 3.0 specification.

Tag attributes

Table 8.2 describes the attributes that can be used with the table tags, as proposed in the draft HTML 3.0 specification.

TABLE 8.1

Table tags	Purpose
<TABLE> . . . </TABLE>	Defines the encapsulated content as a table. Any table tags not encapsulated with these will be ignored.
<TR> . . . </TR>	Defines the encapsulated content as a table row.
<TD> . . . </TD>	Defines the encapsulated content as table data and specifies a standard cell. Cells that do not contain data will be padded with blank cells.
<TH> . . . </TH>	Defines the encapsulated text as a table header. By default, table headers are boldface and centered across the cell.
<CAPTION> . . . </CAPTION>	Defines the encapsulated content as a caption for the table. Although captions do not fall within rows or cells, they are contained within the TABLE tags. By default, captions are centered across the width of the table.

TABLE 8.2

Attribute	Purpose
BORDER	Used within the TABLE tag, this attribute puts a border around all table cells.
ALIGN	When used inside a CAPTION tag, this attribute controls the placement of the caption above or below the table. The values are TOP and BOTTOM. If not specified, the caption defaults to the top of the table.
	When used inside TR, TH, or TD tags, this attribute controls the horizontal placement of text within table cells. The values are LEFT, CENTER, and RIGHT.
VALIGN	When used inside TR, TH, or TD tags, this attribute controls the vertical placement of text within the cells. It can also be used to specify that all cells in the row be vertically aligned to the same baseline. The values are TOP, MIDDLE, BOTTOM and BASELINE.
NOWRAP	When used in a TH- or TD-tagged table cell, this attribute specifies that the text within the cell not be broken to fit the width of the cell. This attribute is seldom used because it can result in overly wide cells.
COLSPAN	When used in a TH- or TD-tagged table cell, this attribute specifies the number of table columns the cell should span. The default column span for any cell is 1.
ROWSPAN	When used in a TH- or TD-tagged table cell, this attribute specifies the number of table rows the cell should span. The default row span for any cell is 1.

Control attributes

Table 8.3 summarizes the control attributes that can be used in conjunction with the table attributes to add more flexibility to table design.

Creating a Simple Table

Some of the tags and attributes discussed in the foregoing tables are applied in the following HTML-coded table:

```
<HTML>
<BODY>
<TABLE BORDER>
<CAPTION ALIGN=BOTTOM>Table 1. This is an illustration of a simple
table.</CAPTION>
<TR><TH>Header 1</TH><TH>Header 2</TH><TH>Header 3</TH><TH>Header
4</TH> <Header 5</TH></TR>
<TR><TD>Cell 1a</TD><TD>Cell 2a</TD><TD>Cell 3a</TD><TD>Cell
4a</TD><TD> Cell 5a</TD></TR>
   <TD>Cell 1b</TD><TD>Cell 2b</TD><TD>Cell 3b</TD><TD>Cell
4b</TD><TD>Cell 5b</TD></TR>
   <TD>Cell 1c</TD><TD>Cell 2c</TD><TD>Cell 3c</TD><TD>Cell
4c</TD><TD>Cell 5c</TD></TR>
   <TD>Cell 1d</TD><TD>Cell 2d</TD><TD>Cell 3d</TD><TD>Cell
4d</TD><TD>Cell 5d</TD></TR>
</TABLE>
</BODY>
</HTML>
```

Figure 8.1 shows how this table appears when using Netscape Navigator.

Notice how the <TH> . . . </TH> tags put the column headings in bold-face, eliminating the need for separate <B> . . . </B> tags. The <TH> . . . </TH> tags also center the heads within the cells, eliminating the need for separate <CENTER> . . . </CENTER> tags. If you do not want the heads centered within their cells, but want to keep them in boldface, you can replace the <TH> . . . </TH> tags with <TD><B> . . . </B></TD>.

As far as style goes, you might not like how the cells crowd the headers and data, or that the table itself appears too small when viewed with a browser. Furthermore, you might prefer that the table appear centered when viewed with a browser instead of aligning left by default. All this can be fixed by using the CENTER tag and by encapsulating the CELL-PADDING, CELLSPACING, and WIDTH attributes within the <TABLE BORDER> . . . </TABLE> tags.

TABLE 8.3

Control attribute	Purpose
BORDER=(value)	This attribute specifies the width of the border, allowing more variation between tables than if they all used the same default border width. Values of 1 to 8 may be used. Higher values might result in a distorted table border.
CELLSPACING=(value)	This attribute specifies the amount of space between table cells. Netscape uses a default cell spacing of 2.
CELLPADDING=(value)	This attribute specifies the amount of space between the border of the cells and their contents. Netscape uses a default cell spacing of 1.
WIDTH=(value or percent)	When used with the TABLE tags, this attribute specifies the width of the table, either as an absolute width in pixels, or as a percentage of screen width. Care must be used to select a value that will accommodate all of the table cells. When used within TH- or TD-tagged cells, this attribute specifies the width of the cell, either as an absolute width in pixels, or as a percentage of table width.

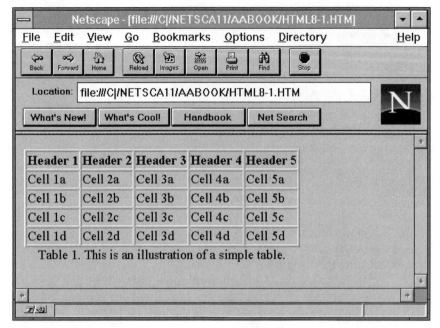

Figure 8.1

Let's add the CENTER tag and these table attributes to Table 8.1. Also, let's move the caption from the bottom of the table to the top and center the contents of each cell. These modifications appear in boldface as follows:

```
<CENTER>
<TABLE BORDER=4 CELLPADDING=5 CELLSPACING=5 WIDTH="75%">
<CAPTION ALIGN=TOP>Table 1. This is an illustration of a simple
table.</CAPTION>
<TR><TH>Header 1</TH><TH>Header 2</TH><TH>Header 3</TH><TH>Header 4
</TH><TH>Header 5 </TH></TR>
<TR ALIGN=CENTER>
   <TD>Cell 1a</TD><TD>Cell 2a</TD><TD>Cell 3a</TD><TD>Cell
4a</TD><TD>Cell 5a</TD></TR>
<TR ALIGN=CENTER>
   <TD>Cell 1b</TD><TD>Cell 2b</TD><TD>Cell 3b</TD><TD>Cell
4b</TD><TD>Cell 5b</TD></TR>
<TR ALIGN=CENTER>
   <TD>Cell 1c</TD><TD>Cell 2c</TD><TD>Cell 3c</TD><TD>Cell
4c</TD><TD>Cell 5c</TD></TR>
<TR ALIGN=CENTER>
   <TD>Cell 1d</TD><TD>Cell 2d</TD><TD>Cell 3d</TD><TD>Cell
4d</TD><TD>Cell 5d</TD></TR>
</TABLE>
</CENTER>
```

This is how the revised Table 8.1 appears when using Netscape Navigator.

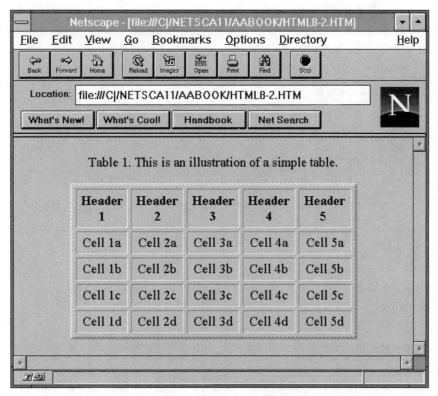

Figure 8.2

Amortization Table

You can experiment with the values for CELLSPACING, CELLPADDING, and WIDTH to achieve exactly the right look for your tables. Your selection of values may be influenced largely by the kind of data you intend to portray in your tables. Now that you have the basic concept down, let's code something a bit more practical and familiar—an amortization table:

```
<HTML>
<BODY>
<CENTER><H2>Amortization Table</H2>
<TABLE BORDER=4 CELLPADDING=5 CELLSPACING=5 WIDTH="80%">
<CAPTION ALIGN=BOTTOM>Note: This table depicts only the first 8
payments of a 48.month car loan.</CAPTION>
<TR><TH>No.</TH><TH>Payment Date</TH><TH>Beginning
Balance</TH><TH>Interest</TH><TH>Principal</TH><TH>Ending
Balance</TH><TH>Cumulative Interest</TH></TR>
<TR ALIGN=CENTER>
<TD>1</TD><TD>1/1/94</TD><TD>20000.00</TD><TD>183.33</TD><TD>333.58
</TD><TD>19666.42</TD> <TD>183.33</TD></TR>
<TR ALIGN=CENTER>
<TD>2</TD><TD>2/1/94</TD><TD>19666.42</TD><TD>180.28</TD><TD>336.63
```

```
</TD><TD>19329.79</TD><TD>363.61</TD></TR>
<TR ALIGN=CENTER>
<TD>3</TD><TD>/1/94</TD><TD>19329.79</TD><TD>177.19</TD><TD>339.72
</TD><TD>18990.07</TD> <TD>540.8</TD></TR>
<TR ALIGN=CENTER>
<TD>4</TD><TD>4/1/94</TD><TD>18990.07</TD><TD>174.08</TD><TD>342.83
</TD><TD>18647.23</TD><TD>714.87</TD></TR>
<TR ALIGN=CENTER>
<TD>5</TD><TD>5/1/94</TD><TD>18647.23</TD><TD>170.93</TD><TD>345.98
</TD><TD>18301.25</TD><TD>885.81</TD></TR>
<TR ALIGN=CENTER>
<TD>6</TD><TD>6/1/94</TD><TD>18301.25</TD><TD>167.76</TD><TD>349.15
</TD><TD>17952.11</TD><TD>1053.57</TD></TR>
<TR ALIGN=CENTER>
<TD>7</TD><TD>7/1/94</TD><TD>17952.11</TD><TD>164.56</TD><TD>352.35
</TD><TD>17599.76</TD> <TD>1218.13</TD></TR>
<TR ALIGN=CENTER>
<TD>8</TD><TD>8/1/94</TD><TD>17599.76</TD><TD>161.33</TD><TD>355.58
</TD><TD>17244.18</TD><TD>1379.46</TD></TR>
</TABLE>
</CENTER>
</BODY>
</HTML>
```

Figure 8.3 shows how the amortization table appears when using Netscape Navigator.

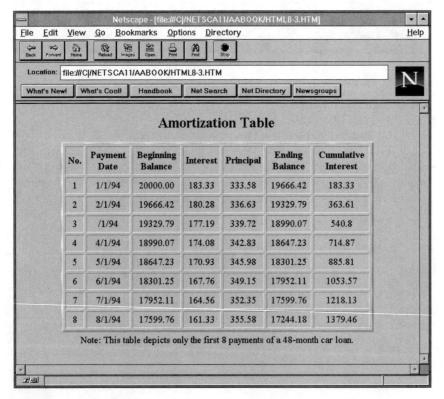

Figure 8.3

You can add as many rows as you like; there is no limit. Keep in mind, though, that Web users may not have a tolerance for viewing overly long tables. Sticking to tables that can be displayed in a single screen or two is probably the safest way to go.

Text Tables

Tables can contain more than just numbers or simple terms. Entire sentences and paragraphs can be used in tables, as the following coding example shows:

```
<HTML>
<BODY>
<CENTER>
<TABLE BORDER CELLPADDING=5 WIDTH="80%">
<CAPTION ALIGN=BOTTOM>Note: it is best to keep the number of bridged
protocols to a minimum and route as many protocols as possible.
</CAPTION>
   <TR><TH>Bridges</TH><TH>Routers</TH></TR>
   <TR><TD>Offer best solution for point-to-point simple mesh
topologies. Bridges are not very scalable. </TD><TD>Accommodate
several data links and can exploit complex mesh topologies in cases
of link failure and congestion. Routers are highly scalable.</TD>
   <TR><TD>Are easier to install and maintain than routers.</TD><TD>
Support multiple network and router layer protocols at the same
time.</TD>
   <TR><TD>Operate independently of higher level protocols.</TD><TD>
Offer advanced administration and control services based on network
and subnetwork addresses.</TD>
   <TR><TD>Offer a flexible method for filtering traffic according to
source-destination addresses, protocol type, and application.</TD>
<TD>Do not have the problem of "broadcast storms", as do bridges.
<TD></TD>
   <TR><TD>Cost: $6,000 to $30,000</TD><TD>Cost: up to $75,000 (even
more for a backbone router)</TD>
   </TR>
</TABLE>
</CENTER>
</BODY>
</HTML>
```

Figure 8.4 shows how the text table appears when using Netscape Navigator.

Text Table with Side Heads

So far, all of the table examples have featured headings at the top of each column. Tables also can be organized with a heading for each row, as in the following coding example:

```
<HTML>
<BODY>
<CENTER>
<TABLE BORDER=4 CELLPADDING=5 CELLSPACING=5 WIDTH="75%">
<CAPTION ALIGN=TOP><H3>Router Selection Criteria</H3></CAPTION>
   <TR>
        <TH>Multiprotocol Support</TH><TD>The ability to route all of
```

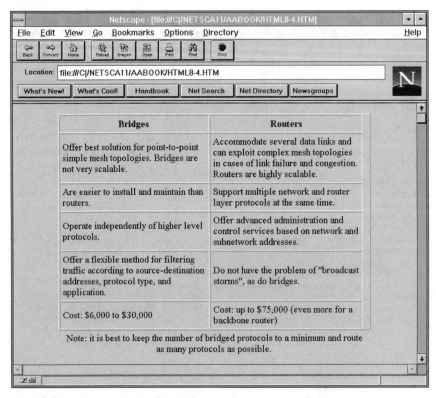

Figure 8.4

the protocols present in the internetwork, including LAN and legacy
data.</TD> </TR>
   <TR>
         <TH>Bridging</TH><TD>Not all protocols are routable; therefore,
routers should possess the ability to bridge protocols.</TD></TR>
   <TR>
         <TH>Verified Throughput</TH>
   <TD>Demonstrated results of benchmark testing, as defined in RFC
1242.</TD></TR>
   <TR>
         <TH>Reliability</TH>
   <TD>Hot-swapping of boards, redundancy of critical components such
as power supplies, plus easy upgrades.</TD></TR>
   <TR>
         <TH>Modularity</TH>
   <TD>The ability to include additional local- or wide-area network
interfaces as requirements or new technologies emerge.</TD></TR>
   <TR>
         <TH>Scalability</TH>
   <TD>The degree to which the new system can meet the requirements of
a network that is continually growing and expanding.</TD></TR>
   <TR>
         <TH>Price/Performance</TH>
   <TD>Buy only the features needed without under- or over-estimating
system requirements.</TD></TR>
   <TR>
         <TH>Vendor Support</TH>

```
   <TD>Around-the-clock telephone support, extended service
agreements, remote diagnostics, upgrade assistance and off-hours
support are essential to keep the network up and running.</TD></TR>
</TABLE>
</CENTER>
</BODY>
</HTML>
```

Figure 8.5 shows how the text table with side heads appears when using Netscape Navigator.

If you prefer the side heads to be centered within their cells, but want to keep them in boldface, you can use the `<TH>` . . . `</TH>` tags instead of the `<TD><B>` . . . `</B></TD>` tags.

Product Comparison Table

On occasion, you might have to develop a matrix table that compares many products in terms of the features they provide or the services they support.

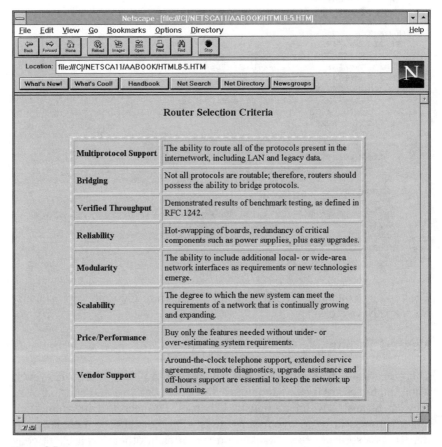

Figure 8.5

The next example provides the coding for this type of table. Notice the use of the COLSPAN=1 attribute within the <TH> tag, which allows each head to span only a single column:

```
<HTML>
<BODY>
<CENTER>
<H3>Comparison of Middleware Service Support Options</H3>
<TABLE BORDER=4 CELLPADDING=5 CELLSPACING=5 WIDTH="85%">
<CAPTION ALIGN=BOTTOM>Adapted from: Data Communications Magazine,
March 21, 1995</CAPTION>
   <TR>
         <TH COLSPAN=1>Vendor/Product</TH>
         <TH COLSPAN=1>ARDIS</TH>
         <TH COLSPAN=1>RAM</TH>
         <TH COLSPAN=1>CDPD</TH>
         <TH COLSPAN=1>Circuit Cellular</TH>
         <TH COLSPAN=1>Wireline Dialup</TH>
         <TH COLSPAN=1>Paging</TH></TR>
   <TR ALIGN=CENTER>
<TD><B>AirSoft/AirAccess</B></TD><TD>N</TD><TD>Y</TD><TD> N</TD>
<TD>Y</TD><TD>Y</TD> <TD>N</TD></TR>
   <TR ALIGN=CENTER>
         <TD><B>DEC/Roamabout
Mobile</B></TD><TD>Y</TD><TD>Y</TD><TD>Y</TD><TD>Y</TD><TD>Y</TD><TD>
Y</TD></TR>
   <TR ALIGN=CENTER>
         <TD><B>IBM/Wireless Mobile
Enabler</B></TD><TD>Y</TD><TD>Y</TD><TD>Y </TD><TD>N</TD><TD>N</TD>
<TD>N</TD></TR>
   <TR ALIGN=CENTER>
         <TD><B>Moda Systems/Via</B></TD>
<TD>Y</TD><TD>Y</TD><TD>Y</TD><TD>Y</TD><TD>Y</TD><TD>N</TD></TR>
   <TR ALIGN=CENTER>
         <TD><B>Oracle/Oracle in Motion</B></TD><TD>N</TD><TD>Y</TD>
<TD>N</TD><TD>N</TD><TD>Y</TD><TD>N</TD></TR>
   <TR ALIGN=CENTER>
         <TD><B>Racotek/KeyWare</B></TD>
<TD>Y</TD><TD>Y</TD><TD>Y</TD><TD>N</TD><TD>N</TD><TD>N</TD></TR>
<TR ALIGN=CENTER>
      <TD><B>Teknique/Transnet
II</B></TD><TD>Y</TD><TD>Y</TD><TD>Y</TD><TD>Y</TD><TD>Y</TD><TD>Y
</TD></TR>
</TABLE>
</CENTER>
</BODY>
</HTML>
```

The product comparison table appears as shown in Figure 8.6 when using Netscape Navigator.

Nested Tables

There are times when information will require multiple tables. However, when the tables are related and not really big enough to stand on their own, they can be nested within a single table border. The secret to designing such tables is to visualize the layout of the finished table and code it crosswise—that is, as a series of rows stacked on top of each other. Even blank cells must be accounted for in the coding.

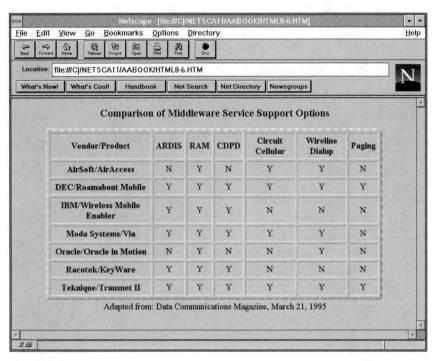

Figure 8.6

Basic concept

Provided below is the coding for a nested table that summarizes different file extensions. Note how the coding consists of 15 major sections. Each of these sections corresponds to an entire table row, including spaces. To help you follow the pattern, the table row tag is highlighted in boldface.

```
<HTML>
<BODY>
<CENTER>
<H2>Common File Extensions</H2>
<TABLE BORDER=6 CELLPADDING=3 CELLSPACING=3>
<TR ALIGN=CENTER><TH COLSPAN=2>Programs and Drivers</TH><TD></TD>
<TH COLSPAN=2>Sound and Video</TH><TD></TD><TH COLSPAN=2>Compressed
Archives</TH><TD></TD><TH COLSPAN=2>Data and Related</TH></TR>
<TR ALIGN=CENTER>
<TD>386</TD><TD>fmt</TD><TD></TD><TD>avi</TD><TD>mpg</TD><TD></TD>
<TD>arc</TD><TD>lzh</TD><TD></TD><TD>asc</TD><TD>txt</TD></TR>
ALIGN=CENTER
<TD>asm</TD><TD>fon</TD><TD></TD><TD>mid</TD><TD>snd</TD><TD></TD><TD
>arj</TD><TD>zip</TD><TD></TD><TD>db</TD><TD>wk1</TD></TR>
<TR ALIGN=CENTER>
<TD>atm</TD><TD>fot</TD><TD></TD><TD>mov</TD><TD>wav</TD><TD></TD>
<TD></TD><TD></TD><TD></TD><TD>dbf</TD> <TD>wk3</TD></TR>
<TR ALIGN=CENTER>
<TD>bas</TD><TD>hlp</TD><TD></TD><TD></TD><TD></TD><TD></TD><TD></TD>
<TD></TD><TD></TD><TD>dic</TD><TD>wk4</TD></TR>
<TR ALIGN=CENTER>
<TD>bat</TD><TD>inf</TD><TD></TD><TD></TD><TD></TD><TD></TD><TD></TD>
```

```
<TD></TD><TD></TD><TD>doc</TD><TD>wk5</TD></TR>
<TR ALIGN=CENTER>
<TD>bin</TD><TD>ini</TD><TD></TD><TD></TD><TD></TD><TD></TD><TD></TD>
<TD></TD><TD></TD><TD>dot</TD><TD>wp</TD></TR>
<TR ALIGN=CENTER>
<TD>cbt</TD><TD>ovl</TD><TD></TD><TD></TD><TD></TD><TD></TD><TD></TD>
<TD></TD><TD></TD><TD>idx</TD><TD>wpm</TD></TR>
<TR ALIGN=CENTER> <TD>cfg</TD><TD>pif</TD><TD></TD><TH
COLSPAN=2>Graphics</TH><TD></TD><TH
COLSPAN=2>Temporary/Backup</TH><TD></TD><TD>mdb</TD><TD>wri</TD></TR>
<TR ALIGN=CENTER>
<TD>com</TD><TD>reg</TD><TD></TD><TD>ai</TD><TD>ico</TD><TD></TD><TD>
bak</TD>
<TD>syd</TD><TD></TD><TD>ndx</TD><TD>xla</TD></TR>
<TR ALIGN=CENTER>
<TD>cpl</TD><TD>scr</TD><TD></TD><TD>bmp</TD><TD>jpg</TD><TD></TD>
<TD>chk</TD> <TD>tmp</TD><TD></TD><TD>rtf</TD><TD>xlm</TD></TR>
<TR ALIGN=CENTER>
<TD>dll</TD><TD>sys</TD><TD></TD><TD>cdr</TD><TD>pcx</TD><TD></TD><TD>
</TD><TD></TD><TD>sam</TD><TD>xls</TD></TR>
<TR ALIGN=CENTER>
<TD>drv</TD><TD>ttf</TD><TD></TD><TD>fxr</TD><TD>pm4</TD><TD></TD>
<TD></TD><TD></TD><TD>sty</TD><TD>xlt</TD></TR>
<TR ALIGN=CENTER>
<TD>exe</TD><TD>vbx</TD><TD></TD><TD>fxs</TD><TD>pm5</TD><TD></TD>
<TD></TD><TD></TD> <TD></TD><TD></TD></TR>
<TR ALIGN=CENTER>
<TD>flt</TD><TD>vxd</TD><TD></TD><TD>gif</TD><TD>tif</TD><TD></TD>
<TD></TD><TD></TD> <TD></TD><TD></TD></TR>
</TABLE>
</CENTER>
</BODY>
</HTML>
```

Figure 8.7 shows how the nested table appears in Netscape Navigator.

With each row represented by its own section of code, you can easily add or revise the information.

Practical application

Now let's put the concept of nested tables to work in a more useful and compelling way. In the next example, several items have been combined in a single table border: a top caption, text box, and several tables. The coding for this example is:

```
<HTML>
<BODY>
<CENTER>
<TABLE BORDER=5 CELLPADDING=6 CELLSPACING=6 WIDTH="80%">
  <TR>
       <TH COLSPAN=4 ALIGN=LEFT><H2>Traffic-Cop/2000</H2></TH></TR>
  <TH COLSPAN=4><H3>A Cross-Platform Networking Server</H3></TH></TR>
       <TR ALIGN=LEFT>
       <TD COLSPAN=4> Traffic-Cop/2000 is a 2-port, multiprotocol
Internet router and remote access server for branch offices. Use it
to access the Internet, link one office to another, allow users to
remotely access the LAN, and give users the ability to dial out to
remote services.</TD> </TR>
  <TR ALIGN=CENTER>
       <TH>WAN Interface Options</TH> <TH>WAN
Protocols</TH><TH>Security Features</TH><TH>Hardware</TH></TR>
```

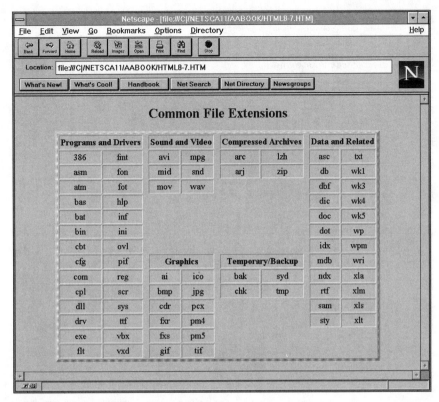

Figure 8.7

```
   <TR ALIGN=CENTER>
        <TD>RS-232</TD>  <TD>PPP</TD><TD>CHAP</TD>
<TD>MC68306 processor</TD></TR>
   <TR ALIGN=CENTER>
        <TD>V.35 Synch</TD>  <TD>LCP</TD>
<TD>PAP</TD><TD>1MB DRAM</TD></TR>
   <TR ALIGN=CENTER>
        <TD>V.34</TD><TD>IPCP</TD><TD>Static Routes</TD><TD>1 MB
flash RAM</TD></TR>
        <TR><TH>
   <TR ALIGN=CENTER>
        <TH COLSPAN=2>Management Features</TH> <TH COLSPAN=2>Benefits
</TH> </TR>
<TD COLSPAN=2>Define access levels</TD><TD COLSPAN=2>Software can be
remotely upgraded</TD></TR>
   <TR ALIGN=CENTER>
        TD COLSPAN=2>Examine routing information</TD><TD COLSPAN=2>Plug
and play installation</TD></TR>
   <TR ALIGN=CENTER>
        TD COLSPAN=2>Configure ports</TD><TD COLSPAN=2>Works with all
network operating systems</TD></TR>
   </TABLE>
   </CENTER>
   </BODY>
   </HTML>
```

Figure 8.8 shows how the table appears in Netscape Navigator:

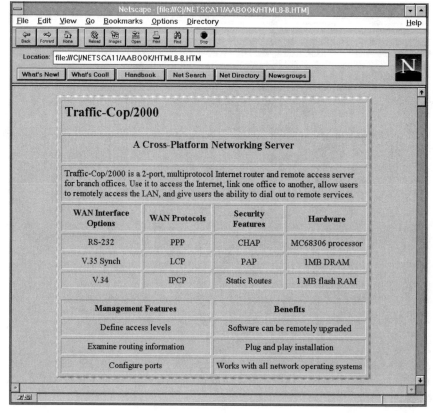

Figure 8.8

If you think the coding is starting to get too complicated, you can call up these files from HTMLdisk for display in Netscape. From Netscape, print the file and use it to plan a table of your own. The printout of the Traffic-Cop/2000 product sheet is shown in Figure 8.9. Just edit the table and use your word processor's find-replace feature to make changes to the file.

In the next example, a top caption, text box, several tables, and a bottom caption are combined within a single table border. The coding for this example is:

```
<HTML>
<BODY>
<CENTER>
<TABLE BORDER=4 CELLPADDING=5 CELLSPACING=5 WIDTH="60%">
   <TR>
        <TH COLSPAN=1>Email Rates</TH></TR>
        <TR ALIGN=LEFT>
        <TD COLSPAN=3>You can choose from among the following service
plans and value-added features. Not included in the prices below are
the $99 activation fee and the cost of a wireless modem.</TD> </TR>
```

Traffic-Cop/2000			
A Cross-Platform Networking Server			
Traffic-Cop/2000 is a 2-port, multiprotocol Internet router and remote access server for branch offices. Use it to access the Internet, link one office to another, allow users to remotely access the LAN, and give users the ability to dial out to remote services.			
WAN Interface Options	**WAN Protocols**	**Security Features**	**Hardware**
RS-232	PPP	CHAP	MC68306 processor
V.35 Synch	LCP	PAP	1MB DRAM
V.34	IPCP	Static Routes	1 MB flash RAM

Management Features		Benefits	
Define access levels		Software can be remotely upgraded	
Examine routing information		Plug and play installation	
Configure ports		Works with all network operating systems	

Figure 8.9

```
<TR ALIGN=CENTER>
        <TH>Plan</TH> <TH>Monthly Fee</TH><TH>Max. Volume (in kilobytes
</TH></TR>
<TR ALIGN=CENTER>
        <TD>Economy</TD> <TD>$49</TD> <TD>50</TD></TR>
<TR ALIGN=CENTER>
        <TD>Frequent User</TD> <TD>$79</TD> <TD>300</TD></TR>
<TR ALIGN=CENTER>
        <TD>Mobile
Professional</TD><TD>$99</TD><TD>700</TD></TR>
        <TR><TH>
<TR ALIGN=CENTER>
        <TH COLSPAN=2>Value-Added Features</TH><TH
COLSPAN=1>Fee</TH></TR>
<TR ALIGN=CENTER>
        <TD COLSPAN=2>Mobile News</TD><TD COLSPAN=1>$18 per
month</TD></TR>
<TR ALIGN=CENTER>
        <TD COLSPAN=2>Fax Services</TD><TD COLSPAN=1>$0.75 per
page</TD></TR>
<TR ALIGN=CENTER>
        <TD COLSPAN=2>Paging Services</TD><TD COLSPAN=1>$0.50 per
page</TD></TR>
  <TR>
        <TD COLSPAN=3><EM>In effect as of June 1995. All rates
subject to change without prior notice.</EM></TD></TR>
</TABLE>
```

```
</CENTER>
</BODY>
</HTML>
```

Note the use of the COLSPAN= attribute to set the column widths of the headings. Also note the use of the <H2> . . . </H2> tags to set off the first head, E-mail Rates, with a level 2 heading. By nesting these tags within the <TH> . . . </TH> tags, the term E-imail Rates is centered across the top of the table using the least amount of coding. Both of these tag sets provide boldface text, but using both of them at the same time does not result in bolder text.

Figure 8.10 shows how the table appears in Netscape Navigator.

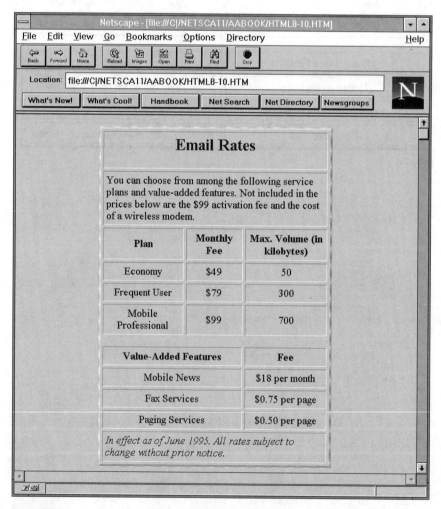

Figure 8.10

Embedding Lists within Tables

Ordered, unordered, or definition-style lists can be embedded into tables. The following tags/attributes are used to create these lists:

Tags/Attributes	Purpose
<OL> . . . </OL>	Used for arranging items in numerical order.
<UL> . . . </UL>	Used for arranging items in no particular order.
<LI>	When used in ordered lists, consecutively numbers each item. When used in unordered lists, provides a bullet for each item.
<DL> . . . </DL>	Normally used for definition lists—a term, followed by a definition—but can be used for any type of list when numbers or bullets are not wanted.
<DD>	When used in definition lists, provides an indent instead of a number or bullet.

A variation of the previously used Traffic-Cop/2000 product sheet is used to demonstrate the use of an unordered list within a table. The use of the <LI> tag in conjunction with the <UL> . . . </UL> tags, creates bullets that are used to summarize the important product features. Below that, the features are broken out in greater detail under separate headings. The coding for this example is:

```
<HTML>
<BODY>
<CENTER>
<TABLE BORDER=5 CELLPADDING=6 CELLSPACING=6 WIDTH="80%">
   <TR>
        <TH COLSPAN=5 ALIGN=LEFT><H2>Traffic-Cop/2000</H2></TH></TR>
        <TH COLSPAN=5><H3>A Cross-Platform Networking
Server</H3></TH></TR>
        <TR ALIGN=LEFT>
        <TD COLSPAN=5> Traffic-Cop/2000 is a 2-port, multiprotocol
Internet router and remote access server for branch offices. Use it to
access the Internet, link one office to another, allow users to
remotely access the LAN, and give users the ability to dial out to
remote services.
<UL>
<LI>Provides multiple WAN interfaces
<LI>Supports multiple WAN protocols
<LI>Supports current security standards
<LI>Offers remote management features
<LI>Uses state-of-the-art hardware
</UL>
</TD> </TR>
   <TR ALIGN=CENTER>
        <TH>WAN Interface Options</TH> <TH>WAN Protocols</TH><TH>
Security Features</TH><TH>Management</TH><TH>Hardware</TH></TR>
   <TR ALIGN=CENTER>
        <TD>RS-232</TD> <TD>PPP</TD><TD>CHAP</TD><TD>Define access
levels</TD><TD>MC68306 processor</TD></TR>
   <TR ALIGN=CENTER>
        <TD>V.35 Synch</TD> <TD>LCP</TD> <TD>PAP</TD><TD>Examine
routing information<TD>1MB DRAM</TD></TR>
   <TR ALIGN=CENTER>
```

```
        <TD>V.34</TD><TD>IPCP</TD><TD>Static Routes</TD><TD>Configure
ports</TD><TD>1 MB flash RAM</TD></TR>
</TABLE>
</CENTER>
</BODY>
</HTML>
```

The table appears in Netscape as shown in Figure 8.11.

The next example makes use of all three types of lists within the same table. It is coded as follows:

```
<HTML>
<BODY>
<CENTER>
<TABLE BORDER=5 CELLPADDING=6 CELLSPACING=6 WIDTH="80%">
  <TR>
        <TD COLSPAN=5><H1>Traffic-Cop/2000</H1><DL><DD>It's a cross-
platform networking server<DD>It's a multiprotocol Internet
router<DD>It's a remote control node<DD></DL><EM>It's everything LAN
managers have been waiting for!</EM></TD>
<TR ALIGN=LEFT>
```

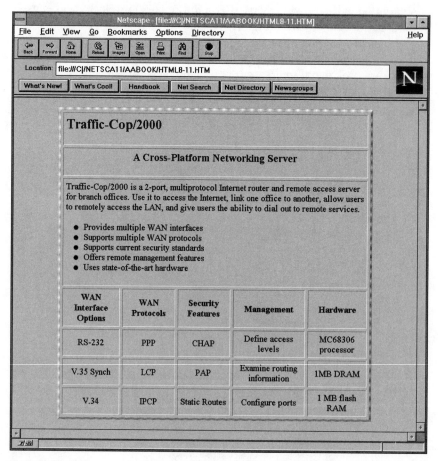

Figure 8.11

```
<TD COLSPAN=5><B>Traffic-Cop/2000 is a compact, software-
configurable, network managed node for branch offices. It allows
users to:</B>
<OL>
<LI>Access the corporate LAN
<LI>Access the Internet
<LI>Link one office to another
<LI>Dial out to remote services.
<OL>
</TR>
<TR ALIGN=LEFT>
<TD COLSPAN=5><B>Traffic-Cop/2000 has the features and capabilities
you need for connectivity in today's distributed work
environment:</B>
<UL>
<LI>Provides multiple WAN interfaces
<LI>Supports multiple WAN protocols
<LI>Supports current security standards
<LI>Offers remote management features
<LI>Uses state-of-the-art hardware
</UL>
</TD> </TR>
<TR ALIGN=CENTER>
     <TH>WAN Interface Options</TH> <TH>WAN Protocols</TH><TH>Security
Features</TH><TH>Management</TH><TH>Hardware</TH></TR>
  <TR ALIGN=CENTER>
       <TD>RS-232</TD> <TD>PPP</TD><TD>CHAP</TD><TD>Define access
levels</TD><TD>MC68306 processor</TD></TR>
  <TR ALIGN=CENTER>
       <TD>V.35 Synch</TD> <TD>LCP</TD> <TD>PAP</TD><TD>Examine
routing information<TD>1MB DRAM</TD></TR>
  <TR ALIGN=CENTER>
       <TD>V.34</TD><TD>IPCP</TD><TD>Static Routes</TD><TD>Configure
ports</TD><TD>1 MB flash RAM</TD></TR>
</TABLE>
</CENTER>
</BODY>
</HTML>
```

The table appears in Netscape Navigator as shown in Figure 8.12.

Embedding Graphics within Tables

In the same way that graphics can be embedded into text using the <IMG
SRC= . . . > tag, graphics can be embedded into the cells of tables. In the
following coding example, images of flags are embedded in the first column
of cells in the table. The IMG tag is highlighted as well as the ALIGN attribute.

```
<HTML>
<HEAD>
<BODY>
<CENTER>
<TABLE BORDER=4 CELLPADDING=5 CELLSPACING=5 WIDTH="70%">
  <TR>
       <TH COLSPAN=1>Country</TH>
       <TH COLSPAN=1>Capital</TH>
       <TH COLSPAN=1>Population</TH>
       <TH COLSPAN=1>GNP</TH></TR>
       <TR ALIGN=LEFT>
```

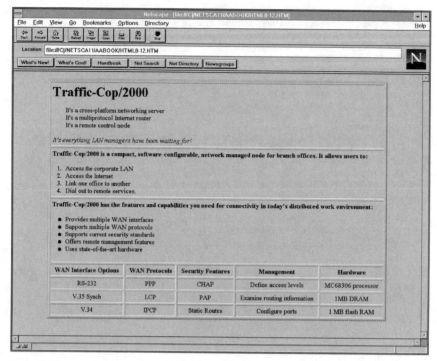

Figure 8.12

```
     <TD><IMG SRC="flag_no.gif" ALIGN=MIDDLE> Norway</TD><TD
ALIGN=MIDDLE>Oslo</TD><TD ALIGN=MIDDLE>4 million</TD><TD
ALIGN=MIDDLE>$95 Billion</TD></TR>
         <TR ALIGN=LEFT>
     <TD><IMG SRC="flag_fr.gif" ALIGN=MIDDLE> France</TD><TD
ALIGN=MIDDLE>Paris</TD><TD ALIGN=MIDDLE>60 million</TD><TD
ALIGN=MIDDLE>$750 Billion</TD></TR>
         <TR ALIGN=LEFT>
     <TD><IMG SRC="flag_gb.gif" ALIGN=MIDDLE> England</TD><TD
ALIGN=MIDDLE>London</TD><TD ALIGN=MIDDLE>55 million</TD><TD
ALIGN=MIDDLE>$1 Trillion</TD></TR>
         <TR ALIGN=LEFT>
     <TD><IMG SRC="flag_us.gif" ALIGN=MIDDLE> United States</TD><TD
ALIGN=MIDDLE>Washington, DC</TD><TD ALIGN=MIDDLE>260 million</TD><TD
ALIGN=MIDDLE>$5.5 Trillion</TD></TR>
         <TR ALIGN=LEFT>
     <TD>IMG SRC="flag_ca.gif" ALIGN=MIDDLE Canada</TD><TD
ALIGN=MIDDLE>Ottawa</TD><TD ALIGN=MIDDLE>30 million</TD><TD
ALIGN=MIDDLE>$700 Billion</TD></TR>
     </TABLE>
     </CENTER>
     </BODY>
     </HTML>
```

In Netscape, the table appears as in Figure 8.13.

The flag images in each row can be coded as hypertext links that take the reader to additional information about each country. For example, to make the flag of Canada a hypertext link to a file called canada.htm, use the following format between the table data tags:

```
<A HREF="canada.html"><IMG SRC="flag_ca.gif"
ALIGN=MIDDLE></A>
```

Changing the control variable from LEFT to MIDDLE vertically centers Canada next to the flag image. Using graphics in this way enables tables to be used as menus. In the next example, a table is used as a menu for Usenet newsgroups on various data communications topics. The coding is as follows:

```
<HTML>
<HEAD>
<BODY>
<CENTER>
<TABLE BORDER=4 CELLPADDING=5 CELLSPACING=5 WIDTH="70%">
  <TR>
        <TH COLSPAN=2><<H3>The Usenet News*Desk</H3></TH></TR>

        <TR ALIGN=LEFT>
  <TD><A HREF="news:comp.dcom.isdn"><IMG SRC="news.gif" ALIGN=MIDDLE>
</A> ISDN</TD><TD><A HREF="news:comp.dcom.telecom"><IMG
SRC="news.gif" ALIGN=MIDDLE></A> Telecom (general)</TD></TR>

        <TR ALIGN=LEFT>
  <TD><A HREF="news:comp.dcom.lans.fddi"><IMG SRC="news.gif"
ALIGN=MIDDLE></A> FDDI</TD><TD><A HREF="news:comp.dcom.frame-relay"><IMG
SRC="news gif" ALIGN=MIDDLE></A> Frame Relay</TD></TR>
```

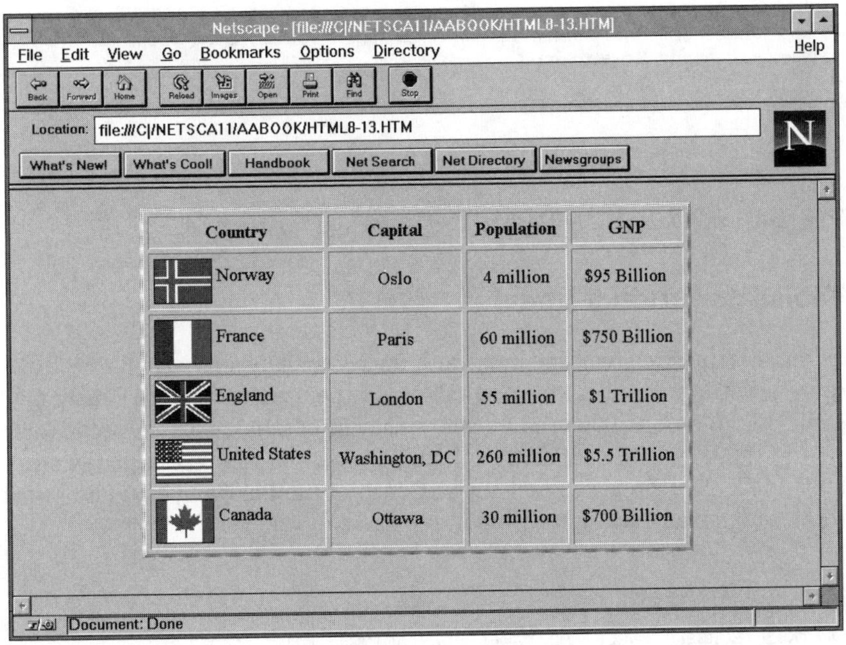

Figure 8.13

```
        <TR ALIGN=LEFT>
    <TD><A HREF="news:comp.dcom.net-management"><IMG SRC=news gif" ALIGN=
MIDDLE></A> Network Management</TD>
    <TD><A HREF="news:comp.std.wireless"><IMG SRC="news.gif"
ALIGN=MIDDLE></A> Wireless/Mobile</TD></TR>

        <TR ALIGN=LEFT>
    <TD><A HREF="news:comp.dcom.cell-relay"><IMG SRC="news.gif"
ALIGN=MIDDLE></A> Cell Relay</TD><TD><A HREF="news:comp.dcom.lans.
ethernet"><IMG SRC="news.gif" ALIGN=MIDDLE></A> Ethernet</TD></TR>

        <TR ALIGN=LEFT>
    <TD><A HREF="news:comp.dcom.lans.misc"><IMG SRC="news.gif" ALIGN=
MIDDLE></A> LAN Hardware/Software</TD><TD> <A HREF="news:comp. dcom.
lans.token-ring"><IMG SRC="news.gif" ALIGN=MIDDLE></A> Token-Ring
</TD></TR>

        <TR ALIGN=LEFT>
    <TD><A HREF="news:comp.dcom.servers"><IMG SRC="news.gif" ALIGN=
MIDDLE></A> Servers</TD><TD><A HREF="news:comp.dcom.videoconf">
<IMG SRC="news gif" ALIGN=MIDDLE></A> Videoconferencing</TD></TR>

        <TR ALIGN=LEFT>
    <TD><A HREF="news:comp.dcom.modems"><IMG SRC="news.gif" ALIGN=MIDDLE>
</A> Modems</TD><TD><A HREF="news:comp.dcom.cabling"><IMG
SRC="news.gif" ALIGN=MIDDLE></A> Cabling</TD></TR>

        <TR ALIGN=LEFT>
    <TH COLSPAN=2><FONT SIZE=4><A HREF="http://www.cen.uiuc.edu/
cgi-bin/ find-news"><IMG SRC="question.gif" ALIGN=MIDDLE></A> <I>If
you don't see your favorite topic, search Usenet here.</I></FONT>
</TH></TR>

        <TR ALIGN=LEFT>
    <TH COLSPAN=2><FONT SIZE=4><A HREF="news:comp.dcom.*"><IMG
SCR="sheet gif" ALIGN=MIDDLE></A> <I>Subscription form for data
communications News groups.</I></FONT></TH> </TR>

</TABLE>
</CENTER>
</BODY>
</HTML>
```

The table, as rendered by Netscape, is shown in Figure 8.14.

Tables as Product Sheets

Different font sizes, colored text, and an abstract design can be used to dress up otherwise bland-looking tables. In the case of our previously described Traffic-Cop/2000 product sheet, the use of font size 6, navy blue text (as indicated by RGB code 23238E), and a two-color ribbon design give the table the look of a real product sheet. Consider the following example, with these added elements highlighted in boldface:

```
<HTML>
<BODY TEXT="23238E">
<CENTER>
<TABLE BORDER=7 CELLPADDING=6 CELLSPACING=6 WIDTH="80%">
  <TR>
```

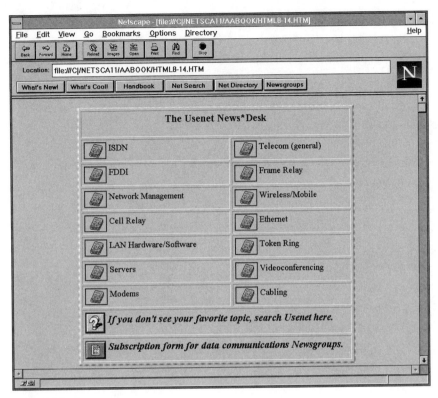

Figure 8.14

```
        <TH COLSPAN=5 ALIGN=LEFT><FONT SIZE=6>Traffic-
Cop/2000</FONT><IMG SCR="ribbon.gif" ALIGN=RIGHT>
   <I><FONT SIZE=4>Cross-Platform Networking
Server</FONT></I><BR><ALIGN=CENTER><FONT=3>from Streamer
Corp.</FONT></TH></TR>
   <TR ALIGN=LEFT>
        <TD COLSPAN=5> Traffic-Cop/2000 is a 2-port, multiprotocol
Internet router and remote access server for branch offices. Use it
to access the Internet, link one office to another, allow users to
remotely access the LAN, and give users the ability to dial out to
remote services.
<P>
<UL>
<LI>Provides multiple WAN interfaces
<LI>Supports multiple WAN protocols
<LI>Supports current security standards
<LI>Offers remote management features
<LI>Uses state-of-the-art hardware
</UL>
</TD> </TR>
   <TR ALIGN=CENTER>
        <TH>WAN Interface Options</TH> <TH>WAN Protocols</TH><TH>
Security Features</TH><TH>Management</TH><TH>Hardware</TH></TR>
   <TR ALIGN=CENTER>
        <TD>RS-232</TD> <TD>PPP</TD><TD>CHAP</TD><TD>Define access
levels</TD><TD>MC68306 processor</TD></TR>
   <TR ALIGN=CENTER>
```

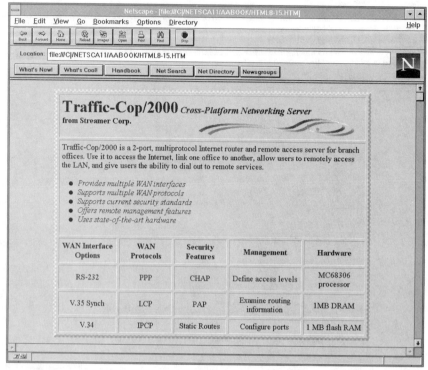

Figure 8.15

```
        <TD>V.35 Synch</TD> <TD>LCP</TD> <TD>PAP</TD><TD>Examine
routing information<TD>1MB DRAM</TD></TR>
   <TR ALIGN=CENTER>
        <TD>V.34</TD><TD>IPCP</TD><TD>Static Routes</TD><TD>Configure
ports</TD><TD>1 MB flash RAM</TD></TR>
</TABLE>
</CENTER>
</BODY>
</HTML>
```

The table appears in Netscape as in Figure 8.15 above.

Instead of an abstract design, you could easily use a corporate logo or a scanned photo of a product—anything that seems appropriate. Keep in mind that when graphics are used in tables, they can be somewhat disruptive, causing cells to become larger, for example. This applies as well to the use of different font sizes. You might have to experiment to keep all of the elements in the table balanced.

Embedding Hypertext Links within Tables

Hypertext links can be embedded in any or all cells of a table using the anchor tags, which are structured as <A HREF="file.name"> . . . </A>.

In the following coding example, hypertext links are embedded in the Periodic Table of Elements (several versions, including this one, are posted on the World Wide Web). In this case, the links take the user to other files that provide additional information about each element, such as its atomic number, atomic weight or mass number, density, discoverer's biography, and date of discovery.

```
<HTML>
<BODY>
<HR>
<H3>Select an element by clicking on it.</H3>
<CENTER>
<TABLE BORDER>
<CAPTION> <B>The Periodic Table of Elements</B> </CAPTION>
<TR>
<TD ALIGN=CENTER>1</TD>
<TD ALIGN=CENTER>2</TD>
<TD ALIGN=CENTER>3</TD>
<TD ALIGN=CENTER>4</TD>
<TD ALIGN=CENTER>5</TD>
<TD ALIGN=CENTER>6</TD>
<TD ALIGN=CENTER>7</TD>
<TD ALIGN=CENTER>8</TD>
<TD ALIGN=CENTER>9</TD>
<TD ALIGN=CENTER>10</TD>
<TD ALIGN=CENTER>11</TD>
<TD ALIGN=CENTER>12</TD>
<TD ALIGN=CENTER>13</TD>
<TD ALIGN=CENTER>14</TD>
<TD ALIGN=CENTER>15</TD>
<TD ALIGN=CENTER>16</TD>
<TD ALIGN=CENTER>17</TD>
<TD ALIGN=CENTER>18</TD>
</TR>
<TR>
<TD ALIGN=CENTER><A HREF="H.HTML">H</A></TD>
<TD COLSPAN=16></TD>
<TD ALIGN=CENTER><A HREF="HE.HTML">He</A></TD>
</TR>
<TR>
<TD ALIGN=CENTER><A HREF="LI.HTML">Li</A></TD>
<TD ALIGN=CENTER><A HREF="BE.HTML">Be</A></TD>
<TD COLSPAN=10></TD>
<TD ALIGN=CENTER><A HREF="B.HTML">B</A></TD>
<TD ALIGN=CENTER><A HREF="C.HTML">C</A></TD>
<TD ALIGN=CENTER><A HREF="N.HTML">N</A></TD>
<TD ALIGN=CENTER><A HREF="O.HTML">O</A></TD>
<TD ALIGN=CENTER><A HREF="F.HTML">F</A></TD>
<TD ALIGN=CENTER><A HREF="NE.HTML">Ne</A></TD>
</TR>
<TR>
<TD ALIGN=CENTER><A HREF="NA.HTML">Na</A></TD>
<TD ALIGN=CENTER><A HREF="MG.HTML">Mg</A></TD>
<TD COLSPAN=10></TD>
<TD ALIGN=CENTER><A HREF="AL.HTML">Al</A></TD>
<TD ALIGN=CENTER><A HREF="SI.HTML">Si</A></TD>
<TD ALIGN=CENTER><A HREF="P.HTML">P</A></TD>
<TD ALIGN=CENTER><A HREF="S.HTML">S</A></TD>
<TD ALIGN=CENTER><A HREF="CL.HTML">Cl</A></TD>
<TD ALIGN=CENTER><A HREF="AR.HTML">Ar</A></TD>
</TR>
<TR>
```

```
<TD ALIGN=CENTER><A HREF="K.HTML">K</A></TD>
<TD ALIGN=CENTER><A HREF="CA.HTML">Ca</A></TD>
<TD ALIGN=CENTER><A HREF="SC.HTML">Sc</A></TD>
<TD ALIGN=CENTER><A HREF="TI.HTML">Ti</A></TD>
<TD ALIGN=CENTER><A HREF="V.HTML">V</A></TD>
<TD ALIGN=CENTER><A HREF="CR.HTML">Cr</A></TD>
<TD ALIGN=CENTER><A HREF="MN.HTML">Mn</A></TD>
<TD ALIGN=CENTER><A HREF="FE.HTML">Fe</A></TD>
<TD ALIGN=CENTER><A HREF="CO.HTML">Co</A></TD>
<TD ALIGN=CENTER><A HREF="NI.HTML">Ni</A></TD>
<TD ALIGN=CENTER><A HREF="CU.HTML">Cu</A></TD>
<TD ALIGN=CENTER><A HREF="ZN.HTML">Zn</A></TD>
<TD ALIGN=CENTER><A HREF="GA.HTML">Ga</A></TD>
<TD ALIGN=CENTER><A HREF="GE.HTML">Ge</A></TD>
<TD ALIGN=CENTER><A HREF="AS.HTML">As</A></TD>
<TD ALIGN=CENTER><A HREF="SE.HTML">Se</A></TD>
<TD ALIGN=CENTER><A HREF="BR.HTML">Br</A></TD>
<TD ALIGN=CENTER><A HREF="KR.HTML">Kr</A></TD>
</TR>
<TR>
<TD ALIGN=CENTER><A HREF="RB.HTML">Rb</A></TD>
<TD ALIGN=CENTER><A HREF="SR.HTML">Sr</A></TD>
<TD ALIGN=CENTER><A HREF="Y.HTML">Y</A></TD>
<TD ALIGN=CENTER><A HREF="ZR.HTML">Zr</A></TD>
<TD ALIGN=CENTER><A HREF="NB.HTML">Nb</A></TD>
<TD ALIGN=CENTER><A HREF="MO.HTML">Mo</A></TD>
<TD ALIGN=CENTER><A HREF="TC.HTML">Tc</A></TD>
<TD ALIGN=CENTER><A HREF="RU.HTML">Ru</A></TD>
<TD ALIGN=CENTER><A HREF="RH.HTML">Rh</A></TD>
<TD ALIGN=CENTER><A HREF="PD.HTML">Pd</A></TD>
<TD ALIGN=CENTER><A HREF="AG.HTML">Ag</A></TD>
<TD ALIGN=CENTER><A HREF="CD.HTML">Cd</A></TD>
<TD ALIGN=CENTER><A HREF="IN.HTML">In</A></TD>
<TD ALIGN=CENTER><A HREF="SN.HTML">Sn</A></TD>
<TD ALIGN=CENTER><A HREF="SB.HTML">Sb</A></TD>
<TD ALIGN=CENTER><A HREF="TE.HTML">Te</A></TD>
<TD ALIGN=CENTER><A HREF="I.HTML">I</A></TD>
<TD ALIGN=CENTER><A HREF="XE.HTML">Xe</A></TD>
</TR>
<TR>
<TD ALIGN=CENTER><A HREF="CS.HTML">Cs</A></TD>
<TD ALIGN=CENTER><A HREF="BA.HTML">Ba</A></TD>
<TD ALIGN=CENTER>*</TD>
<TD ALIGN=CENTER><A HREF="HF.HTML">Hf</A></TD>
<TD ALIGN=CENTER><A HREF="TA.HTML">Ta</A></TD>
<TD ALIGN=CENTER><A HREF="W.HTML">W</A></TD>
<TD ALIGN=CENTER><A HREF="RE.HTML">Re</A></TD>
<TD ALIGN=CENTER><A HREF="OS.HTML">Os</A></TD>
<TD ALIGN=CENTER><A HREF="IR.HTML">Ir</A></TD>
<TD ALIGN=CENTER><A HREF="PT.HTML">Pt</A></TD>
<TD ALIGN=CENTER><A HREF="AU.HTML">Au</A></TD>
<TD ALIGN=CENTER><A HREF="HG.HTML">Hg</A></TD>
<TD ALIGN=CENTER><A HREF="TL.HTML">Tl</A></TD>
<TD ALIGN=CENTER><A HREF="PB.HTML">Pb</A></TD>
<TD ALIGN=CENTER><A HREF="BI.HTML">Bi</A></TD>
<TD ALIGN=CENTER><A HREF="PO.HTML">Po</A></TD>
<TD ALIGN=CENTER><A HREF="AT.HTML">At</A></TD>
<TD ALIGN=CENTER><A HREF="RN.HTML">Rn</A></TD>
</TR>
<TR>
<TD ALIGN=CENTER><A HREF="FR.HTML">Fr</A></TD>
<TD ALIGN=CENTER><A HREF="RA.HTML">Ra</A></TD>
<TD ALIGN=CENTER>**</TD>
<TD ALIGN=CENTER><A HREF="RF.HTML">Rf</A></TD>
<TD ALIGN=CENTER><A HREF="HA.HTML">Ha</A></TD>
```

```
<TD ALIGN=CENTER><A HREF="SG.HTML">Sg</A></TD>
<TD ALIGN=CENTER><A HREF="NS.HTML">Ns</A></TD>
<TD ALIGN=CENTER><A HREF="HS.HTML">Hs</A></TD>
<TD ALIGN=CENTER><A HREF="MT.HTML">Mt</A></TD>
</TR>
</TABLE>
<P>
<UL>
<TABLE BORDER>
<TR>
<TD ALIGN=CENTER>*</TD>
<TD ALIGN=CENTER><A HREF="LA.HTML">La</A></TD>
<TD ALIGN=CENTER><A HREF="CE.HTML">Ce</A></TD>
<TD ALIGN=CENTER><A HREF="PR.HTML">Pr</A></TD>
<TD ALIGN=CENTER><A HREF="ND.HTML">Nd</A></TD>
<TD ALIGN=CENTER><A HREF="PM.HTML">Pm</A></TD>
<TD ALIGN=CENTER><A HREF="SM.HTML">Sm</A></TD>
<TD ALIGN=CENTER><A HREF="EU.HTML">Eu</A></TD>
<TD ALIGN=CENTER><A HREF="GD.HTML">Gd</A></TD>
<TD ALIGN=CENTER><A HREF="TB.HTML">Tb</A></TD>
<TD ALIGN=CENTER><A HREF="DY.HTML">Dy</A></TD>
<TD ALIGN=CENTER><A HREF="HO.HTML">Ho</A></TD>
<TD ALIGN=CENTER><A HREF="ER.HTML">Er</A></TD>
<TD ALIGN=CENTER><A HREF="TM.HTML">Tm</A></TD>
<TD ALIGN=CENTER><A HREF="YB.HTML">Yb</A></TD>
<TD ALIGN=CENTER><A HREF="LU.HTML">Lu</A></TD>
</TR>
<TR>
<TD ALIGN=CENTER>**</TD>
<TD ALIGN=CENTER><A HREF="AC.HTML">Ac</A></TD>
<TD ALIGN=CENTER><A HREF="TH.HTML">Th</A></TD>
<TD ALIGN=CENTER><A HREF="PA.HTML">Pa</A></TD>
<TD ALIGN=CENTER><A HREF="U.HTML">U</A></TD>
<TD ALIGN=CENTER><A HREF="NP.HTML">Np</A></TD>
<TD ALIGN=CENTER><A HREF="PU.HTML">Pu</A></TD>
<TD ALIGN=CENTER><A HREF="AM.HTML">Am</A></TD>
<TD ALIGN=CENTER><A HREF="CM.HTML">Cm</A></TD>
<TD ALIGN=CENTER><A HREF="BK.HTML">Bk</A></TD>
<TD ALIGN=CENTER><A HREF="CF.HTML">Cf</A></TD>
<TD ALIGN=CENTER><A HREF="ES.HTML">Es</A></TD>
<TD ALIGN=CENTER><A HREF="FM.HTML">Fm</A></TD>
<TD ALIGN=CENTER><A HREF="MD.HTML">Md</A></TD>
<TD ALIGN=CENTER><A HREF="NO.HTML">No</A></TD>
<TD ALIGN=CENTER><A HREF="LR.HTML">Lr</A></TD>
</TABLE>
</UL>
</CENTER>
</BODY>
</HTML>
```

In Netscape, the table appears as in Figure 8.16.

Creating a Decision Tree

Another type of table is the decision tree. This, too, can be coded in HTML. Keep in mind that there usually will be a lot of blank space in the decision tree, which must be accounted for when coding.

In the following coding example, the reader is being stepped through a sequence of decision points that will lead to the selection of the most appro-

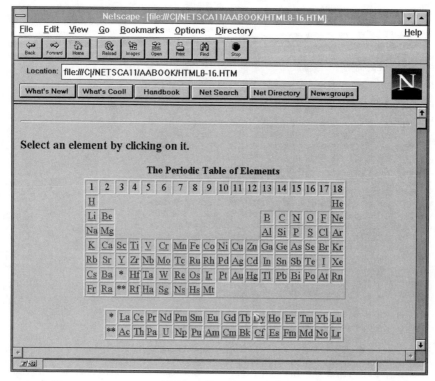

Figure 8.16

priate windows platform for his or her needs. The three items in boldface are the starting points of the decision tree:

```
<HTML>
<BODY>
<H2>Decision Tree</H2>
<P>
<STRONG>Choose the right Windows.</STRONG> Start on the left. Choose
from among the three factors that are most important to you. Keep
going to the right until you have narrowed down the best windows
operating system for you.
<P>
<TABLE BORDER CELLPADDING=4 CELLSPACING=2 WIDTH="85%">
<CAPTION ALIGN=BOTTOM>Source: <I>PC Computing</I> June
1995.</CAPTION>
<CENTER>
<TR><TD ALIGN=LEFT><TD ALIGN=LEFT><TD ALIGN=LEFT><TD ALIGN=LEFT><TD
ALIGN=LEFT><TD ALIGN=LEFT><TD ALIGN=LEFT><TD ALIGN=LEFT><TD
ALIGN=LEFT><TD ALIGN=LEFT></TR>

<TR><TD ALIGN=LEFT><TD ALIGN=LEFT><TD ALIGN=LEFT><TD ALIGN=LEFT><TD
ALIGN=LEFT>Service &amp; Support<TD ALIGN=LEFT><TD ALIGN=LEFT><TD
ALIGN=LEFT>Windows for Workgroups<TD ALIGN=LEFT><TD ALIGN=LEFT></TR>

<TR><TD ALIGN=LEFT><TD ALIGN=LEFT><TD ALIGN=LEFT>Performance<TD
ALIGN=LEFT><TD ALIGN=LEFT><TD ALIGN=LEFT><TD ALIGN=LEFT><TD
ALIGN=LEFT><TD ALIGN=LEFT><TD ALIGN=LEFT></TR>
```

```
<TR><TD ALIGN=LEFT><TD ALIGN=LEFT><TD ALIGN=LEFT><TD ALIGN=LEFT><TD
ALIGN=LEFT>Low Hardware Requirements<TD ALIGN=LEFT><TD ALIGN=LEFT><TD
ALIGN=LEFT>Windows 3.1<TD ALIGN=LEFT><TD ALIGN=LEFT></TR>

<TR><TD ALIGN=LEFT><B>Compatibility</B><TD ALIGN=LEFT><TD
ALIGN=LEFT><TD ALIGN=LEFT><TD ALIGN=LEFT><TD ALIGN=LEFT><TD
ALIGN=LEFT><TD ALIGN=LEFT><TD ALIGN=LEFT><TD ALIGN=LEFT></TR>

<TR><TD ALIGN=LEFT><TD ALIGN=LEFT><TD ALIGN=LEFT><TD ALIGN=LEFT><TD
ALIGN=LEFT>Service &amp; Support<TD ALIGN=LEFT><TD ALIGN=LEFT><TD
ALIGN=LEFT>Windows for Workgroups<TD ALIGN=LEFT><TD ALIGN=LEFT></TR>

<TR><TD ALIGN=LEFT><TD ALIGN=LEFT><TD ALIGN=LEFT>Networking<TD
ALIGN=LEFT><TD ALIGN=LEFT><TD ALIGN=LEFT><TD ALIGN=LEFT><TD
ALIGN=LEFT><TD ALIGN=LEFT><TD ALIGN=LEFT></TR>

<TR><TD ALIGN=LEFT><TD ALIGN=LEFT><TD ALIGN=LEFT><TD ALIGN=LEFT><TD
ALIGN=LEFT>Ease of Installation<TD ALIGN=LEFT><TD ALIGN=LEFT><TD
ALIGN=LEFT>Windows 95<TD ALIGN=LEFT><TD ALIGN=LEFT></TR>

<TR><TD ALIGN=LEFT><TD ALIGN=LEFT><TD ALIGN=LEFT><TD ALIGN=LEFT><TD
ALIGN=LEFT><TD ALIGN=LEFT><TD ALIGN=LEFT><TD ALIGN=LEFT><TD
ALIGN=LEFT><TD ALIGN=LEFT></TR>

<TR><TD ALIGN=LEFT><TD ALIGN=LEFT><TD ALIGN=LEFT><TD ALIGN=LEFT><TD
ALIGN=LEFT><TD ALIGN=LEFT><TD ALIGN=LEFT><TD ALIGN=LEFT><TD
ALIGN=LEFT><TD ALIGN=LEFT></TR>

<TR><TD ALIGN=LEFT><TD ALIGN=LEFT><TD ALIGN=LEFT><TD ALIGN=LEFT><TD
ALIGN=LEFT>Multimedia<TD ALIGN=LEFT><TD ALIGN=LEFT><TD
ALIGN=LEFT>Windows 95<TD ALIGN=LEFT><TD ALIGN=LEFT></TR>

<TR><TD ALIGN=LEFT><TD ALIGN=LEFT><TD ALIGN=LEFT>Ease of
Installation<TD ALIGN=LEFT><TD ALIGN=LEFT><TD ALIGN=LEFT><TD
ALIGN=LEFT><TD ALIGN=LEFT><TD ALIGN=LEFT><TD ALIGN=LEFT></TR>

<TR><TD ALIGN=LEFT><TD ALIGN=LEFT><TD ALIGN=LEFT><TD ALIGN=LEFT><TD
ALIGN=LEFT>Low Hardware Requirements<TD ALIGN=LEFT><TD ALIGN=LEFT><TD
ALIGN=LEFT>Windows 3.1<TD ALIGN=LEFT><TD ALIGN=LEFT></TR>

<TR><TD ALIGN=LEFT><B>Performance</B><TD ALIGN=LEFT><TD
ALIGN=LEFT><TD ALIGN=LEFT><TD ALIGN=LEFT><TD ALIGN=LEFT><TD
ALIGN=LEFT><TD ALIGN=LEFT><TD ALIGN=LEFT><TD ALIGN=LEFT></TR>

<TR><TD ALIGN=LEFT><TD ALIGN=LEFT><TD ALIGN=LEFT><TD ALIGN=LEFT><TD
ALIGN=LEFT>Service &amp; Support<TD ALIGN=LEFT><TD ALIGN=LEFT><TD
ALIGN=LEFT>OS/2, Version 3<TD ALIGN=LEFT><TD ALIGN=LEFT></TR>

<TR><TD ALIGN=LEFT><TD ALIGN=LEFT><TD ALIGN=LEFT>Internet Support<TD
ALIGN=LEFT><TD ALIGN=LEFT><TD ALIGN=LEFT><TD ALIGN=LEFT><TD
ALIGN=LEFT><TD ALIGN=LEFT><TD ALIGN=LEFT></TR>

<TR><TD ALIGN=LEFT><TD ALIGN=LEFT><TD ALIGN=LEFT><TD ALIGN=LEFT><TD
ALIGN=LEFT>Flexibility<TD ALIGN=LEFT><TD ALIGN=LEFT><TD
ALIGN=LEFT>Windows 95<TD ALIGN=LEFT><TD ALIGN=LEFT></TR>

<TR><TD ALIGN=LEFT><TD ALIGN=LEFT><TD ALIGN=LEFT><TD ALIGN=LEFT><TD
ALIGN=LEFT><TD ALIGN=LEFT><TD ALIGN=LEFT><TD ALIGN=LEFT><TD
ALIGN=LEFT><TD ALIGN=LEFT></TR>

<TR><TD ALIGN=LEFT><TD ALIGN=LEFT><TD ALIGN=LEFT><TD ALIGN=LEFT><TD
ALIGN=LEFT><TD ALIGN=LEFT><TD ALIGN=LEFT><TD ALIGN=LEFT><TD
ALIGN=LEFT><TD ALIGN=LEFT></TR>

<TR><TD ALIGN=LEFT><TD ALIGN=LEFT><TD ALIGN=LEFT><TD ALIGN=LEFT><TD
ALIGN=LEFT>Service &amp; Support<TD ALIGN=LEFT><TD ALIGN=LEFT><TD
ALIGN=LEFT>Windows for Workgroups<TD ALIGN=LEFT><TD ALIGN=LEFT></TR>
```

```
<TR><TD ALIGN=LEFT><TD ALIGN=LEFT><TD ALIGN=LEFT>Compatibility<TD
ALIGN=LEFT><TD ALIGN=LEFT><TD ALIGN=LEFT><TD ALIGN=LEFT><TD
ALIGN=LEFT><TD ALIGN=LEFT><TD ALIGN=LEFT></TR>

<TR><TD ALIGN=LEFT><TD ALIGN=LEFT><TD ALIGN=LEFT><TD ALIGN=LEFT><TD
ALIGN=LEFT>Scalability<TD ALIGN=LEFT><TD ALIGN=LEFT><TD
ALIGN=LEFT>Windows NT 3.5<TD ALIGN=LEFT><TD ALIGN=LEFT></TR>

<TR><TD ALIGN=LEFT><B>Networking</B><TD ALIGN=LEFT><TD ALIGN=LEFT><TD
ALIGN=LEFT><TD ALIGN=LEFT><TD ALIGN=LEFT><TD ALIGN=LEFT><TD
ALIGN=LEFT><TD ALIGN=LEFT><TD ALIGN=LEFT></TR>

<TR><TD ALIGN=LEFT><TD ALIGN=LEFT><TD ALIGN=LEFT><TD ALIGN=LEFT><TD
ALIGN=LEFT>Internet Support<TD ALIGN=LEFT><TD ALIGN=LEFT><TD
ALIGN=LEFT>Windows 95<TD ALIGN=LEFT><TD ALIGN=LEFT></TR>

<TR><TD ALIGN=LEFT><TD ALIGN=LEFT><TD ALIGN=LEFT>NetWare Support<TD
ALIGN=LEFT><TD ALIGN=LEFT><TD ALIGN=LEFT><TD ALIGN=LEFT><TD
ALIGN=LEFT><TD ALIGN=LEFT><TD ALIGN=LEFT></TR>

<TR><TD ALIGN=LEFT><TD ALIGN=LEFT><TD ALIGN=LEFT><TD ALIGN=LEFT><TD
ALIGN=LEFT>Ease of Installation<TD ALIGN=LEFT><TD ALIGN=LEFT><TD
ALIGN=LEFT>Windows 95<TD ALIGN=LEFT><TD ALIGN=LEFT></TR>

<TR><TD ALIGN=LEFT><TD ALIGN=LEFT><TD ALIGN=LEFT><TD ALIGN=LEFT><TD
ALIGN=LEFT><TD ALIGN=LEFT><TD ALIGN=LEFT><TD ALIGN=LEFT><TD
ALIGN=LEFT><TD ALIGN=LEFT></TR>
</TABLE>
</CENTER>
</BODY>
</HTML>
```

In Netscape, the decision tree looks like that in Figure 8.17.

As you can see, the amount of coding is quite large and would probably discourage anyone from developing a decision tree in the first place. Actually, this decision tree was not manually coded. It was generated by a macro that works with Microsoft's Excel spreadsheet program. The macro, called XL2HTML and created by Jordan Evans, is freeware and may be freely distributed. It is posted on the Internet at:

```
http://www.710.gsfc.nasa.gov/704/dgd/xl2html.html
```

For convenience this macro is included in HTMLdisk. Just load it into your Excel directory and follow the instructions contained in the README.TXT file, which also is on HTMLdisk.

The advantage of using a spreadsheet is that its inherent cell structure allows you to easily visualize and map out tables, unencumbered by HTML code. You can use such methods as cut-and-paste to easily design any type of table. When you are satisfied with the layout of your table, you can apply the XL2HTML macro to translate it into the HTML format.

Figure 8.18 shows how the decision tree looks as designed in Excel 5.0.

The XL2HTML macro does not do all the work for you—just the basics. For example, if you want to use colored text or specify attributes for the table, you have to do it yourself. Also, tables that are coded by such HTML converters tend to use more code than is really necessary. On the positive side, the results are the same and with a lot less work.

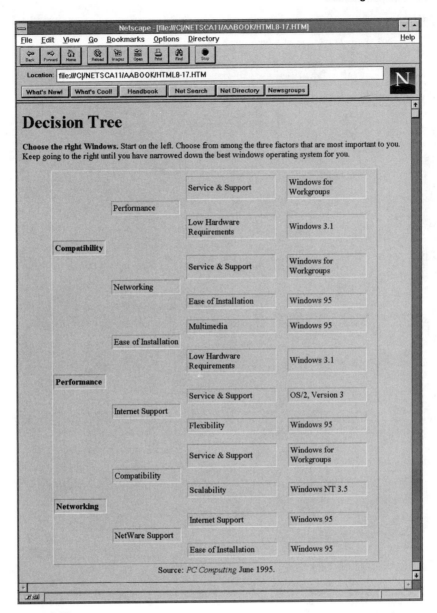

Figure 8.17

Embedding Forms within Tables

Using the information in chapter 7 about creating forms and the information in this chapter about creating tables, let's combine a form and table in a single structure. What follows is a front-end HTML-coded form for the Web-Crawler search engine, which is encapsulated in a table. WebCrawler, originally developed at the University of Washington, is now owned and op-

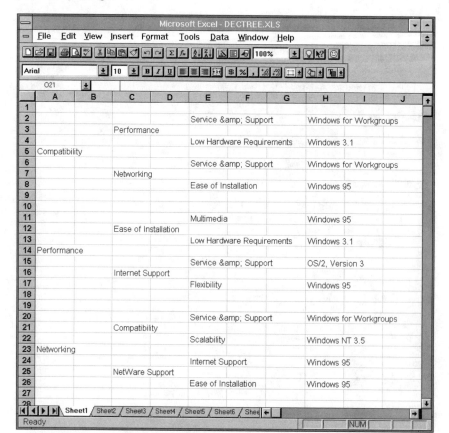

Figure 8.18

erated by America Online as a service to the Internet. I call my front-end form Web*Crawler Jr.

```
<HTML>
<HEAD>
<BODY>
<CENTER>
<TABLE BORDER=8 CELLPADDING=6 CELLSPACING=6 WIDTH="60%">
<TR>
        <TH COLSPAN=1><FONT SIZE=6><I>Web*Crawler
Jr.</I></FONT></TH></TR>
        <TR ALIGN=LEFT>
        <TD COLSPAN=1>Type in your search keywords here. Use as many
relevant keywords as possible:</TD></TR>
<FORM ACTION="http://webcrawler.com/cgi-bin/WebQuery" METHOD="POST">
<TR ALIGN=LEFT>
        <TD><INPUT NAME="searchText" SIZE=65,4></TD></TR>
<TR ALIGN=LEFT>
        <TD><INPUT TYPE="submit" VALUE="Search> <INPUT TYPE= RESET
VALUE=" Clear "></TD></TR>
<TR ALIGN=LEFT>
        <TD><INPUT type="checkbox" NAME="andOr" VALUE="and" CHECKED>
use <B>AND</B> to separate multiple words.</TD></TR>
<TR ALIGN=RIGHT>
```

```
        <TD>Number of results to return: <SELECT NAME="maxHits"><OP-
TION>50<OPTION>100<OPTION>500<OPTION>1000</SELECT></TD></TR>
</FORM>
</TABLE>
</CENTER>
</BODY>
</HTML>
```

The "search table" appears in Netscape as shown in Figure 8.19.

The front-end form to WebCrawler is included in HTMLdisk and, when loaded, is fully functional.

Table Design Tips

Before concluding this chapter, it is worth summarizing a few design tips that make for better tables in general:

- Lay out the basic design for complex tables before attempting to code them. Remember to code horizontally from left to right, rather than vertically from top to bottom. Blank space must be accounted for in the coding.

- Using a spreadsheet to visualize the finished table helps the coding process go a lot easier and faster, even if you do not want to use conversion utilities that tend to inflate the amount of code.

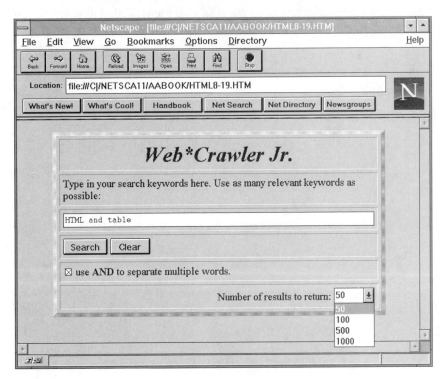

Figure 8.19

- Printing out your table from Netscape provides a cell-based map that can be used for further editing, or as a starting point for creating new tables.

- Tables are intended to convey a lot of information in a minimum amount of space. Coding long tables that span several screens defeats the purpose of using tables.

- One way to avoid a long or crowded table is to embed hypertext links within cells to allow the reader to obtain additional information in other files. This allows the table to convey basic information, while taking on the functionality of a menu.

Finally, creating an attractive as well as informative table requires a sense of balance. For example, in most cases it is not a good idea to mix table data that flushes left in one row of cells and right in another. Likewise, if you start with table heads centered in their cells, do not suddenly change to heads that are aligned left or right in other cells. Concerning the use of RGB color codes, they should be used to add impact to tables, not distract the reader from the table's content. For example, select colors that make the text easier to read, not more difficult to read.

This chapter has presented some ways of creating different types of tables using some of the tags, attributes, and values proposed in the draft HTML 3.0 specification. The draft specification provides much more flexibility in the design of tables than is available under HTML 2.0, allowing you to be much more creative in displaying information.

Server-Side Includes

The term "server-side includes" refers to the ability of the server to auto-matically modify a file as it is served, such as by inserting one file into an-other, according to the special instructions embedded in your HTML documents. In addition to other files, server-side includes can be used to in-sert other types of information at specified places in your files, such as a counter for keeping track of the number of times a particular document has been accessed. Even the current day of the week, date, and time can be dis-played in a variety of formats using server-side includes. As demonstrated in chapter 7, a variation of the server-side include (structured as environmen-tal variables) can be used in CGI programs to return useful information as part of the e-mail output from processed forms. (See the highlighted por-tions of the Perl script for processing a help request form and the e-mail out-put illustrated in Figure 7.23.)

Before actually embedding server-side includes in your documents, you should determine whether your server supports them. The easiest way to determine if server-side includes are supported is to ask the system admin-istrator. Most Web servers support this feature, but for one reason or another the system administrator may have disabled it for system-wide implementa-tion, preferring instead to implement it on a selective basis. In addition, there may be particular server-side includes that the system administrator will not support at all because of potential performance or security concerns.

If the Web site is very busy, the system administrator may decide not to turn on server-side includes at all because they can place a heavy process-ing burden on the server. Overuse of server-side includes can noticeably im-pact server performance. However, at normal Web sites server-side includes will not usually present a problem.

Security is another concern of the system administrator. Many system ad-ministrators are not comfortable with average users executing server-based commands and will not turn on the server-side include as a matter of policy. Even if the execute (exec) option is disabled to reduce the security risk, the potential performance drain remains an issue for busy Web sites.

File Naming Conventions

Another thing to be aware of when using server-side includes is that every file that contains an include statement must be renamed with the .shtml file extension. This is typically done after the file is loaded to the UNIX or Windows NT server via FTP or telnet, because most Windows- and DOS-based computers do not recognize file extensions of more than three characters. If you are just beginning to develop your Web pages, this is not a real concern. But if you have a large amount of hyperlinked documents and your Web site has been operating for a long time, suddenly adding include statements into your documents can cause three major problems:

- First, when renaming an HTML document with the .shtml extension, you also must rename any references to it in your other documents or the hypertext links will not work. The hypertext links you already have are looking for files with the .html extension, not the .shtml extension.

- Second, if you use include statements on your home page, it too must be renamed with the .shtml extension. This can pose problems when others try to access your home page through bookmarks and Web search engines—all of which may still be referencing the original .html extension for your home page.

- Finally, if other Web sites reference any of your documents with hypertext links, those links will become invalid, because they are keyed to the .html file extension and not the .shtml extension.

Does all this mean you should avoid using server-side includes? The short answer is no. A long-term solution would be to phase them in when adding new documents, which minimizes your exposure to problems with existing hypertext links.

With regard to the home page, there is an effective solution that automates the redirection of users from the old page to the new page. (Other uses of meta-information are discussed at the end of this chapter.) Depending on how it is set up, the transfer can be entirely transparent to users or display a brief message. To accomplish this, you must create a new file that contains instructions as meta-information that appears in the first line.

The following HTML coding example is a complete file containing such meta-information:

```
<META HTTP-EQUIV="Refresh" CONTENT="1;
URL=http://iquest.com/~nmuller/index.shtml">
<HTML>
<HEAD>
```

```
<TITLE>Strategic Information Resources</TITLE>
</HEAD>
<BODY BACKGROUND="back04.gif" TEXT="#0000FF" LINK="#9F5F9F">
</BODY>
</HTML>
```

This file is renamed with the same file name users would normally access, keeping the .html extension. The META tag attributes redirect the request to the new URL with the .shtml extension. In this case, the redirection takes the shortest amount of time, as specified by the number 1. If you would like to display a short message, before the redirection occurs, you should increase this value to 4 or 5, or even more. Some experimentation might be necessary to arrive at an appropriate value for the size of the message you want to display.

Another application for this redirection is when you have to change the location of your files from one server to another. Instead of users encountering error messages when they try to access your old URL, you can momentarily display a message explaining that you have moved and reminding them to set new bookmarks—all before the redirection occurs. When users arrive at your new location, they can bookmark it for future reference. Of course, the same goal can be achieved by creating a temporary file that contains a hypertext link to your new URL, but you risk the user changing his or her mind.

Including Another File within a Document

One of the most useful implementations of server-side includes is the ability to specify the appearance of another file within a document as it is being loaded. Let's say that you have a large collection of documents that contains a fairly lengthy standard message at the beginning or end of each document. Instead of typing that message into each and every document, all you need to do is type it once and save it as a separate file. Then all you have to do is put a simple include statement in each of your documents that references that file. When a particular document is accessed, the standard message(s) will appear automatically, and in the desired place.

For example, I use the following standard message at the end of some of the documents I write for my Web page, which is called Strategic Information Resources (http://iquest.com/~nmuller/index.shtml):

```
Source: Strategic Information Resources
Copyright 1995 by Nathan J. Muller
All rights reserved.
E-mail: nmuller@ddx.com
```

Whenever one of my documents is displayed or printed, this standard message will appear at the bottom. This message is saved in a file called copyr.html. The HTML coding for the message is:

```
<HTML>
<BODY>
<B>Source:</B> Strategic Information Resources<BR>
Copyright &copy; by 1995 Nathan J. Muller<BR>
```

```
All rights reserved.<BR>
E-mail: <A HREF="mailto:nmuller@ddx.com">nmuller@ddx.com</A><BR>
</BODY>
</HTML>
```

The message includes a hypertext link to a simple pop-up e-mail form (via `mailto`), making it easier for users to send me comments or ask questions about anything in the document. You should be aware that not all browsers support mailto, but you can substitute a link to any e-mail form.

The server-side include that calls up the message file is very simple and is written as:

```
<!--#include FILE="copyr.html"-->
```

This statement appears as the last line in the body of my document files so that the message appears as the last item. I could just as easily move it to the top portion of my documents to have the message displayed there, or I could vary the location of the message based on the type of document.

Figure 9.1 shows how the message appears at the end of a document when rendered by Netscape Navigator.

Server-side includes also make it easier to update standard information. For example, I might want to add the following statement to my standard message: "Permission to excerpt is granted, provided that the source is cited." Instead of updating all of my documents with this new line, I just

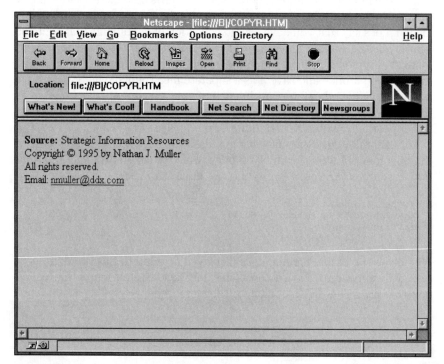

Figure 9.1

have to update one file and the change will be carried through to all of my documents automatically whenever they are displayed or printed.

Including Multiple Files within a Document

You can specify the appearance of multiple files within a document. One include can be used to provide a standard header and another include can be used to provide a standard footer. For example, a header include can call up a file with the author's name, e-mail address, and copyright information. The footer can provide subscription information and a hypertext link to a subscription order form.

The following HTML coding provides a sample document footer, which contains a hypertext link to an order form:

```
<HTML>
<BODY>
Technology Abstracts is published weekly by the ABC Company. If you
would like to subscribe to the full-text version of this service,
which includes in-depth analysis by leading industry experts, you can
place your order now, using our convenient <A HREF="ordform.html">
e-mail order form. </A>
</BODY>
</HTML>
```

The server-side include for this footer is written in the same way as the one used in the previous example, except that it references the file name of the HTML-coded message above:

```
<!--#include FILE="subscrib.html"-->
```

Another application of this type of server-side include is for logically connecting multiple files of a long document. Let's say that you have a long document and you want to break it up into three files so they load faster. This method of optimization introduces several problems:

- First, to read the whole document the user is forced to use a hypertext link to call up the next file. This introduces delay.

- Second, if the user wants to print the entire document or save it to disk, he or she must call up each file in turn and issue separate save or print commands.

- Third, if the user loses the connection before the next document is loaded, the process must be started again at the point of interruption after reestablishing the connection.

Using server-side includes to automate multifile document integration on the fly provides the load performance everyone wants, but without sacrificing convenience. As the first file is loaded, the user can scroll through the text as the remaining files load. When loading stops, the files can be saved to disk or printed with a single command.

Including a File from Another Directory

There may be times when the file you want to include in your document resides on the same server, but in a different directory.

The include is written in the following format:

```
<!--#include virtual="/~dirname/filename.html"-->
```

If the file you are specifying to include in your own document has inline images, they will not show up in your file unless your directory has the same image files. This can be overcome if all image files are assigned a single directory so that all HTML documents can reference them in the same way. Assigning image files to one directory also frees up valuable disk space on the server, because it eliminates the need for all users to have their own set of image files.

Displaying Date and Time within a Document

There are several possible server-side includes for dislaying the date and time, two of which are shown below; they provide the same information in different formats:

```
<!--#exec cmd="date"--> gives this format: Thu Jul 6 22:33:41 CDT 1995
<!--#echo var="DATE_LOCAL"--> gives this format: Friday, 07-Jul-95
09:08:40 CDT
```

The time zone that will be displayed is the one in which your server is located. If you are using these includes in the eastern time zone of the U.S., for example, the time zone designation will be EDT, for eastern daylight-saving time.

Time can also be expressed as GMT, as in the following server-side include:

```
<!--#echo var="DATE_GMT"-->, which gives this format: Wednesday,
19.Jul-95 02:42:04
```

Displaying Visitor Count within a Document

You can display a count of the visitors to your home page by inserting a server-side include that will display the number of accesses. There are several ways to write the include, one of which is shown below, along with text that puts the count into a context:

```
You are visitor number <!--#exec cgi="/cgi-bin/count.cgi"--> since
June 21, 1995.
```

Displaying Browser Type within a Document

For each visitor to your Web pages, you can echo back the type of browser they are using. This is accomplished as follows:

```
<!--#echo var="HTTP_USER_AGENT"-->
```

If the visitor happens to be using Netscape Navigator, the message echoed back reads as:

```
Mozilla/1.1N (Windows; I; 16bit)
```

Displaying Remote Identification within a Document

It is possible to display a greeting to visitors that includes an echo of their e-mail address. The include that accomplishes this is written as:

```
<!--#echo var="REMOTE_IDENT"--> or <!--echo var="cgi-bin/REMOTE_IDENT"-->
```

This include should be encapsulated with appropriate text, as in the following example:

```
Welcome <!--#echo var="REMOTE_IDENT"-->
```

An example of how the message might be displayed is:

```
Welcome nmuller@iquest.com
```

Be aware, however, that the REMOTE_IDENT variable may not always work. Some Web site system administrators turn off IDENT support entirely because it can cause performance problems for corporate users whose systems are behind network firewalls. A firewall is used for establishing security, and it may be configured to block the IDENT connections as part of that security.

If you use the REMOTE_IDENT variable in your Web home page and it does not work, the following message will be displayed to the user:

```
Welcome (none)
```

Displaying Remote Host within a Document

Alternatively, you can display a greeting to visitors by echoing back just their remote host name. One way to do this is with an include written as:

```
<!--#echo var="REMOTE_HOST"-->
```

For this include to make sense, it should be encapsulated with appropriate text, as in the following example:

```
Welcome <!--#echo var="REMOTE_HOST"-->!
```

An example of how the message would be displayed is:

```
Welcome nmuller.iquest.com!
```

Displaying Server Name within a Document

Sometimes it may be useful to display the name of the server that the current document resides on within the document itself. For example, if a company operates a private Web comprised of servers at each corporate location, it might be useful for users to know which server has the documents they are viewing—and in a more friendly format than the URL displayed by the browser.

The include is written as shown below, along with text that puts the server name in a context:

```
This document resides on server: <!--#echo var="SERVER_NAME"-->
```

When displayed, the message might reads as follows:

```
This document resides on server: iquest.com
```

Displaying Server Software and Version within a Document

The include for displaying server software (and version) is written as:

```
<!--#echo var="SERVER_SOFTWARE"-->
```

When the document containing this include is rendered, it might say something like this:

```
Apache/0.6.5
```

Displaying Server Port within a Document

The include for displaying the server's port is written as:

```
<!--#echo var="SERVER_PORT"-->
```

When the document containing this include is rendered, it might say 80, which is a standard Web port number. Other standard port numbers are 21 for FTP, 23 for Telnet, and 70 for Gopher. If a server is using a nonstandard port, that port will be echoed back to the user.

Displaying Server Administrator within a Document

The include for displaying the server administrator (e-mail address) is written as:

```
<!--#echo var="SERVER_ADMIN"-->
```

When rendered, the return for this include might be:

```
webmaster@iquest.com
```

Displaying Remote Address within a Document

The include for displaying the remote IP address of a user is:

```
<!--#echo var="REMOTE_ADDR"-->
```

When rendered, a remote IP address might look something like this:

```
204.177.193.22
```

Displaying Accepted Graphics Files within a Document

To return a listing of supported graphics files, the include is written as:

```
<!--#echo var="HTTP_ACCEPT"-->
```

When rendered, the return for this include might be:

```
*/*, image/gif, image/x-xbitmap, image/jpeg
```

Displaying Document URL within a Document

To echo back the URL of a document, the include is written as:

```
<!--#echo var="DOCUMENT_URI"-->
```

This include might be rendered as:

```
/~nmuller/filename.shtml
```

Displaying Document Name within a Document

To echo back the name of a document, the include is written as:

```
<!--#echo var="DOCUMENT_NAME"-->
```

This include might be rendered as:

```
filename.html
```

Displaying File Modification Date within a Document

Another useful application of the include is for displaying the file modification date of your Web documents. The include is written as shown below, along with text that puts the date in a context:

```
Last modified on:<BR>
<!--#flastmod file="filename.shtml"-->
```

When displayed, the message shows up as:

```
Last modified on:
Saturday, July 8, 1995
```

Displaying File Size within a Document

The size of a file, in bytes, can be displayed within the document. This information might be useful to provide, especially for long documents. It can give the user an idea of how long the document might take to download. The include is written as:

```
The size of this file is: <!--#fsize file="filename.shtml"-->
```

This include generally is not very accurate, but it provides a close enough approximation of file size.

Using Meta-Information

Meta-information is specified with the META tag. The META tag(s) is used within the HEAD tags to embed document meta-information not defined by other HTML tags. They can also be used to implement a special Netscape Navigator capability called client-pull.

Indexing

Meta-information can be extracted by servers/clients for use in identifying, indexing, and cataloging documents. For example, programs like ALIWEB (Archie-Like Indexing for the WEB), periodically scan Web sites and retrieve information about the various Web pages that reside there.

For ALIWEB to index your Web pages, the following tags must be present:

```
<META name="resource-type" content="document">
<META name="description" content="a sentence to a paragraph describing
your document">
<META name="keywords" content="key words">
<META name="distribution" content="global">
<META name="copyright" content="a sentence to a paragraph declaring
copyright and conditions of use">
```

The first four tags are required for ALIWEB to index your pages. Only the "copyright" tag is optional.

Screen refresh

In addition to URL redirection (mentioned earlier, under file naming conventions), another use of the META tag is for screen refresh. This can be used to provide updates to fast-changing information such as stock quotes, election results, and sports scores. This is implemented by a special capability supported by Netscape Navigator, (starting with version 1.1), which is called client-pull. With client-pull, the server sends to the browser data that includes a directive in the HTTP response or the document header. The directive might say "reload this data in 10 seconds," or "load this other URL in

10 seconds." The client does what it is told after the specified amount of time has elapsed; it either reloads the current data or gets new data from the server. In either case, a new HTTP connection is established.

Such an instruction might be written using the META tag as follows:

```
<META HTTP-EQUIV="refresh" content=10>
```

Normally, the user has to point and click to "reload" the document. This META tag reloads the document automatically. In the example above, the screen is refreshed at 10-second intervals. You can set the refresh rate to a longer or shorter interval, depending on how much information is displayed on the screen at one time.

If you have more than one document to refresh, you can add the URL of a second document to the META tag. This would cause the current document to reload and then specify the next document to be loaded in its place. To accomplish this, the META tag would be written as follows:

```
<META HTTP-EQUIV="refresh" content="10;
URL=http://iquest.com/newdoc.html">
```

Notice that the complete URL of the next document is required, even though it may be located in the same directory.

The second document can have a META tag that specifies the first document to load in its place. The user's browser will then flip back and forth between them indefinitely at the specified time interval, providing updates or new information as it does so. This client-pull capability can be used for other applications, such as running canned presentations.

Self-running presentations

Using the META tag in this fashion gives you the ability to design and implement self-running presentations. When accessed, the first screen is displayed for a specified time before being replaced by the next screen, and the next and the next, until the entire presentation has run its course. To automatically restart the presentation, the last document's META tag would contain the URL of the first document.

What follows is a sequence of document headers (which would normally appear in separate documents, of course) that make use of the META tags to automate a document presentation. The refresh rate is five seconds. Notice how each META tag points to the URL of the next document and how the last META tag points back to the first document—in effect, restarting the entire presentation.

```
<META HTTP-EQUIV="refresh" content="5; URL=http://iquest.com/~nmuller/
doc2.html">
<META HTTP-EQUIV="refresh" content="5; URL=http://iquest.com/~nmuller/
doc3.html">
<META HTTP-EQUIV="refresh" content="5; URL=http://iquest.com/~nmuller/
```

```
doc4.html">
<META HTTP-EQUIV="refresh" content="5; URL=http://iquest.com/~nmuller/
doc5.html">
<META HTTP-EQUIV="refresh" content="5; URL=http://iquest.com/~nmuller/
doc6.html">
<META HTTP-EQUIV="refresh" content="5; URL=http://iquest.com/~nmuller/
doc7.html">
<META HTTP-EQUIV="refresh" content="5; URL=http://iquest.com/~nmuller/
doc8.html">
<META HTTP-EQUIV="refresh" content="5; URL=http://iquest.com/~nmuller/
doc1.html">
```

Instead of an endlessly running presentation, you might want to give the user the option of returning to the main menu when the last document is called up. This can be accomplished by leaving out the META tag entirely and putting a hypertext link at the bottom of the document, which points to the file containing the main menu.

Another strategy would be to put a META tag in the last document and specify a refresh rate of 20 seconds (or longer), and to also provide a hypertext link back to the main menu. That way, if the user does not activate the hypertext link within the allotted time, the presentation will automatically start again from the beginning.

Summary

You can dress up your presentations with graphical objects and specify background color and text color. You can even use the fade-in/fade-out technique described in chapter 4. Keep in mind, however, that the more graphic-intensive you make your documents, the longer they will take to load.

Chapter 6 provides information on a related capability supported by Netscape Navigator, called server-push. Unlike client-pull, which establishes a new connection every time the screen is refreshed, server-push keeps the connection open indefinitely. This offers the opportunity to do animations within static documents.

Contents of HTMLdisk

HTMLdisk contains all of the HTML documents, tables, forms, and Perl scripts discussed in this book, plus an extensive collection of such graphical objects as backgrounds, icons, buttons, bars, and other items that can be used to dress up your Web pages. As you roam the Web, you will have numerous opportunities to add to this collection as your needs change. Meanwhile, HTMLdisk will help you get a professional Web page up and running fairly quickly.

You should copy the contents of HTMLdisk into a single directory. Do this by typing A:INSTALL from the directory you wish to use. (This assumes, of course, that HTMLdisk is in drive A:). The reason for dumping all of the files in a single directory is that if you want to view the HTML documents offline with a browser such as Netscape Navigator, all of the graphical objects, tables, and forms will show up the way they are illustrated throughout the book.

Graphics

There are 200 files on HTMLdisk, most of them are GIFs. Many of the GIFs have file names that are somewhat descriptive of their contents. For example, *bltred.gif* means bullet, red, and *graphbut.gif* is a button of a graph. The GIF files that begin with *bg* are backgrounds. Unfortunately, it is not easy to come up with short descriptions that can be used as file names for all of the images. An easy way to find what you want is to use an image viewer.

If you do not already have an image viewer, there are a number of shareware products that can be downloaded from the Web. For example, Paint Shop Pro comes with an image viewer called PSP Browser. The software can be found at *ftp://winternet.com/users/jasc/psp301.zip* or *http://www*

.winternet.com/~jasc. In addition to displaying the GIF images as thumbnails, PSP Browser lets you rename them, copy them, move them to another directory, or delete them. In addition, PSP Browser provides useful information about each GIF, including its file size, GIF version, compression, width and height, bits per plane, number of planes, maximum number of colors, and unpacked size. PSP Browser also lets you sort the GIFs for viewing by such criteria as file name, extension, date, and size. Alternatively, you can sort by image width, height, bits per pixel, or size. Regardless of the sort method, you can specify ascending or descending order.

Forms

HTMLdisk contains all of the forms discussed in chapter 7, both the HTML coding (*.htm*) for the form itself and the Perl script (*.pl*) for processing each form. The following forms and scripts are provided:

- Evaluation form (*evalform.htm* and *evalform.pl*)
- Guest book form (*guestfrm.htm* and *guestfrm.pl*)
- Catalog request form (*catreq.htm* and *catreq.pl*)
- Single-product order form (mailord.htm and mailord.pl)
- Multiproduct order form (ordersht.htm and ordersht.pl)
- Subscription form (newsub.htm and newsub.pl)
- Seminar registration form (regform.htm and regform.pl)
- Help request form (helpreq.htm and helpreq.pl)

You should read chapter 7 before trying to use the forms. The chapter contains information on how to alter the forms so they will work properly.

Animation Files

Chapter 6 discussed a simple animation that flashed the words "Welcome to my home page" in sequence before stopping on the full sentence. Each word in the sentence, as well as the full sentence, is really a separate GIF. Three files are needed to make this animation run:

- An HTML document where the animation will appear (home.htm)
- An ASCII file containing the list of GIFs to be displayed in sequence (giflist.txt)
- A Perl script that implements the animation (nph-home.pl)

Before running the script, you should read the relevant portion of chapter 6 to find out where to place these files and how to alter them so the animation will work properly. You can experiment with these files to run your own animation. For example, you can substitute any number of your own GIFs in the giflist.txt file. Admittedly, this is a crude animation, but its intent is only to illustrate the concept without resorting to multimedia authoring tools.

Macro for Building Tables

HTMLdisk contains a macro written by Jordan Evans that allows you to lay out a table in an Excel spreadsheet and convert it to HTML. A spreadsheet is a useful way to plan and visualize a complex table. This macro is activated from a "smiley face" button that gets installed on the Excel toolbar. The macro is contained in a file called x12html.xls, and the installation instructions are contained in a file called readme.txt.

HTML Documents

All of the illustrations in this book that rely on HTML code, including forms and tables, are included in HTMLdisk. Just refer to the figure numbers in the book and match them to the file names in HTMLdisk. You can view these files offline in Netscape Navigator. The only figures not included in HTMLdisk are drawings, examples of e-mail, and the acknowledgment messages that are the result of forms processing.

Support

Many of the concepts discussed in this book have been implemented on my own Web page, called Strategic Information Resources. It can be reached at:

```
http://iquest.com/~nmuller/index.shtml
```

You may e-mail questions, comments, and suggestions about this book to me at nmuller@ddx.com. I will try to answer all e-mail in as timely a manner as possible. You can also obtain tips on HTML by joining the newsgroup located at:

```
comp.infosystems.www.author.html
```

Colors and RGB Codes

Starting with Netscape 1.1, the HTML document writer can decide the color of different page elements: specifically, the background color, text color, link color, active link color, and visited link color. The following list provides the RGB codes, not including gradients, for some of the colors that are supported.

Color	RGB#	Color	RGB#
White	FFFFFF	Copper	B87333
Red	FF0000	Coral	FF7F00
Green	00FF00	Cornflower blue	42426F
Blue	0000FF	Dark brown	5C4033
Magenta	FF00FF	Dark green	2F4F2F
Cyan	00FFFF	Dark green copper	4A766E
Yellow	FFFF00	Dark olive green	4F4F2F
Black	000000	Dark orchid	9932CD
Aquamarine	70DB93	Dark purple	871F78
Baker's chocolate	5C3317	Dark slate blue	6B238E
Blue violet	9F5F9F	Dark slate grey	2F4F4F
Brass	B5A642	Dark tan	97694F
Bright gold	D9D919	Dark turquoise	7093DB
Brown	A62A2A	Dark wood	855E42
Bronze	8C7853	Dim grey	545454
Bronze II	A67D3D	Dusty rose	856363
Cadet blue	5F9F9F	Feldspar	D19275
Cool copper	D98719	Firebrick	8E2323

Color	RGB#	Color	RGB#
Forest green	238E23	New tan	EBC79E
Gold	CD7F32	Old gold	CFB53B
Goldenrod	DBDB70	Orange	FF7F00
Grey	C0C0C0	Orange red	FF2400
Green copper	527F76	Orchid	DB70DB
Green yellow	93DB70	Pale green	8FBC8F
Hunter green	215E21	Pink	BC8F8F
Indian red	4E2F2F	Plum	EAADEA
Khaki	9F9F5F	Quartz	D9D9F3
Light blue	C0D9D9	Rich blue	5959AB
Light grey	A8A8A8	Salmon	6F4242
Light steel blue	8F8FBD	Scarlet	8C1717
Light wood	E9C2A6	Sea green	238E68
Lime green	32CD32	Semi-sweet choc.	6B4226
Mandarian orange	E47833	Sienna	8E6B23
Maroon	8E236B	Silver	E6E8FA
Medium aquamarine	32CD99	Sky blue	3299CC
Medium blue	3232CD	Slate blue	007FFF
Medium forest green	6B8E23	Spicy pink	FF1CAE
Medium goldenrod	EAEAAE	Spring green	00FF7F
Medium orchid	9370DB	Steel blue	236B8E
Medium sea green	426F42	Summer sky	38B0DE
Medium slate blue	7F00FF	Tan	DB9370
Medium spring green	7FFF00	Thistle	D8BFD8
Medium turquoise	70DBDB	Turquoise	ADEAEA
Medium violet red	DB7093	Very dark brown	5C4033
Medium wood	A68064	Very light grey	CDCDCD
Midnight blue	2F2F4F	Violet	4F2F4F
Navy blue	23238E	Violet red	CC3299
Neon blue	4D4DFF	Wheat	D8D8BF
Neon pink	FF6EC7	Yellow green	99CC32
New midnight blue	00009C		

Glossary

Absolute URL A reference to a document or service located on another server on the Internet. (See also Relative URL.)

alias A shorthand method of referring to directories. (See also bin alias.)

anchor In HTML parlance, an anchor defines the position of an inline image or text which is a hypertext link. Clicking on the anchor brings the user to another file or service to which the link points.

anti-aliasing A method of removing rough edges in bitmapped images. This is accomplished by creating pixels that average the color values between two or more adjacent colors.

ASCII American Standard Code for Information Interchange offers a standard for representing computer characters. There are 128 standard ASCII character codes, each of which can be represented by a 7-digit binary number: 0000000 through 1111111. ASCII files often have the .txt file extension.

aspect ratio The relationship between the height and width of an image.

BBS A bulletin board system, usually offering dialup access to local users. However, BBSs are accessible from anywhere over the public telephone network. BBSs also can be set up for corporate use, which can be reached via their private data networks, as well as the public telephone network.

bin alias A shorthand method of referring to the cgi-bin directory. For example, instead of typing out /user/home/nmuller/public_html/cgi-bin, the user can type a bin alias, such as /nmullerbin. A bin alias must be set up at the server to become functional.

bitmap An image composed of individual dots (pixels).

browser A computer application that is used to view documents on the World Wide Web. The browser renders documents that are coded in the HyperText Markup Language (HTML). Although browsers cannot edit the documents they display, browsers can be used to save the documents to disk where they can be edited by word processors.

byte A common unit of computer file size, with one byte usually consisting of eight bits. A bit consists of one character whose value can be 1 (on) or zero (off).

cache A location in memory where data is temporarily stored for easy retrieval. Most Web browsers make use of cache, allowing users to view previously loaded HTML documents without having to return to the Web to retrieve them again.

CERN The European Laboratory for Particle Physics, where HTML was developed in the late 1980s to provide researchers with a means to access and display documents stored on servers anywhere on the Internet.

CGI Common Gateway Interface, a method of interfacing Web servers with programs, allowing them to process information based on forms and other user inputs.

cgi-bin directory A directory in which CGI scripts are held, such as those that process HTML forms.

client A program that requests information from a server. Web browsers like Netscape and Mosaic are client applications, because they request documents from servers on the World Wide Web, Gopher documents from Gopher servers, files from FTP servers, and articles from Usenet news servers.

cyberspace A term used to describe the universe of networked computers on the Internet.

CYMK The color model that uses the four subtractive primary colors: cyan, magenta, yellow, and black. Generally, CYMK is used in print processing, whereas another color model—RGB—is used for screen display. (See also RGB.)

database A collection of files, such as HTML documents.

dedicated line A full-time, high-speed connection to the Web server. This is the most expensive type of Internet connection, the cost of which is usually justified by a high volume of traffic.

dither A method of creating the illusion of a color by placing dots of other colors very close together. A color is dithered when the display adapter does not support that color.

document source The ASCII version of a document being rendered by the browser, showing all HTML tags used to code the document. Many browsers include the capability to view the document source through a pop-up window.

domain name server A computer that matches domain names to numeric addresses, making them easier to remember. All Web servers have this capability.

download The transfer of a file from a remote system to a local system. For example, documents rendered by a browser can be downloaded from the remote Web server to the local client computer via the "save as" command (or something similar) accessed from File on the menu bar.

e-mail An abbreviation for "electronic mail," which refers to the ability of a system to send and receive addressed messages from user to user over a network.

en A typographical unit equal to half the point size.

encryption A process whereby data is scrambled to protect it from unauthorized access. At the opposite end, the data is decrypted to its original form so it can be read.

external image An image in a separate file that is specifically requested by activating a hypertext link. (See also Inline Image.)

FAQ Short for Frequently Asked Questions. A FAQ file contains the answers to commonly-asked questions to expedite the handling of routine inquiries, while freeing up disk space on a news server or bulletin board system (BBS).

finger A command that is used to display information about a user on a remote system, such as when he or she last logged on. To use Finger, you must know the user name and host name of that individual. In addition, the remote system must be configured to accept remote Finger requests.

fire wall   Software and/or hardware that provides security to a system connected to the Internet, preventing intruders from gaining access to private information.

FTP   File Transfer Protocol, used to transfer files between systems. A special use of FTP is "anonymous FTP," which provides public access for file transfers to a computer system that would otherwise require special authorization, such as a username and password.

gateway   A program that translates information between different computer systems or different applications.

GIF   Graphics Interchange Format, a type of file format widely used on the Internet, especially in HTML documents accessible on the Web. This file format was originally developed by CompuServe.

gopher   A menu-based system, usually text only, for finding information on the Internet. Unlike HTML documents on the Web, Gopher documents do not contain hypertext links.

gopherspace   A term used to describe the worldwide network of Gopher systems.

gradient   A gradual fade in color intensity, or the gradual blend of one color into another.

guest book   A form that is used to collect information about users who browse through your home page.

home page   The first HTML file that is usually accessed at a particular WWW site. A home page typically includes a menu of hypertext links which are used by readers to access related files and/or other resources on the Web.

host   A computer, particularly one that is the source or destination of messages on a communications network. On the Internet, a host can be any type of computer with its own IP address.

hotlist   A selection of interesting URLs compiled by the user, providing an easy way to return to various resources on the Internet.

hotspot   A portion of an image that changes the mouse cursor, indicating the location of a hypertext link.

HTML   HyperText Markup Language, a coding specification that relies on tags to indicate how documents on the World Wide Web should be rendered by browsers. HTML documents are portable from one platform to another. HTML documents are essentially SGML documents with generic semantics that are appropriate for representing information from a wide range of applications. HTML has been in use on the World Wide Web since 1990. (See also SGML.)

HTML editor   A program that facilitates the creation of HTML documents. HTML editors are available as standalone products or as add-ins to word processors.

HTTP   HyperText Transfer Protocol, used for transferring hypertext documents, such as those used on the World Wide Web, across the Internet.

hypertext   A method of interlinking collections of documents so that users can go from one topic to another as their interests or information needs change from moment to moment.

hypertext link   A connection between two documents (or resources) built from HTML anchor tags, an example of which is `<A HREF="filename.html">...</A>`.

IDDD   International Direct Dialing Designator, a reference to how users dial international calls without operator assistance. IDDD is used in the remote-printer application for specifying the fax number of an addressee when sending e-mail to a fax machine.

IETF   Internet Engineering Task Force, a volunteer group that researches and solves technical problems and makes recommendations to the Internet Architecture Board (IAB). The HTML Working Group of the IETF is in the process of refining HTML 3.0 into a formal standard.

image map   A graphic image containing hypertext links. The user clicks on a specific area of the image to go to another document.

inline image   An image that appears within the text of a document. When the document is retrieved, the appropriate image file is automatically retrieved as well. The browser displays the image as if it were part of the text. (See also External image.)

Internet   A world-wide network of computers offering many types of services, include the World Wide Web.

IP address   A set of numbers uniquely identifying a particular computer connected to the Internet (such as 127.127.127.11). Because IP addresses can be difficult to remember, Internet software uses the Domain Name System (DNS) to translate these numeric addresses into easier-to-remember names, like "iquest.com," "whitehouse.gov," or "buchanan.org." (See also Domain name server.)

IRC   An acronym for Internet Relay Chat, a method of exchanging text messages in real time over the Internet, as opposed to merely posting messages via e-mail or news.

ISDN   An acronym for Integrated Services Digital Network, which is a carrier-provided, switched digital service that can handle voice and data at the same time.

ISINDEX   The ISINDEX element informs the HTML user agent (browser) that the document is an index document, which can be navigated by using a keyword search. Simply adding ISINDEX to an HTML document does not make it searchable. The server must have a search engine.

ISMAP   An HTML attribute that identifies an image as an image map. An image map is a graphical map through which users can navigate transparently from one information resource to another.

ISO   International Organization for Standardization, a worldwide organization that issues international standards, such as SGML. (See also SGML.)

JPEG   Joint Photographic Experts Group, the international standards body that developed the compression/decompression algorithms for photographic image files. This file format can be much more compressed than, say, GIF, but high compression causes some loss of detail. Such files use the .jpg file extension.

LAN   Short for local area network, over which groups of computers are connected within an office or building. LANs can be interconnected over greater distances via carrier-provided lines and services, which also are referred to as WANs—wide area networks.

lynx   A full-screen, character-based Web browser developed at the University of Kansas as part of an effort to build a campus-wide information system.

META   An element used within the HEAD element to embed document meta-information not defined by other HTML elements. Such information can be extracted by servers/clients for use in identifying, indexing, and cataloging specialized document information.

MIME Multipurpose Internet Mail Extension, a standard used by Internet e-mail applications that enables users to send virtually any type of data across the Internet, including text, graphics, sound and video clips, and many other types of files.

Mosaic A browser that provides access to documents on the World Wide Web. Mosaic is written and maintained at the National Center for Supercomputing Applications (NCSA) at the University of Illinois.

MPEG Moving Pictures Experts Group, the international standards body that developed the compression/decompression algorithms for video files. Such files use the .mpg file extension.

NCSA National Center for Supercomputer Applications at the University of Illinois, where the Mosaic Web browser was developed.

newsgroup A collection of articles on a specific topic that are posted on a news server. There are approximately 4,000 newsgroups accessible from the Web, covering a wide range of topics.

NHTML Netscape HTML refers to the HTML-like tags recognized by Netscape Navigator, a popular browser offered by Netscape Communications. These HTML-like tags are proprietary and are not part of HTML 2.0 or HTML 3.0 specifications. Two examples are the CENTER and BLINK tags.

NNTP An acronym for Network News Transfer Protocol, which runs on a news server, enabling users to subscribe to newsgroups, as well as post and receive articles.

object Any graphical element that appears within an HTML document, including a hypertext link.

Perl Practical Extraction and Report Language, a popular scripting language used for all kinds of processing tasks on the Web, especially forms processing.

pixel A picture element, which is the smallest unit (dot) of a bitmapped image.

POP Server A server that uses the Post Office Protocol, which holds incoming e-mail until the recipient is ready to read or download it.

ppi Pixels per inch, a unit of measurement used to describe the width and height of graphic images.

PPP Point-to-Point Protocol is used to establish connections to remote networks via a PC's COM port and modem. When the user dials into a remote network, the PC becomes a node on that network. PPP supports multiple types of data transmission protocols, such as TCP/IP and IPX/SPX. PPP is expected to supplant SLIP as the preferred method of establishing dialup connections to the Internet.

prologue A prologue is a statement that identifies the type of document. To identify documents as HTML 3.0, it is recommended that they start with the following prologue: `<doctype HTML public "-//W3O//DTD W3 HTML 3.0//EN">`. When absent, this prologue is implied by the MIME content type for HTML 3.0, together with the associated version parameter.

protocol A set of rules and conventions for exchanging data over a network. The term also refers to the software and/or hardware implementation of these rules.

RGB The color model in which all colors are composed of varying intensities of red, green and blue—the primary additive colors. Another color model—CYMK—is used for print processing. (See also CYMK.)

relative URL A reference to a document or service on the same server. (See also Absolute URL.)

script A series of commands that perform a specified function, such as establish a connection or process a form.

server A computer that handles requests for data, e-mail, file transfer and other network services. A server at a remote site is often called a "host."

server-side includes The ability of the Web server to automatically modify a file as it is being served to include information from other files, or environment variables, such as date and time.

SGML A standard since 1986, the Standard Generalized Markup Language is an ISO standard for document markup for both print and online publication. HTML 2.0 is based on some of the concepts of SGML. HTML 3.0 will be fully compliant with SGML.

SLIP Serial Line Internet Protocol is used to establish connections to remote networks via a PC's COM port and modem. When the user dials into a remote network, the PC becomes a node on that network. Whereas SLIP supports only TCP/IP, PPP supports multiple data transmission protocols.

SMTP server A server that uses the Simple Mail Transfer Protocol to send and route e-mail over the Internet.

syntax The syntax of an HTML document defines what is permissible in terms of the tags, names, attributes, and values that describe document elements.

tags In HTML documents, tags define the start and end of headings, paragraphs, lists, character highlighting, links and other document elements. Most HTML document elements are identified with a start tag, which gives the element name and attributes, followed by the content, and then the end tag. Start tags are encapsulated by < and >, while end tags are encapsulated by </ and >.

TCP/IP Transmission Control Protocol/Internet Protocol, the de facto protocol suite for data transmission over the Internet.

telnet A type of program that is used to access a remote computer over the Internet, requiring a user name and password.

texture Bitmapped images used to create repeating patterns, which are referred to as tiles. Applying texture lays the tiles side by side. Depending on the image selected, the seam between the tiles may not be noticeable.

TIFF Tagged Image File Format, a common format for storing color and grayscale images, which is not currently supported by Web browsers.

UNIX A multiuser, multitasking operating system that is used by most Web servers. UNIX was originally developed by AT&T Bell Laboratories.

upload The process of transferring files from the local computer to a remote system over the network.

URL Uniform Resource Locator, a string of characters that uniquely identifies each page of information on the World Wide Web. An example is http://iquest.com/~nmuller /index.html.

usenet An electronic forum on the Internet of several thousands of different topical discussion groups, or newsgroups.

UUCP UNIX to UNIX Copy Protocol, a method of transferring files between computers, including electronic mail. An alternative is the Simple Mail Transfer Protocol. (See also SMTP.)

variable In HTML, the portion of a tag that a user can change to influence how text or images in a document are rendered by the browser.

Veronica A client/server system that provides a way to search for a keyword in all Gopher menus at all Gopher sites known to the Veronica server database.

viewer A specialized program that is launchable from a browser; it allows the user to access multimedia files, such as audio and video clips.

W3C World Wide Web Consortium, created by the Massachusetts Institute of Technology (MIT) and CERN to direct the development of the Web. When CERN pulled out of further Web development in 1995, it appointed INRIA, France's national computing research institute, to take its place.

WAIS Short for Wide Area Information Service, a network service that is used to search for information by key words or phrases in specially indexed files.

WAN An acronym for Wide Area Network, which connects computers over long distances via carrier-provided lines and services.

webmaster A person who manages a Web site and who also may have responsibility for retrieving and responding to e-mail messages concerning the content of the site's Web pages. Whether or not the Webmaster actually manages the Web server, the term implies a high degree of expertise in HTML, forms, and associated programs.

Winsock A commonly used network stack that implements network functions within Windows.

WWW World Wide Web, also known as the Web, is a service on the Internet that weaves information and resources together through the use of hypertext links.

Index

ABOUT THE AUTHOR

Nathan Muller is an independent consultant in Huntsville, Alabama, specializing in advanced technology marketing and education.

In his 24 years of industry experience, he has held numerous technical and marketing positions with such companies as Control Data Corporation, Planning Research Corporation, Cable Wireless Communications, ITT Telecom, and General DataComm Inc. He has an M.A. in Social and Organizational Behavior from George Washington University.

Muller has written extensively on many aspects of computers and communications, having published over 800 articles and ten books on such diverse topics as frame relay, the synchronous optical network, LAN interconnection, intelligent hubs, network management, document imaging, and wireless data networking.

Muller is a regular contributor to the technical reports published by Datapro Information Services Group, one of The McGraw-Hill Companies, as well as Faulkner Technical Reports and Auerbach's Data Communications Management and Information Management reports. He also writes frequently for Unisphere, an independent magazine for Unisys computer users. He is on the editorial board of the International Journal of Network Management published by John Wiley & Sons, Ltd. His many editorials on technology and management issues have appeared in Communications Week and Network World.

DISK WARRANTY

This software is protected by both United States copyright law and international copyright treaty provision. You must treat this software just like a book, except that you may copy it into a computer in order to be used and you may make archival copies of the software for the sole purpose of backing up our software and protecting your investment from loss.

By saying "just like a book," McGraw-Hill means, for example, that this software may be used by any number of people and may be freely moved from one computer location to another, so long as there is no possibility of its being used at one location or on one computer while it also is being used at another. Just as a book cannot be read by two different people in two different places at the same time, neither can the software be used by two different people in two different places at the same time (unless, of course, McGraw-Hill's copyright is being violated).

LIMITED WARRANTY

Windcrest/McGraw-Hill takes great care to provide you with top-quality software, thoroughly checked to prevent virus infections. McGraw-Hill warrants the physical diskette(s) contained herein to be free of defects in materials and workmanship for a period of sixty days from the purchase date. If McGraw-Hill receives written notification within the warranty period of defects in materials or workmanship, and such notification is determined by McGraw-Hill to be correct, McGraw-Hill will replace the defective diskette(s). Send requests to:

McGraw-Hill, Inc.
Customer Services
P.O. Box 545
Blacklick, OH 43004-0545

The entire and exclusive liability and remedy for breach of this Limited Warranty shall be limited to replacement of defective diskette(s) and shall not include or extend to any claim for or right to cover any other damages, including but not limited to, loss of profit, data, or use of the software, or special, incidental, or consequential damages or other similar claims, even if McGraw-Hill has been specifically advised of the possibility of such damages. In no event will McGraw-Hill's liability for any damages to you or any other person ever exceed the lower of suggested list price or actual price paid for the license to use the software, regardless of any form of the claim.

McGRAW-HILL, INC. SPECIFICALLY DISCLAIMS ALL OTHER WARRANTIES, EXPRESS OR IMPLIED, INCLUDING, BUT NOT LIMITED TO, ANY IMPLIED WARRANTY OF MERCHANTABILITY OR FITNESS FOR A PARTICULAR PURPOSE.

Specifically, McGraw-Hill makes no representation or warranty that the software is fit for any particular purpose and any implied warranty of merchantability is limited to the sixty-day duration of the Limited Warranty covering the physical diskette(s) only (and not the software) and is otherwise expressly and specifically disclaimed.

This limited warranty gives you specific legal rights; you may have others which may vary from state to state. Some states do not allow the exclusion of incidental or consequential damages, or the limitation on how long an implied warranty lasts, so some of the above may not apply to you.

Diskette Instructions

The diskette that accompanies this book contains graphics files, HTML code, Perl scripts, and associated files for setting up World Wide Web pages. The diskette does **not** contain any programs for accessing the WWW or doing any actual HTML coding. For these purposes you need a Web browser program (such as Netscape Navigator or Mosaic). Such programs are available from software distributors, or can be downloaded from a variety of on-line sites for evaluation or purchase.

The files on this diskette are stored in a self-extracting compressed archive file, INSTALL.EXE. To access the files, you must first unpack the files. Do this by putting the diskette in drive A:, then typing A:INSTALL at a DOS command line. The files will unpack into your current directory.

Chapter 10 of this book provides detailed information on the diskette's files and how they can be used.

IMPORTANT

Read the Disk Warranty terms on the previous page before opening the disk envelope. Opening the envelope constitutes acceptance of these terms and renders this entire book-disk package nonreturnable except for material defect.